The Hunter's World

Photographers:
Erwin A. Bauer
Bill Browning
Charley Dickey
W. J. Kenner
George Laycock
Karl H. Maslowski
Steve & Dolores McCutcheon
Paul D. McLain
Leonard Lee Rue III
Scott-Swedberg
John Turner
Joseph Van Wormer
Lewis W. Walker
Charles F. Waterman
and others.
Photography compiled and edited by Bill Browning.

The Hunter's World

by Charles F. Waterman

WINCHESTER PRESS
An Imprint Of
NEW CENTURY PUBLISHERS, INC.

Prepared and produced by The Ridge Press, Inc.

Editor-in-Chief: Jerry Mason
Editor: Adolph Suehsdorf
Art Director: Albert Squillace
Consulting Editor: Robert Elman
Associate Editor: Moira Duggan
Associate Editor: Barbara Hoffbeck
Art Associate: David Namias
Art Assistant: Neil R. Leinwohl
Art Production: Doris Mullane

Printing code
11 12 13 14 15 16 17
Library of Congress Catalog Card Number: 83-60105

ISBN 0-8329-0290-X

Printed in the Netherlands by Royal Smeets Offset B.V., Weert

To my wife, Debie—who can
climb all day with an eight-pound rifle,
walk into a cold tent and
warm up a stew in eleven minutes.

Contents

Acknowledgments

These people have helped me with this book. More important, they have added greatly to my personal Hunter's World:

Louis H. Nordmann, the Florida quail gunner; Walter J. Kenner, Florida Park Service naturalist; Don Williams, Rocky Mountain guide; Ben Williams, Montana hunter-naturalist; Steve Gallizioli, chief of research, Arizona Game & Fish Department; Oliver Glimsdale, Alberta Fish & Wildlife officer; Forrest Ware, biologist of the Florida Game & Fresh Water Fish Commission; Grits Gresham, Louisiana writer and television director; Warren McGowan, chukar chaser of Vale, Oregon; Max Stevenson and his fellow woodchuck experts of Pennsylvania; Don Anderson, recreation director of Sun Valley, Idaho; Pete McLain, biologist, writer, and shotgunner of Barnegat Bay, New Jersey; John Gilpatrick, writer-conservationist of Hilger, Montana; Neil Martin, sage-country biologist; Maurice Peterson, Kansas coyote hunter; Garry Vince and Blair MacDougall of British Columbia, sheep hunters extraordinary; John P. Weigand, Hungarian partridge researcher; Dr. Robert Weeden of the Alaska Department of Fish & Game, grouse and ptarmigan authority; Captain Ted R. Smallwood, swamp navigator and pintail finder; Jack Ward and Red Monical, who know about mule deer; Bud Baker, who pointed out my first buck; W. S. Steerman, who interprets hound talk; V. M. Gowdy, who knows the midwestern hedgerows; Milton Culp, wood duck student; the late Ed Welch, mountain horseman and rifleman; Don Anderberg, Canadian goose expert; the late Orville Spork, California wildfowler; George Radel, sheep hunter.

1.
All life in the hunter's world is governed by law which the hunter himself must learn, utilize, and respect.

12 A hunter's life, although dedicated in part to the killing of game, is inevitably involved in the whole world of nature. The hunter's pleasures, excitement, and, to a large degree, his success—all are influenced by his role as a naturalist, his awareness of his surroundings and of how the over-all pattern of wildlife affects his days in the field.

Each game species has its own ecology. That is to say, each species closely relates to other creatures and to specific habitats. It is plentiful or scarce, migrant or stationary, erratic or predictable—all as factors of feed, game cover, and hunting pressure dictate. Thus a hunter's skills must go well beyond merely sighting and cleanly killing his game. He must be able to identify its habitat through knowledge of the appropriate vegetation and terrain. He must be woodsman enough to recognize the signs of game presence before he sees the game itself. He looks for the things his game will feed upon and the things that will feed upon his game. He knows how game species are affected by the activities of their nongame neighbors.

To consider hunting in these terms is the basic, practical purpose of this book. But beyond this, the reader will experience the world of nature through the eyes and ears of a hunter-naturalist, observing wildlife as it really lives—by the ancient laws of tooth and claw, despite the changes that man has imposed.

Some of the happiest hunting is hopeless. The mule deer hunter turns away from the big buck's toe-dragged print in fresh snow and traces the route of a cougar, knowing from long experience that he will sight the cat only by coincidence and that before the day ends the cougar probably will be trailing him. Perhaps he has grown up with that particular lion and has never considered whether he would actually shoot it if he had the chance; but he is firmly drawn to the unfolding story of his unseen co-hunter's travel through the wilderness.

A hunter's world may be small in geography, but still be complete. A watchful squirrel hunter who spends fall days in the same woodlot each year can learn more of the wild world than the unobservant fellow who fills a trophy room from the ends of the earth under others' guidance, but who has seen little besides his targets.

The squirrel has been called the "smallest of big game" because of the hunting methods used. In his eastern woodlot the hunter may find the dark side of an overturned oak leaf that marks the cache of a nut, and the powdery siftings of shell fragments beneath a branch favored and used repeatedly by his subject. In spring, when the acorns are gone, he may find shredded cones in the conifers farther up the slope. He studies the mysterious tide of natural life—the periods when game is active and the silent times when nothing moves. The squirrel hunter uses his ears for the rustle of movement, a sound that in other environments might mean moose or leopard; he holds as still for the squirrel as he must for a grizzly. The blue jay that betrays his quarry in the woodlot might indicate the passage of a bull elk in other forests.

The edge of his woodlot is a transition area from mature forest to marshy areas, with a skirting border of weeds, grasses, and bushes. It is a main street of wildlife, where only a few steps separate one life zone from another. At the edge of the oaks, where the land slopes downward to moist earth, he will find more rumpled leaves, often many of them very close together: the dawn feeding area of a woodcock. When he brushes them aside there is a small probe hole instead of a buried nut, and the find is confirmed by the white chalk marks of woodcock droppings. The hoof tracks he sees have such rounded toe imprints he knows they were made by a foraging hog instead of deer. On down the gentle slope there is a sudden change to the boggy border of a slough, with bunches of willows and a little flat of mud that carries a sheen of wetness on

Opening pages: Western hunter explores transitional area, where weeds and grasses border cultivated land, for Hungarian partridge and pheasants. Abandoned buildings are gathering place for small game and predators. This page: Familiar elements of American hunting environment. Clockwise from top: Mallards, jackrabbit, ring-necked pheasant, silvertip grizzly, pronghorn antelope.

2

3

4

5

6

14

1

2

3

4

5

Seasons and Environments:
Beaver dam (1) changes
entire ecology of game area.
Golden aspens (3) decorate
wide and rugged spaces
where elk (2) bugle
challenges during autumn rut.
Startled mallards (4)
demonstrate quick
takeoff and steep climb
typical of their kind.
Tracks in snow (5)
are continuing story of
wildlife activity
for experienced hunter who
can interpret them.

15

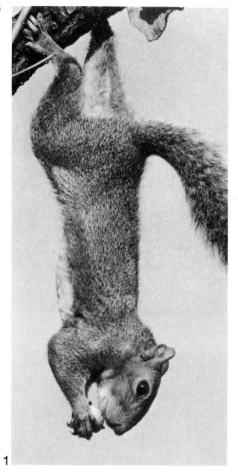

1

2

3

Gray squirrel sometimes dines head down. Cougar predation helps keep mule deer herds to proper size for range. Growth rings of ram's horns record seasons of plenty and of want.

its surface. Here there is a new patch of turned leaves among those that have blown from the oaks sixty yards away. This time there are more probe marks, but they were made by a Wilson's snipe; the student knows that the lower ground is too wet for woodcock.

Put to a different scale, the squirrel hunter's art can fit almost any game. A similar relationship is explained by the veteran hunter who said the cock pheasant provides the best features of whitetail deer pursuit, with a lighter load to carry after a successful day. Both the deer and the bird are likely to be residents of the close cover that borders grainfields and forests—both live in the brushy draws. The two employ similar escape tactics, holding to cover when possible, and then breaking forth in sudden departure when all ruses have failed. Both species of game

are found by careful spying at dawn and dusk. It is often claimed that pheasant are the wisest of game birds and that the whitetail is the cleverest of game animals. The studious and successful hunter of one will be on familiar ground when he undertakes pursuit of the other.

Although life zones may be catalogued, the nature student learns that habitat boundaries are changeable and usually altered with good reason. He may find that Hungarian partridge have forsaken the grainfields and valley creeks to live in the high mountains. Has early cold weather made the half-frozen grasshoppers easier to catch at eight thousand feet than at three thousand? And if grasshoppers are thick will the ruffed grouse be seeking open grass patches? Looking for the unusual as well as the routine, makes the hunter a part of the outdoor world.

In the South the quail hunter dallies over his morning coffee, for the night has been clear and cold. He knows the birds will be slow in leaving their roosts and are likely to feed late on the weed seeds of the sunny slopes. In Alberta the hunting camp does not stir until nearly noon. It has snowed during the night and the bighorn sheep will rest in the buckbrush patches until the weather clears. Moving southward the Canadian storm changes to rain. In New Mexico the scaled quail hunter moves very slowly, for he knows the birds lie close in wet weather and will put out little scent for his dog.

Although his time in the woods may be limited, the most successful sportsman takes greatest advantage of the privilege of hunting—a privilege that becomes more and more valuable as game fields shrink and wildlife competes at an increasing disadvantage with the expanding environment of mankind. The hunter's bag and shooting season are limited by law, but if he knows his hunting grounds he hunts better and enjoys it more. He may find more game and kill less of it.

So we speak of hunting rather than killing. Most of the true sportsman's bag is his presence in the natural world, and he feels he is a part of it while his hunt lasts. His joy is largely in escape from his more artificial environment and his absorption in a world of elemental needs, but complex relationships. As hunter he is predator—a part of nature's balance, helpful in some instances, but a predator who must regulate his own impact upon his surroundings.

As he learns to find game and to read the symbol messages of the trails, the browsed bushes, the scuffed ground, the antler-peeled sapling, and the half-eaten nut, the outdoorsman learns something of how he can preserve his sport for other years. He learns the parts of the forest and plains that are essential to the game species, and he can plan his civilized world around them. He learns from the wild environment and its residents that

sound game management must be substituted for unguided effort if hunting in any form is to continue. Invariably, man's failure with game management has resulted from too shallow an awareness of the subject's way of life. The chukar, a recent and successful introduction from India, failed at first because we assumed the bird would be happy in the lush grainfields of the Midwest. Not until we allowed him to scatter through the arid wastelands of the West—in dry hills like those of his native land—did he thrive.

In this book we follow hunting seasons from northern Alaska to southern Florida. Along the way we note the behavior, both characteristic and sometimes puzzling, of mountain goats and sheep, moose and bear, the migratory pattern of geese and ducks and woodcock, the interrelationships among such species as the rabbit, the fox, and the coyote, the life cycle of quail, the feeding requirements of grouse and pheasants, elk and antelope. We look closely at all of the game species, major and minor, as well as at a host of nongame animals and birds that merit the hunter's attention, not only because they affect what he hunts, but because they are intriguing in themselves. We attempt to present many observations and insights that may be new even to those who are familiar with the woods and fields, and we report many facts we cannot fully explain. But we shall serve our purpose if we point to a thousand of the things that multiply hunting pleasure and make hunting more successful. If we produce more questions than answers, it is all to the good; one of the successful hunter's most important traits is a continuing curiosity. For unless a man inquires into the many factors that have brought him and his game together, he is only a gunner and not a hunter. If he does not know his quarry—its life cycle, the process of its reproduction, the course of its migrations, and the subtlety of its relationship to other creatures and its environment—its death means only marksmanship. Such a man reads only the last chapter of a mystery.

2.
The serene, slab-sided goat shares a windswept, vertiginous world with the golden eagle and the rock ptarmigan.

It is only August, but in the North the world of the hunter is restless. The salmon have been running without intermission all summer, the dying bodies of one generation drifting downstream to meet the rush of new spawning migrations. Each new contingent moves powerfully in the lower reaches of the streams and then weakens, its thrust dwindling to desperate wrigglings as the plunging coastal rivers pinch to shallow creeks. The final objective of each dying fish, a certain plot of spawning gravel, is finally reached only by the few that have survived a thousand hazards.

Guides along the Alaska coast watch the mouths of glacial streams, for there are black bear hunters among their clients and the tons of spent salmon are an irresistible attraction to bruin. Brown bear hunting is not so predictable, but along some salmon streams enormous tracks can be seen, and many observers believe it is the yearly salmon feast that has made the coastal giant much bigger than his cousin, the mountain grizzly. I put one foot in the palm of a great track on a smooth gravel bar and note that the imprint of the claws extends several inches ahead of my boot toe, the deep mark of a brownie which must weigh more than a thousand pounds.

Already there has been a regrouping of the caribou and ptarmigan, movements noted by bush pilots and carefully observed by Indians and Eskimos. The restless gatherings of late summer are the prelude to short migrations that will begin with the autumnal weather changes. Some caribou marches leave their marks for years in the slow-growing vegetation of the tundra.

Hunters moving along the coast in small boats are far outnumbered by sports fishermen working the silver salmon (coho) run. Many of the anglers are tourists, almost ready to head back south; ferry bookings to what Alaskans call the "lower states" already have slackened as the weather cools. The main crush of summer visitors has eased, for man's seasonal migrations are most complex of all.

Along the cliffs our boat slows beneath a nesting colony of Arctic terns which could well symbolize all migratory creatures. There are thousands of them: adults, the very young, and uncertain flight students which will soon begin the longest migration known on earth—from the Arctic to the Antarctic. And through some undeciphered impulse, part of them will take the long way around, bending their flight across North America, along the coast of Europe and the African continent, to a resting place in a southern latitude that roughly matches their northern nesting range in climate. It is believed that instincts of an Old World ancestry still bind them to that course. The trip for some will be 22,000 miles. A few, spanning both Arctic and Antarctic summers, will live in constant daylight for eight months of the year.

Although the colony changes the appearance of an entire mountainside, it might easily be missed. From a distance, resting terns seem to be lifeless dots. There are so many birds they give the cliffs a speckled look, as if some light-colored stone were only partly covered by vegetation, and they have chosen a section divided by what Alaskans might call a creek, but which is really an interrupted waterfall, mostly spray, fed by an invisible glacier higher up.

Most fishermen in the awesome fjords see the vertical cliffs and the sky-lined glaciers only as a backdrop to the bit of water where their lures work, but goat and sheep hunters look for other, less obvious things. They scan the jagged terrain for specks that can easily escape the unpracticed eye, specks that may be trophies.

A mountain goat never seems the size or color you expect. His world is on so large a scale that he himself is no more than a speck—dirty if seen against snow, white if against grass, yellow-tinged if he is an old hermit billy of the sort that trophy hunters look for. Most hunters will judge more by the animal's aloofness and the yellow tinge of his coat than by the size of his horns, for the difference between a commonplace six-inch spike and a remarkable ten-inch stiletto is hard to discern from a great distance. Undulating mirages may distort the image in the spotting scope, and the animal's outline wiggles as if something needed tuning.

Looking for goats from the Alaska bays is not the easiest way to get them. The goats are there, but the climbs can be formidable. The coastal mountains are so immense that what appears to be a grassy slope develops into head-high vegetation thrust out from a vertical precipice.

The goat's manner is sometimes offensive to sweating hunters below him. He stands as if he had just completed the universe and is surveying it before taking a brief rest, but probably he is just a little detached and does not associate the view with himself. He is generally credited with only fair eyesight; he seldom seems to study any distant thing minutely. He is probably not listening intently for sounds of danger, either, as he poses on a windswept pinnacle but, since goats have a good sense of smell, he may be testing the air for the presence of predators, including man.

Mountain goats and mountain sheep differ significantly in certain fundamental characteristics. The goat is not a dashing leaper like the sheep, but seems more a part of the mountain, climbing slowly to impossible heights as if this were his duty. His occasional jumps are measured carefully, without the sheep's seeming recklessness. He is American, with no close foreign relatives, although his ancestors are believed to have crossed the ancient land bridge from Asia. His nearest kin are said to be the Asian serow and the Alpine chamois, but his lineage has been confused by the scholar's statement that he isn't a goat at all but an antelope (while the pronghorn "antelope" is really a species of goat).

Goat range can overlap that of mountain sheep, and many goat hunters are concurrently sheep hunters. But goats and sheep are not close associates, since they require slightly different terrain and forage. Sheep on the same mountains with goats will prefer the more rounded ridges and broader pastures. The species usually come into disinterested contact only when weather or food causes a wild-country population shift.

Early explorers called the goat a "white buffalo," because of the prominence of his fleecy hump, but he is a much smaller animal. A very large goat probably weighs no more than three hundred pounds. He is generally hunted in conjunction with other game, and the labors involved protect him from man as well as from other predators. Long after other big-game animals had been studied carefully, the Rocky Mountain goat remained almost unknown, for he was too hard to reach either for meat or sport.

A hunter-naturalist friend shot the first dead mountain goat I ever saw. With enormous effort he had brought it down from the snowy mountain intact. It had been a late-season kill and the animal was not old enough to be discolored; it was gleaming white and the fleece was heavy, the insulating undercoat fully developed. My friend reverently placed the animal on a level rock where it not only looked surprisingly large, but lay so close to the flat stone that it appeared to have been carved in relief, like a frieze. The goat is a slab of bone and muscle, fitted to the vertical cliffs and the tiny trails, capable of standing hard against a stone wall without bulges to unbalance or topple him. The greatest dangers he encounters are landslides and snowslides. The rolling rocks and noisy winds are so common in his land that he is not too sensitive to their sound, but he stiffens instantly if a twig is snapped.

Goats are found in western Canada, Alaska, and a northwestern segment of the contiguous states, including Washington, Idaho, and Montana, and they may yet be introduced successfully elsewhere. Their habitat must have vegetation, and it does, even though the tilted meadows, crevice growths, and stunted conifers may be

*Goat country is a
land of upended splendor.
Quarry's ability to
walk tiny trails on steep
slopes makes it hard
to track. Spotting may be
done from forest (right)
but stalk will be
above timberline. Packing
out may be arduous.*

hard to discern from a distance among tumbled rocks, bare cliffs, and peaks. The goat is a ruminant, feeding on buds and twigs, as well as the grasses, mosses, and lichens of high country. When heavy snows cover their preferred foods, goats will move to wind-cleaned grass ridges somewhat below their usual range. Cold does not force them lower, however, and to find snow-free spots they are as likely to go up as down. In hard winters their rations may be short, indeed. Even in moderate weather, nannies and kids will condescend to feed on lower slopes and often appear in good-sized herds, but the old billies generally stay nearer to the crags.

Predators seeking goats find it literally an uphill proposition. Only the golden eagle, seeking the younger kids, can reach the hunting ground easily. Furred meat eaters must be opportunists, catching their prey on its way between mountains or grazing a bit too far from the precipices. A bear, wolf, cougar, lynx, or wolverine will occasionally attempt an attack, but unless luck is with him he is likely to find himself with a sheer cliff on one side, an abyss on the other, and the menacing black bayonets of a goat ahead. Even grizzlies are said to have died this way.

In mating season the billies may spar a bit, but they cannot afford pitched battles since their horns are too deadly for romantic jousting. Instead, they scrub their horns against rocks and plants, leaving an oily substance which comes from glands located at the bases of the weapons. The rut is in late fall and the kids are born six months later, in April or May. A nanny usually bears a single kid each spring, twins being unusual. The young are able to join the herd and walk the tiny ledges within three weeks.

Spring in that land is not a butterfly-and-daisy time, for April can be bitterly cold. Newborn kids are secluded in a sheltered area and their mothers visit them frequently for nursing. Born with insulating fleece, the seven-pound youngsters appear as blobs of snow, but camouflage is not their sole protection. Their mothers are terrible adversaries of predators and carry horns as long as those of the billies. In fact, record heads have come from females.

Wind may help the stalking hunter by covering the sounds of his climbing and by establishing a positive scent drift. When all is calm the rock formations distort thermal movements and cause subtle, scent-carrying air changes to warn the game.

A goat hunter may come upon his trophy by accident, but this is not the way of the expert, who traditionally sights and judges his animal from a distance. To stalk, one must first study the game's location through a glass and then be able to recognize the area as he enters it, hours later. At close range the site never appears as it did from miles away. If the animal is feeding when first sighted, the hunter knows it is likely to bed nearby, and he tries to guess the probable spot. But if he sights the goat in its bed his reasoning must be reversed, and he looks for a logical grazing area. All of this is tied to an estimate of stalking time and the availability of daylight hours. And always the rules of early and late feeding and midday rest may be suspended by individual animals.

The stalk is made upwind if possible. If that approach is denied by terrain, the hunter may gamble that the architecture of the mountain will divert his scent from the game. Initial surveys of the situation may take ten minutes or several days. The stalk is nearly always long and generally longer than expected, and there is the possibility of warning being given by unwanted goats in unseen notches. There may be a startled ptarmigan to raise the alarm or a dislodged stone that makes a really noisy descent. There may be an impossible crevasse, invisible from the planning site, lying athwart the route from hunter to quarry.

In September in northern British Columbia, four of us saw herds of goats in an area I

*Secret of goat's
phenomenal ability as
mountaineer (above) lies in
formation of hooves
(right), which operate both
as claws and suction cups.*

had heard was poor country for them. Judgment of goat populations is difficult because they gather in loose communities in ideal terrain and may be present year after year, while similar areas a few miles away are goatless. Because of these concentrations, it is possible for seasoned hunting parties to pass through a region, study what appears to be ideal habitat, find no goats, and write off an entire mountain range. Looking through one more valley, they might have found peaks dotted with game.

In our invasion of "poor goat country," we rode horses from a base camp, following a stream upward into a narrowing valley, unable to keep a constant view of the cliffs and slides because the streamside willows and tree clumps obscured them. Game trails scalloped the creek, the rounded tracks of elk mixed with the longer-toed marks of moose, and I was not sure which of the two big deer species had shredded a sapling while polishing antlers.

A guide, whose business is to see everything that moves, stopped us with a cautioning hand and pointed to elk on a rise near an aspen grove. Standing in high grass and brush, the animals were plainly visible as a bunch of elk. There was an occasional antler, glimpses of light-colored rumps, and now and then a flapping ear as they milled restlessly, but to say that I had seen an entire animal or that the antlers were good was impossible. They crossed the creek close ahead of us, four fat young bulls in single file, but they were raghorned animals and I was not surprised, for we were in an area noted for elk roasts instead of elk antlers. Prize heads come from soil of just the right mineral content, and from just the right combination of forage plants. So far the game record books have been more accurate than science in locating perfect antler habitat.

Our brush and timber cover fell away suddenly and we saw goat country ahead. Five minutes later we were watching a yellow-white trophy billy, as we took turns at the high-powered spotting scope and also found more than twenty other goats, mostly nannies and kids, with our binoculars. The big billy, well separated from the lesser·citizens, was grazing on an outcropping near the top of a weathered ridge that pointed almost straight at us and sharpened as it receded in the distance, sloping higher until it ended in

Opposite: On uncertain footing of Alaskan slope, hunter aims at rock ptarmigan as pointing dog crouches. Above: Ptarmigan plumage (1, 2, 3) is shifting mixture of summer brown and winter white. Small mountain lake (4) may be gathering place for sheep, goats, ptarmigan.

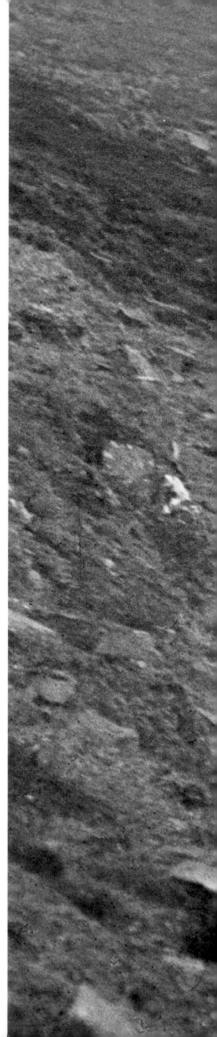

Franklin's grouse unused to man (above) will act like "fool hen," but hunting pressure will make it wary.
Right: Message in snow says ptarmigan landed with primaries extended and walked off on feathered feet.

a series of ragged spires. The goat's position was almost perfect. No other spot would give so wide a view of approaches; no other would give so many avenues of retreat. But it was the very perfection of his stronghold that had caused us to scan it first. It was the logical spot.

We memorized the point where the billy grazed. Our plan was to scale the ridge beyond the goat, approach him from above, and be back in the valley before dark. When the canyon narrowed and the horses could be used no farther, we started up the slope on foot.

At noon we reached the top and saw the mountains again, endless peaks and ridges, proceeding toward the Pacific, but we turned down the ridge toward the big billy's meadow. The breeze was still favorable, walking was easy, and we moved cautiously, racking our memories for every detail of the outcropping where we had watched him feed. There were goat tracks and droppings everywhere and we stopped at a barricade of boulders, the final obstruction between

us and the little green slope where he had grazed. I looked across the boulders by degrees, climbing gently about them so that no inch of the meadow would be missed, and I studied the shadows beneath the few scrubby conifers at its edge.

The goat had moved and certainly was bedded nearby, but I scoured the area while the others held back, and I saw and heard nothing. The ground was trampled in some spots and the tracks were big. "This is where he lives!" said the other hunter, like an infantryman who has finally overrun the enemy's position and actually looks at the spot from which he has been fired on. Once we heard a movement and froze for a long minute, but we never found our goat, so we plodded back up the great ridge to peer down into steep pockets.

We saw others that afternoon, one of them like a tiny, carved ivory goat set in the very tip of a pinnacle and evidently sound asleep, but he was too far away to be startled and I have no idea how he got up there or how he could get down.

Such mountaineering seems to be done simply for the climber's satisfaction. The kids and nannies were busy with their evening feeding on the more gentle slopes when we hurried down to reach the horses before dark.

We rode down the creek at a fast walk and trotted in the easy stretches, so it was only dusk when we came to where we had first sighted the big billy. We stopped to blow the horses and looked back curiously to where we had lost him. Beneath his little bench there was an overhanging ledge we had not noticed before. Was that a creamy speck against darker rock? A little evening mist moved in the valley, but it parted to give me a brief, sharp view through my binoculars. The big billy rose slowly to his hind legs, reached to the rocks above him with his front feet, and climbed thirty feet back to the flat where I had searched for him hours before. He had won, for it was the last day of my hunt.

Goat hunters prefer to move early before heavy snows can isolate their quarry. Also, as goat season begins, the rock ptarmigan start flocking-maneuvers in Alaska. They are neighbors of the goat and mountain sheep and when flushed they can ruin a stalk; not that they chase a goat from his bed, but their hasty flight will sharpen his watchfulness. By mid-August the young are ready for strong flight and family groups mingle for fall migrations. The long season opens early in August, but it creates no stir in the sporting-goods stores of Fairbanks or Anchorage, for the ptarmigan is not quite accepted as game in a land where moose weigh almost a ton and Dall sheep can be watched from highways.

The early-season hunter will find the birds near known nesting areas after the family groups begin to flock but before they become nomads for the winter. The ptarmigan has no credentials to prove it a near relative of the treasured red grouse of Scotland, which is gunned by noblemen with handmade shotguns, but like many a "fool hen" (the words are used for almost any grouse at times) it needs only the right circumstances to be a game bird.

Often caught like a simpleton, relying on ptarmigan-colored and ptarmigan-shaped rocks as its only concealment from the hunter seeking camp meat, it is a poor excuse for game. But flailing its white wings down a nearly vertical slope in a sweeping wind it is worthy of its Old World relatives, and Alaska heather smells as sweet as Britain's. Sometimes the bird flushes wild, out of range, and towers through mountain fogs to other mountaintops where the hunter's climb alone is enough to make it a prize.

Associated generally with the Arctic, ptarmigan are also found at high altitudes in the more southerly Rockies. In the North, the three kinds are willow, rock, and white-tailed, and it is the white-tailed bird that ranges far to the south. In appearance, the three are similar, turning white in winter, and even a trained ornithologist may have to check his notebook to tell one from another. Most of the year the willow ptarmigan prefers the creek bottoms, the rock ptarmigan the high slopes, and the white-tailed bird the uppermost peaks, but in dead of winter they may live nearly together. Then they are sometimes picked off because their shiny eyes and beaks show above the protective snow cover. In snow they are easily trailed by the shallow tracks of their feathered feet.

In August the birds were high. Sometimes, climbing on all fours, I saw the swift, sliding shadow of a golden eagle on a sunny mountain face. In ancient times the golden was a hunter for kings; in Alaska, it hunts in freedom, often seeking the little Arctic ground squirrels that pop up and down and deliver squeaky tirades of abuse from the slopes. From a distance, it was often hard to tell whether I was seeing the shadow or the seven-foot spread of the eagle itself, but generally the shadow showed more plainly, unless the bird was against the sky. An

Coexistence: The Alaskan world on whose highest level the mountain goat lives also accommodates the Arctic tern (1), brown bear (2), and cougar (4). The tern, a tireless flier, migrates to Antarctica in fall. Coastal brownie has become world's largest carnivore in part through salmon diet. Cougar track (3) is more readily seen than elusive cat himself, who may trail trailer.

1

2

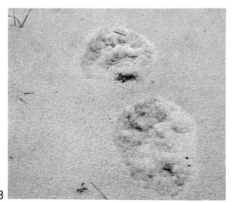

3

4

Golden eagle (6) shares heights with mountain goat and bighorn sheep (9) and may prey on their young, although ground squirrel (11)—a staple of many creatures' diet—is more frequent victim. Willow buds (5) are a favorite food of browsers and birds, particularly ptarmigan. Lichen (7) and mosses are low-lying mountain carpets. Canada jay, or whiskey jack, (10) is wilderness camp follower.

5

7

8

10

9

eagle will take a ptarmigan, but so will a sharp-shinned hawk.

I have found the ptarmigan in summer brown and white where the pointing dog occasionally was surrounded by curious birds, cocking their heads at him and pecking now and then at the ground; where a distraught single, a little separated from the rest of its flock, would run over my feet in a dither to regroup; and where lazily rising coveys offered little challenge except the selection of the individual wanted. This is typical behavior for birds that have not been hunted, and such performance has established the ptarmigan's reputation for being tame.

But I have also gunned rock ptarmigan on Donnelly's Dome. The Dome is an Alaskan mound, dwarfed by great, snowy ranges, and it is set miles from them on a flat plain, easily circled by a motorist willing to travel a bit of gravel road. It seems to rise abruptly from solid ground, but what appears to be short grass and weeds from a distance develops into thick willows, alder, and muskeg at close range. I chose the most difficult route, floundering forward. There had been splay-toed, water-filled moose tracks all the way in, and I finally met their author near the mound's base—startlingly tall and seemingly black as night, sun glancing from his wet sides as he left his wallow and trotted loosely through willows to disappear almost instantly.

Climbing the Dome in a rising gale, I went from underbrush and willows across grassy blobs protruding from muskeg bog and finally to a rocky slope, looking for and finding most of the things that rock ptarmigan need. The buds and twigs of willows make winter food, and above the willows were blueberries and crowberries for the warmer months.

I visited the Dome at the suggestion of a ptarmigan authority, Dr. Robert Weeden, of the Alaska Department of Fish and Game, and it finally dawned that he had sent me because the Dome was a capsule of the rock ptarmigan's world. It contained all that the bird needed for its year and was set apart from similar habitat. Ptarmigan could go from their wind-ripped high ridge to the shelter of thick willows in one short flight. In other areas the transition from plain to peak would be more gradual. Most of the types of cover commonly assigned to rock ptarmigan were here within less than a mile of walking. The Dome's birds could have their own community and were described as a "breeding population" as opposed to casual or occasional visitors; they also had been hunted, and they could be found because their range was small. It is important that they had been hunted, for only a hunted bird becomes a game bird.

I needed just the right height, and already I was above tree line and the minimum altitude expected of the August ptarmigan, but the vegetation changed sharply on the way up and I made short, sidewise forays of fifty yards or so at frequent intervals, because I was not quite certain of the exact level at which the birds would hold. I was confident they would be on a stratum of the slope, not scattered up, down, and over. This is not a fast rule but the altitude that attracts one bird is likely to attract others. The Dome was ideal habitat and quite typical, with the advantage that it was separated from other good areas by miles of level ground, so that its population was unlikely to wander away.

A few hundred feet from the plain level the wind had risen to forty or fifty miles an hour, enough to cause an occasional stagger on poor footing, and the long-haired dog, a Brittany pointing spaniel, was sleek and thin when he faced it, shaggy and unkempt when he turned away. In such a blast, a pigeon-sized bird cannot stand comfortably and one must look with special care in steep, miniature erosions, occasional low bushes, and in the lee of rock outcroppings. There was little bare ground. The earth-hugging, sub-alpine vegetation had matured in such gales and was contoured so that it hardly moved.

I found a weathered, empty shotgun shell, one of the signs the hunter looks for almost as religiously as he watches for game tracks or game foods. Analysis of such expended cartridges for age, gauge, and probable former content approaches a science with many gunners.

At any rate, the ptarmigan of the Dome were at least descendants of birds that had been shot at, and probably some of the current residents had escaped. Man trains birds and animals to become game, partly as individuals learn what man and gun mean, partly as the slow-witted and trusting of the species are survived by the quick and the canny. It is likely the descendants of birds that have escaped hunters are a product of selection, even in the first generation.

Still, expecting the dog to point a co-operative bird that would walk pompously among the scattered rocks and possibly croak conversationally to his friends, I was unprepared for something with flashing white wings that flushed from a rocky pocket and plunged down the slope, caught a full blast of air, turned steeply a hundred yards below me, and swept out of sight around a shoulder of the Dome. The dog gawked in amazement. He had never pointed the bird and simply stood staring at what he only suspected was game.

The bird had been too far away, I thought, but I was a little unsure as to just what area it had left, the wind having killed its sounds, and I gripped the gun too tightly and cautioned the dog to hunt close. He barely made his point when the second and third birds flew, one of them vanishing somewhere up forward and the other swinging back ahead of a clean miss and sailing downhill to alight on a small outcropping, in sight but out of range. I went after that one, trying to stalk but knowing I was in plain view on the open slope and screaming senseless instructions to the dog.

The bird held until I was within easy range and then it fluttered out of sight over the brow of the rimrock ledge where my hastily pointed shot dug up a little dust and powdered stone. But when it soared into view some distance below I killed my first ptarmigan on Donnelly's Dome and stumbled down to retrieve it.

Then I looked uphill, realized I had sacrificed two hundred yards of sweaty altitude, and grimly started back to where the birds were, dog tired, with a pounding pulse and shakily excited. Were these birds the same species caught in long-handled nets by researchers and killed by hungry sourdoughs with rocks and sticks? They were the same, of course, and I marveled at how a species' characteristics can sometimes be affected by even slight gunning pressure.

Not all ptarmigan are game birds and neither are all ruffed grouse, for the king of eastern coverts can be killed with a club in virgin forests. Is there any trick of flight known by Scotland's red grouse that the rock ptarmigan cannot learn or inherit? Were the deer killed with clumsy matchlocks by hungry Pilgrims as clever as the ghostly whitetails of today's hunted woods? Where the ptarmigan has learned that man is as much a predator as the gyrfalcon and the fox, it is a game bird and still holds its own. It simply learns to fly away when man comes near; often it is out of range when it does so.

The Alaska spruce grouse is a roadside fool. When it was late afternoon, the time for game birds to feed and gather grit for their crops, I found a covey strolling in a creek-bottom trail. They squatted a little as if to fly, picked up one more bit of gravel, milled uncertainly, and walked into the weeds where I put them up and killed two for dinner as they fluttered out of the cover like Leghorn pullets. I watched a dozen more bore into the forest, going fast once they had chosen their course.

A campfire delicacy, the spruce grouse is called the most stupid grouse of all, but as I looked at the rounded wings and the bullet shape I wondered if this, too, were a potential forest prize. There may have been a time when the wild turkey was only curious about hunters.

3.
Well above timberline, beyond
the usual range of caribou,
the acrobatic sheep wanders rimrock
ledges in search of pasture.

In Alaska and Canada, mountain sheep range is in the high country, which consists mainly of huge, rounded mountains and big pastures, with some rocky, rugged areas. The sheep, a grazer, prefers tender grasses to the coarse forage of mountain goats, although in hard times he will browse in the buckbrush and willows.

Ideally, sheep prefer a feeding area near a canyon or rocky outcropping, where they can disappear almost instantly. They also take to timbered draws when caught at low altitude, but prefer to feed where visibility is good, and although careful to have an escape route, they make no special effort to hide when feeding or bedding. Their traditional predators are not notably farsighted except for the golden eagle, and he is interested only in lambs. Wolves, bears, and mountain cats depend mainly on scent.

For most of the year rams do not associate closely with ewes and lambs, but generally move about in bands of their own. It is possible to hunt for days without seeing a trophy, then to come upon a dozen together, including several with impressive curls. A startled rifleman may shoot quickly, then find he has picked the wrong sheep and watch as a larger head disappears. His used-up license in his pocket, he stands disconsolately and begins to plan another trip a year or years ahead, for no sheep hunter ever concedes that he has had his last hunt.

These things are true of all American wild sheep, but we speak now of the Dalls and Stones, generally hunted in August, September, and October in Alaska, the Yukon, and British Columbia.

It is October when the rams begin to lose their camaraderie, and crashing duels soon signal the onset of the rut. The opponents, charging head-on from considerable distance, smash each other until one concedes defeat and retires, dazed and wobbly. Scars and dents of combat show plainly on the horns of most trophies, though the pitched battles occur only when adversaries are fairly evenly matched. Otherwise, supremacy is established almost automatically with a few threatening feints.

Winners gather sizable bands of ewes. In the North, the lambs, frequently twins, are born in May or June, generally above timberline, against the base of a cliff or on a hidden ledge. The ewe chooses the spot with care, demanding a clear view of all approaches, and the lambs will follow their mothers to the herd after a week or so of hiding. They nurse until the following fall.

The sheep is a high-strung master of quick movements, a gymnast, whereas the goat is a contortionist. Even a heavy ram can land unharmed from a fifty-foot downhill leap. He cannot always follow the methodical goat, but he races and bounces where the goat plods and pulls. His most spectacular maneuver is best described as a ricochet. He leaps from ledge to minimal ledge, unable to stop on any of the tiny footholds, but maintaining momentum, and with each strike selecting his next landing point, and so on until he reaches firm footing. It is a graceful refinement of a man's system of hopping from rock to rock in crossing a creek. Generally a zigzag pattern, it can work in a rock chimney, the sheep using both sides for his landings. Without speed, the trick could not work.

The mental equipment necessary for such maneuvers was once described by Ernest Thompson Seton as the "quick, calm brain." Seton estimated that the sheep required a foothold every five or six feet going up at high speed, but could safely break a downward plunge by striking only once in twenty feet. Countless hunters have lost trophy rams that seemed to be trapped by gorge, crevasse, or precipice, yet disappeared safely over the edge.

The sheep's feet are suction pads with sharp-edged hooves, similar to those of the goat, and their effect can be clawlike in rough going. The edges of the hooves are fairly straight to make maximum use of outcroppings of only a fraction of an inch, and the animal can travel a steep bank with only the inside edges of the hooves in contact. The dew claws, too, are part of a braking system that can make a dead stop anywhere there is room for the body to be balanced.

There is an early morning feeding period, followed by a cud-chewing rest and some movement and feeding around midday. Another major feeding period comes before dusk. Around these habits the hunter must base his stalk, and it is the skillful spotter who begins the game with much more than luck on his side—whether he is a professional guide or a lone rifleman.

In August, when the hunting season begins in Alaska and northern British Columbia, the hunter is plagued by heat that moves the sheep into shade, driving them downward into timber or buckbrush, or into rocky areas where spotting is extremely difficult.

From a valley of the Kenai Peninsula, I have watched bands of gleaming Dalls disappear almost instantly from their early morning feeding, and have seen several hunters toiling the heights from different directions only to miss sheep shaded in folds of the mountain. Across miles, aided by the prying eye of the long-range telescope, I have watched an exhausted hunter rest at full length, while a few yards beneath him on a similar ledge, a prize ram spent the warm hours unseen, shaded by a boulder.

Canadian Stone sheep country has the most plentiful big game of all America. It is within the range of the great gray wolf. Elk are plentiful, and some of the continent's biggest moose browse at the base of sheep mountains. There are goats in the rougher areas, and both black and grizzly bear are in the lower canyons and on the big burns. The caribou will be almost anywhere during the early hunting season, generally in small, fidgety groups, rather than in the giant herds of the Arctic tundra. It is wolverine country, and meat caches must be mounted on high poles.

It is only a short climb from clinging muskeg to timberline. Most salt licks are at the lower levels and can attract a variety of customers at dusk. Sheep will come great distances to a lick, as will moose, deer, caribou, and elk. The low valleys are made up largely of muskeg bogs, sometimes seeping slowly into open streams, and forming excellent range for moose. From mud and willows a pack train can go up into timber where moss and leaves form a ground cover so thick that even a loaded packhorse's tracks disappear behind him. There the grouse are likely to fly away silently, and moose will be only bulky, drifting shadows. Parts of the timbered area may be felled by forest fires and the new succession of plants is attractive to the browsing animals that may find little to eat in heavy forest.

Just above the timber is the brushy stratum, broken frequently by streams lined with taller willows. As the brush shortens farther up the mountain slopes, grass and moss show more prominently. After most of the buckbrush is passed the climber is in true sheep country and will soon be among year-round snow patches.

Above the tall vegetation, the expert first scans his entire area with binoculars, holding as inconspicuous a position as possible, and ever mindful that game may be very close. If he finds game at a distance, he resorts to a powerful spotting scope for identification and judging, and he may look from the same point many times during his hunt, learning it so well that he becomes acquainted with individual groups and single animals, living within a range of several miles. Hunters who have studied an area thoroughly may speak casually of familiar sheep. Gossip concerning Old Spotty, or Lonesome Joe, or Rock Hopper, would sound idiotic to an eavesdropper but it is hunter talk; a week of watching a ram leaves the watcher with a feeling of some vague rapport, although the game may have no idea of the hunter's presence. Through long observation the hunter may know an individual ram's personal habits of resting and feeding and may have studied the same rocks and grass patches until he knows them almost as well as the ram does. He feels pro-

1

Sheep live in enormous
mountain ranges, such as
those opposite, which
require minute study (2)
with spotting scope.
To determine if trophy
is good, like (1),
or a record, like author's
Stone (3), requires
judgment—and luck.

2

3

jected into the ram's world, although he has remained a mile away.

Even when a desirable ram is located, there are new cautions to be observed, for the eager hunter can be betrayed by the subtle treachery of the telescope. The glass may reveal only the clean, smooth ridges and slopes and ignore the rocky chasms that appear as vague shadows. It oversimplifies the giant landscapes, leaving out the brushy draws and the hidden creeks, and showing only the main features.

Before the snows, the scoper can simply look for something white if he's hunting Dalls; the darker Stone sheep is not so easy. For minutes, the hunter can watch a slope and see nothing but scattered rock, scrubby trees, and grass. Then, suddenly, a sheep is there as if flashed on a screen. One at a time an entire flock may appear. Careful study has finally separated sheep from background and established the correct image size to look for.

As if searching a forest at close hand, the expert studies the entire slope, looking for a

Activities of unpredictable caribou can be read in Ontario snow trails (opposite). Note groups at top and bottom of picture. Bull (below) sports trophy antlers.

41

telltale shadow, a little color that fills in the pattern, a movement that makes a minor change in the scene. With Stone sheep it is most often the lighter parts that appear: a flicker as the white inside of a leg moves in feeding, a dot of white rump patch, possibly a tiny glint of horn.

But much depends on knowing where to look for sheep. In early fall, the perfect spot for big rams is a high basin with rolling grass slopes and a creek to drain it, nearby boulders for bedding shade, a broken rim of rugged bluffs and talus fans for escape. All of this should be set well above timberline, but not so high as to be above fertile soil for banks of grass.

A single ram may be harder to locate, but he is easier to approach. A band of bedded patriarchs is always watchful, and if bedded among rocks the hunter seldom sights all of them at first look. If he plans a stalk, he must count them over and over again, for if he is seen by one at close range, the whole band will ghost into mountain mists or an unseen canyon. A most bitter defeat is

1

2

3

*Whitest of wild
sheep, Dall (opposite) are
easily seen before
snowfall. They prefer
grass to browse.
Above-the-clouds view
of hunter glassing peaks
for Stone rams (1)
may be a good day's climb
away. Packhorses (2)
help—some. Hunters
still walk a lot.
Black bear (3) live in
sheep mountains, but
in burns at lower levels.*

to reach the place where the quarry has been and find the sheep gone without sight or sound. Perhaps they left while the hunter was beginning his stalk, if he revealed himself through misjudgment of terrain. Perhaps a thermal draft took the scent to them. Perhaps he moved a totally different band that spread the alarm, or possibly the trouble was an excited caribou or even a traitorous bear.

There was a time when mountain sheep fed the mining camps and provided dog food, but today they are taken almost invariably for their horns. A ram may live to fifteen years, but his likely span is nearer ten. From seven or eight years on he may have a trophy head. Judging those horns from a great distance or at a fleeting glimpse is a science. The diary of a ram's life is in the yearly growth rings of his horns—wide-spaced in years of plenty, narrow in the bad years of disease or hunger. The latest rings are those near the skull, since growth is from the base.

Once the ram is glassed, the hunter begins a series of comparisons. The curl of the horns comes first—the diameter of their circle should be

nearly one third of the animal's height. They should approach a full curl, and for the true record hunter the full curl is essential. Somehow, they must also be seen from both side and front, for there are various types of horns. The Dalls and more northern Stones tend to have wide-spreading but slender horns, while the bighorns carry more mass and curl closer to the head.

For record hunters, the guess-scoring of a head at long distance takes experience and cool appraisal. "Broomed" tips will effect the final score. These result from a ram rubbing and breaking off the tips of his horns, probably to keep the horns from blocking his side vision. Some horns, of course, are broken at the tips from fighting, and if the two are uneven in length, the final score suffers. Records or not, there are hunters who actually prefer chipped and broomed trophies.

These things are deliberately considered by the hunter at long range, but he may surprise rams suddenly as he rounds a boulder or tops a ridge, and he hopes to see all of these things somehow while unslinging a rifle and taking aim to the tune of thumping hooves and clattering rocks.

The wild sheep of the world live in a curving belt, 15,000 miles long, of almost continuous high country. One end of the belt is in western Mexico; the other stops at the Mediterranean, and 4,500 miles of the belt follow the western mountains of North America. A chosen few sportsmen have hunted almost its entire length.

All of the true wild sheep are in the northern hemisphere and their habits are strikingly similar, although their habitat ranges from the desert to the Arctic. Although they differ in appearance and are divided into several families and dozens of scientific classifications, all of the rams have curving horns. Another thing they have in common is that hunting them requires effort.

The sheep belt sweeps northward from the Mediterranean, crosses Asia, is broken by the Bering Strait, continues through western Canada and the United States, turns southward and ends some-

Good Dall ram and younger companion (opposite) stand on steep slope—which they can ascend at top speed if necessary. Hunters (left) on trail of Dalls wear white camouflage. Wolves (below) supported by snow surface can catch prey unobtainable at other seasons.

46

Flock of young bighorns and their mothers in light spring pelage climb shale rock and grass of mountain home. Ewe (above) nurses young but agile lamb. Trophy rams usually are higher up at this time of year. Hunters must spend considerable effort glassing sheep country before deciding strategy of stalk to bring them within shooting range.

where in scorched, crumbling mountains near the Gulf of California. For trophy records, North American sheep are now recognized in four groups, rather sharply divided geographically. They are the Dall, the Stone, the Rocky Mountain bighorn, and the desert bighorn.

It is believed that American sheep came from Asia, crossing a land bridge to Alaska and working southward in the course of time. Sheep are not great travelers, drifting only very slowly over a span of hundreds of generations. Probably distribution was accomplished through the movements of glaciers that crowded animals from their ranges, then receded unevenly, allowing new population shifts. Although the record book recognizes four varieties of American sheep, there are only two species. *Ovis dalli* includes both the Dalls and Stones of Alaska and Canada, and *Ovis canadensis* includes the Rocky Mountain bighorn and the desert bighorn. There are many subspecies but they are not recognized separately in the records.

The Alaska Dall is white the year around, but his nearest relative, the Stone, which operates a little to the south, is known as a black sheep (despite wide color variations). The bighorns of the northern Rockies are mostly brown, as are the desert bighorns of the south. It is likely that the brown bighorns came first, driven southward by glaciers, and some of them may have then followed the receding ice back northward. The Dalls are believed to be more recent arrivals.

The "true" Dalls are white with yellowish horns which tend to be long and slender. In the southern part of their range, they merge with the somewhat larger Stones. Where the ranges overlap, there is obvious interbreeding, for residents of that sector appear in a wide variety of colors from near-white to a blue-black. For some time, part of the animals along this dividing line were called Fannins, but that designation has been abandoned except as a color phase. Zoologists think the interbreeding has been relatively recent,

since the white remains pure in northern Dall country, and the dark Stone characteristics are less diluted in the southern part of Stone range. The indistinct dividing line between Dalls and Stones runs through the northern Yukon.

One subspecies of Dall lives only on the Kenai Peninsula of Alaska. It has never shown a tendency to spread to the mainland, even when its way was not barred by Anchorage and its environs. The Kenai sheep are somewhat smaller than their neighbors and the horns curl a little closer to the head.

Other hunting may be relaxing, engrossing, or highly exciting; sheep hunting becomes a passion, pursued to the ragged edge of human endurance. Many an expensive sheep expedition, planned for leisure and comfort, ends with the hunters gaunt, grave, and fumble-tongued; not because conditions demanded hardship, but because the desire for a certain ram has driven them to days and nights of man-killing labor. In seeking Asiatic sheep, hunters have crossed hostile lands and even endured capture and torture.

When a man has killed a big ram, he may expect telephone calls from total strangers thousands of miles away. Hunters accept him immediately as a member of the world-wide fellowship, and within seconds he will find himself chattering away without reserve to a man he doesn't know and will never see. Their only bond will be the wild sheep.

Forty is the finest age of the sheep hunter. In his twenties and thirties he chases sheep, pursues them in the knowledge that the ram which eludes him today will have a bigger head next year. But at forty he begins to plan around his physical strength. Still able to scale the slopes, although more slowly, he now feels more sharply the beauty of the high places and recognizes that he cannot have it forever. In his fifties he looks up at the far peaks, smells his camp's wood fire, and thinks long of the tilted grass slopes and the thread-trails of sheep hooves on the high, clean ridges. He knows that though these pleasures may still be savored, they are now to be rationed, and his quota dwindles as the years advance. He weighs his accomplishments against his ambitions, and often decides that he still has work to do.

It was in the area of the Muskwa and Prophet rivers in northern British Columbia, that L. S. Chadwick collected the top Stone sheep head of all time in 1936, with both horns more than fifty inches long. Many other heads from that sector have reached the Boone and Crockett record book. I have been to the Muskwa-Prophet country for a big ram. It is a country where hunting requires some effort and where government-allotted guide areas offer considerable protection to trophies. The horses were located at a base camp where they lived the year around. By the end of winter their manes are rubbed off from the grubbing they've done under tree branches where the snow was not so deep. They were bush horses, born and reared in the back country. They treated a moose as an annoying competitor for food and they only glanced toward a rising ruffed grouse or a curious caribou.

After several days of cool and clear weather, just right for sheep hunting, an early snow changed everything. Until the snow we had sighted sheep almost hourly, but the fall, even after it slackened to small scattered flakes, deprived us of a full day's hunting. Nothing in the mountains seemed to move and all game tracks were covered. But that is the story on the day it snows. The next day the whole wild world may be busy in a rush to feed after fasting through the storm. Within two days the mountains had returned to fall colors, although most of the leaves had fallen from the aspens on lower slopes. Shallow drifts of new snow mingled with crusts of the year before in some shaded gullies.

We climbed to a high ridge for a great black ram sighted from camp and my guide, Blair MacDougall, and I found ourselves where the sheep trails crisscrossed the upper ridge. Where there was a steep slope they were so narrow it was uncomfortable to fit a boot sole into them. Individual tracks were almost like those of whitetail deer, but less rounded. There were dozens of pockets and knolls, ideal for sheep residence. Once we saw a small ram moving far ahead of us on a shoulder of the ridge—a bad sign, for the youngster had seen us and our quarry might have done the same and escaped long ago.

The wind was in our favor, but a sheep's eyes are the equal of a man's aided by powerful binoculars. We went as silently as possible. I walked just a little to the left of the ridge's peak, and MacDougall stayed well on top, hoping to make a find far enough ahead so that we could plan a stalk. He was careful to stay even with me; many a trophy ram has fled successfully when an over-eager guide appeared on the skyline while a hunter plodded upward from behind him.

The ram, aroused from his bed in a little basin, saw MacDougall first and had started flight when he saw me far to one side. He then made a sudden stop, a leaping turn, and headed at top speed on a rocky, familiar trail around a bulge of the ridge. I hit him as he stopped and again as he struck his escape route, and he slid, headlong, downhill for thirty yards, coming to a stop on a small half-bench. There was a tinkle of pebbles going over a small drop-off, then everything was very still. The sun gleamed on the glossy black body and the heavy, corrugated horns. Sheep hunting is a very emotional business and no one said anything for several seconds. It had been a long, hard hunt.

When we left the mountains in early October, the aspen leaves were gone, and on Thanksgiving Day I went back to Fort St. John to receive the guide association's trophy for the largest Stone ram of the year. It was thirty below zero on the Alaska Highway and colder in the mountains. Snow was heavy and I hoped the sheep were faring well along the nameless ridge.

4.
The bulky but capable moose wades the shoreline shallows of northern lakes, not far from the wilderness haunts of bear.

In a northern lake he is a great black form near shore, so large that the hunter does not instantly recognize him as game. He stands with his head submerged for minutes at a time, his enormous muzzle grubbing for choice pieces of bottom growth, especially roots. When finally he needs air he lifts his big, palmated antlers, festooned with lily pads, roots, and stems, and streaming gallons of cool lake water, and looks arrogantly about—a giant left over from a day of giants and almost out of scale with his surroundings.

His immensity is frightening at close range, but he can also be a bumbling clown, given to quixotic attacks on railway locomotives and bulldozers. His death in such charges prompts newspaper reporters to write semicomic paragraphs, but those who have seen him coming in anger reserve a bit of awe for his brute power and malevolent purpose. Bull moose are funny only at long range.

In the lakes of the Northeast, moose hunting is traditionally undertaken from a canoe moved silently through the inshore shallows where slough edges slip upward to conifer forests. The hunter may be tempted to move farther out, so he can watch a longer shoreline, but he knows he must stay near shore for better camouflage as he slides upwind. This tactic works best in warm weather when moose seek to thwart the flies of early autumn by standing in five feet of water. When the flies go, they may retire to shallower ponds and bogs, but generally they are near water in one form or another, and willing to wallow if they cannot wade or swim.

North-woods guides having scant faith in their clients' marksmanship sometimes paddle so close to a shoreline moose that the hunter wishes he could fire from the rear seat instead of the forward one. The paddler moves the boat when the moose's head is down and holds still when it is up. The moose has indifferent eyesight and may not see the canoe when the occupants are quiet, although his donkey-like ears will catch the slightest sound. Probably the tales of wounded moose climbing into canoes are a result of overdoing the stalk, the last thrust of the paddle being a little too strong, and the sportsman finding himself at bayonet range just as the monster's head comes up.

Only four states now have moose seasons. Alaska is the home of the largest beasts of all, and they still are in good supply. Idaho, Montana, and Wyoming have seasons, but the hunter must draw for a permit. Moose hunting extends across Canada from east to west. In Maine the population is now too low to permit hunting. Hunting pressure is generally blamed for the moose's recession. Because his size makes him visible at great distances he is especially vulnerable to the modern scope-sighted rifle, and long-range crippling by inept riflemen has helped reduce numbers.

The moose has one unusual defense. Although prized as a meat animal for centuries, he is so heavy that he becomes a monumental problem when killed far from civilization. The canoe may be a solution, but many a hunter pauses in apprehension when he finds he has collected almost a ton of moose, possibly sunk in several feet of cold water, far from a road, and more than a load for three packhorses even when dressed out and butchered.

The largest of the American moose is the subspecies found in Alaska and in northwestern Canada and known simply as the Alaskan moose. The smaller Shiras moose is located in western Wyoming and parts of Idaho and Montana. The Northwestern moose is in the north central United States and central Canada. The Northeastern moose is in New England and eastern Canada. Except for size and minor color variations, all are similar in appearance.

Moose do not gather in herds and the rutting bulls do not collect harems, but attend one cow at a time. A single cow is sometimes followed by several suitors, the biggest generally nearest to her and others trailing in order of their size and fighting abilities. The scene of a toe-to-toe bull moose battle will be ripped and gouged, the turf

Opening pages: Largest member
of the deer family, the moose may reach
almost eight feet at the shoulder.
He is ungainly, but hunters who encounter
him invariably come away impressed.

ploughed by skidding hooves, and although combatants are seldom killed, their intent is destruction. Only retreat will save a loser from death. Big bulls are not satisfied with mere shoving and butting contests, but fence with grunting passion, seeking a killing thrust from the side. Once defeated, an old bull often prowls the wilderness looking for another match; he seldom retires completely as long as he is able to charge.

In mountain country the old burns are top choice for moose hunting, especially near creeks or mountainside springs. In such a burn I once found unmistakable moose sign in early evening, the droppings larger than those of elk. There were numerous mule deer tracks in the neighborhood, as well as those of a small black bear. I found the first large prints in a patch of soppy snow. They looked like moose, but I studied them to make sure they were not elk. The difference is obvious on firm ground or in textbook sketches, but in snow even a wapiti's rounded toes may make a spread pattern. I have seen sweaty hunters eagerly track a yearling moose, sure they were onto elk.

On the burn the old logs were not yet rotted away, and mosses grew on their shaded parts. A few young conifers and mountain maples, well rooted, had reached three or four feet in height. There was the beginning of an aspen grove, and in several places there were mountain seeps, hummocks of sedge marking boggy spots that would be the favored hangouts of high-country moose. Finally I saw the game, bigger than I had expected, of course, but carrying small antlers. He was slipping through a patch of willows, moving quietly until he realized he had been sighted. Immediately he forgot his caution and trotted off with long strides, smashing against old down timber, throwing mud and striking his shins so hard against the logs that I winced. I watched him for a quarter mile and listened to him going much farther, no longer a crafty woods traveler, but a scrambling fugitive who had abandoned caution.

Encounters with the moose are likely to be various, for he has many moods. Sometimes he becomes so familiar with man that he is a nuisance. Sometimes he is completely unafraid in wilderness country during rutting season. Sometimes he is no more than a grotesque shadow in heavy timber, fitting five feet of antlers through openings that appear too small, and picking his way with his big, splayed hooves almost as silently as a deer a fraction of his size. The first impression of awkwardness never quite disappears, but his five-foot legs put him through heavy snows and up to browse a deer cannot touch, and his big feet are remarkably sure in bogs. Long after deer are yarded up, the moose go where they please; it takes three feet of snow to seriously handicap their travel.

In the far North the moose's principal enemy is the wolf, especially in deep-crusted snow that breaks under the moose's weight but supports that of the pack members. Wolves will attack any moose that is helplessly mired, but at other times their kills are nearly always young, sick, or old animals. An aggressive dog can sometimes drive away a full-grown moose, probably because of its innate respect for wolves.

To "call," or challenge, a completely wild bull at the height of the rut takes no artistry with a birchbark instrument. Almost any low-pitched grunt will do, although moose that have had contact with hunters are much harder to fool. A responding bull may come very slowly and cautiously with little sound, or he may come in a headlong charge. Calling takes two forms. The caller can imitate a trouble-hunting bull, or attempt the whines and gurgles of a lovesick cow. In the wilderness, cows will sometimes come to an imitation of a bull. The cow is seldom aggressive unless she feels her calf is in danger.

A guide, experienced in moose calling, took me to a mineral lick for a Canadian moose ambush. He had not been there for years, yet was somehow able to remember the way along a

Bull feeding in stream
(opposite) is surrounded by
typical moose country.
Since moose spend most time
near water (1), hunters
frequently make approach by
canoe (2). Bark stripped
by moose (3). Fine example of
palmate antlers (4). Wolf
(5) is wintertime enemy.

Moose tracks in snow (above) are often confused with elk's. Calf (right) learns to forage for underwater vegetation. Inevitable problem in hunting moose is packing out (far right). Antlers and cape alone are full load for Rockies packhorse.

game trail marked with a few blazes. We left our horses a quarter mile from the lick and walked in water-filled trails through willow and alder thickets. The paths were well used, probably by caribou as well as moose, but the coarser signs were all we could make out as it was almost sundown and gloom was gathering in the valley. There were trees scarred by antlers, some of the gouging fresh, branches almost stripped; and there were saplings ridden down for browsing convenience. When he browses from a large branch or hauled-down sapling, the moose can take the entire stem in his mouth as if about to bite it in two, then make a wide sweep with his head, stripping away a bundle of twigs and leaves. He catches them at one side of his rubbery lips and secures the gigantic bite with an agile tongue, not losing so much as a single leaf. Branches he has stripped may be at unbelievable height once they have straightened out again.

We stopped frequently to listen because our boots made a gentle sloshing in the water, and we finally heard a shredding, sawing sound that faded into a series of squeaks. The guide turned toward me, put his hands up beside his ears as mock antlers and grinningly tipped his head from side to side, imitating a blustering bull polishing his weapons. The sound was so close that it was a relief when the brush-hemmed water trail opened into a little flat thirty feet across, rimmed by alders and a few evergreens.

We were facing the west and the water, which had appeared black until then, reflected the sky. The water was only six inches deep, but almost unbroken by vegetation. We stood still for a few moments and heard the bull giving his antlers another trial against an unseen tree. The guide gave a guttural grunt and the antler-polishing stopped abruptly. A second grunt brought an answer and the quick, ripping sound of a bull savaging a sapling in a rage. Then there was a rustling and another grunt from a different angle. I stared into the poorly lighted alder jungle,

but made out nothing until a bull's head silently appeared in startling silhouette, high above the area I was watching, towering ten feet and appearing higher, too close for shooting with a scope-sighted rifle although I half-aimed involuntarily.

"Don't shoot. No good!" hissed the guide.

The great head disappeared, the forest was silent, and we walked out of the swamp in near darkness. The antler palms had been too narrow for a trophy, the guide explained.

When the rut has ended the bulls lose their gullibility, and hunting may require the utmost caution.

In winter many of the moose's wallows are covered with snow and some of his favorite streams and lakes are frozen, so he partially changes his diet. He still prefers willows, dogwoods, sedges, and other streamside forage, but he increases his consumption of birch, maple, mountain ash, and the conifers, including fir and balsam.

Accustomed to trout-stream views of valley moose, many hunters in mountainous country are reluctant to believe the moose's fall range may overlap that of the bighorn sheep. I remember a long, hard day's ride into the high Rockies that found four of us near the end of the line. An early snow had brought drifts across the skimpy game trails we rode, and we hesitated to attempt a shallow pass ahead of us before turning back toward camp.

Glassing a steep slope we saw a band of bighorns traveling fast along a ridge, perhaps driven by other hunters miles away. Of the four sheep, one was a big ram, and they ran along what I had thought was a crack in the face of an almost vertical cliff, slanting toward us, only a little out of desperation rifle range. It appeared they were headed for a cul-de-sac, for the ridge ended in a rocky point. That is where they stopped, all but the big ram out of sight, and he watching us without movement, partly hidden by a boulder, but with his head and forequarters

Mountain meadows, marshy ground, and quiet pools (1) mean moose and bear habitat to wilderness hunters. Alaska brown bear portrait (opposite) shows wide brow and broad muzzle of largest bear species. Grizzly (2) is much larger than black (5) and distinguished by shoulder hump. Businesslike claws mark grizzly print (3), black-bear paw (4), and gouges in "bear tree" (a territorial warning).

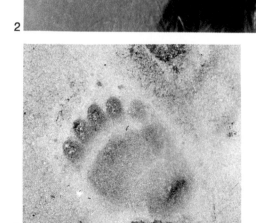

in easy view of the spotting scope.

The ram was still out of range, high above us, and we made a dozen foolish plans for surrounding him. But the slope was icy and impossible to mount without climbing equipment, so we stared back at the big ram for a few minutes, caught our breath, and gave up.

When we turned to go back down the mountain, I sighted the largest Shiras moose I have ever seen, walking through a geological formation of protected pockets and scanty tree growth, and within easy range. When we stopped to consider that none of us had a moose permit, he broke into a trot and went higher, along rimrock where snow was blown away and past a few scrubby whitebark pines that twisted into the sky. He apparently intended to go over the top to another watershed.

Since then I have found bighorn sheep and moose together in my binocular field several times, the sheep grazing on a steep pasture, the moose stripping willows a short distance away.

In nearly all moose range, the moose and the black bear are neighbors with many of the same requirements as to terrain, although they do not compete for food. Especially in the Northeast, hunts frequently are conducted for both animals at the same time. The bear may have casual designs on newborn moose calves, as might the bobcat, puma, or even a coyote, but the predation is nominal.

The black bear (one tribe, though its wide variety of colors has led to numerous descriptive names) is a vegetarian who varies his diet with occasional carrion, rodents, beetles, or honey. For the most part he is a shy comedian; yet his temperament is unreliable. Even half-tamed he is a dangerous playmate. This has been proved repeatedly in public parks, long lists of bear attacks appearing each year. Stern warnings by officials do not deter park visitors from closely approaching, feeding, even teasing the unpredictable bears.

Some hunters confuse the relatively unaggressive black with the grizzly, a completely different fellow, and get a thrill from surrounding the black bear with an aura of imagined ferocity.

Although blacks do not associate with grizzlies and are generally afraid of their larger and more irascible relative, they are found in some of the same regions. In fact, some of the bear sign takes a bit of study, since both species have similar appetites and forage in almost identical habitat. The adult grizzly's tracks are not only larger but display the claw marks much more plainly. Under many circumstances the black's trail shows no claw marks at all. A well-used grizzly route appears as two separate trails, since the feet are set down wide apart.

Both blacks and grizzlies are omnivorous. They will dig for small rodents and dismantle rotten logs for grubs. Larger excavations generally indicate the presence of a grizzly, and an adult will tear up much of a mountainside to unearth a ground squirrel or marmot. The blacks love blueberries and wild cherries, dote on apples and grapes, and consistently dine on acorns and beechnuts. Both species are frequenters of old burns where rotting logs are especially plentiful. They are likely to appear as dark blobs on mountainsides among thick doghair growths of hardwood saplings and buckbrush. Bears have an extremely acute sense of smell and will travel great distances to carrion. The grizzly is noted for dragging away heavy animals and burying them for future use.

Along the Canadian rivers moose and bears share identical habitat, the moose browsing where the bears find berries and roots. In Alaska, too, moose frequently share their habitat with bears, and there both may attain awesome dimensions. The image of one gigantic wide-antlered Alaskan moose—the embodiment and culmination of a unique life cycle—remains as vivid to me as any sight in the wilderness.

The bull moose was moving slowly toward the river's edge when we saw him. He was old and huge, standing nearly eight feet high at the shoulders, and he had lived his life in the back wilderness. If he had ever seen a man, it had made no impression. The bull had been calved twelve years before, a ridiculous juvenile with very long legs and an immature version of the "bell," the pendant of skin and hair which hangs from the throat and has no discoverable function.

For more than a year he lived with his mother, following her even after he began to carry antlers. These did not acquire the mooselike palms with sharp points until his third year. After that he lived alone, except during the rut and when he yarded with other animals during severe winter weather. In his early maturity he was sometimes chased off ignominiously by bigger bulls. Each year after he shed his antlers the new ones that replaced them were broader and heavier, and one year they spread some sixty inches, for he was a member of the Alaskan race and even six-foot antlers are not unheard of in that company. It must have been in the ninth or tenth year that they grew so large. At that time he won all of his battles during the fevered strife of the rut.

It was in his thirteenth year that the bull began to lose his rutting battles. He charged as before, but not so swiftly, and the great neck took the shock, but gave a little before the onslaught of even slightly smaller bulls. The great frame was still there but not the weight. The middle of rutting season, October in that giant land between the Alaskan Highway and the Pacific, found the old bull gaunt when he should have held some of the fat of his summer feed.

In one of the fights (they must have run together in the beast's brain like one nightmare of red fury), the bull received a long gash on his shoulder, and in another he was speared four times in his taut neck muscles. At some time in the endless tournament he lost an eye.

When he approached the river the day I saw him, he was very thin, but from the side there was little change in his appearance. His shovels measured a little less than those of the sixty-inch

year. The tines had been broken off and their places were marked only by ragged stubs. The long shoulder cut was nearly healed. The four deep thrusts in his neck were festering sores; he had parried the death thrusts at the belly. Now he walked a little stiffly toward a new adversary he had not yet encountered.

Across the river, the four horses were strange silhouettes, and the men on the ground beside them were too small for attention. The old bull's kind has never had keen sight, and he had only one eye now, marked where a glancing thrust had grazed it. He saw the outlines downwind, and was prevented by the river from circling to catch their scent. His wits dulled a little by crashing defeats, the old bull gave a deep grunt and received an answering challenge from near the horses—or were they a group of moose? He heard another grunt over the river's gurgle.

There was no doubt now and the old bull walked into the river, swinging his antlers. The channel was almost four feet deep, but the bull paid little attention to the swift current and he paused only once to look for his adversary on the other side. The men were silent now and unmoving, lumpy outlines on the gravel bar, and as the bull stepped onto the edge of the bar, his front hooves just out of the water, the bullet struck its paralyzing blow measured to 3,000 foot-pounds of energy.

The black hulk went down slowly, hindquarters first, and the great head struck last, then moved only a little, still facing the direction the charge must come from; the antlers finally tipping slightly as one palm fell against the gravel.

I ejected the empty cartridge and could hear only the murmur of the water until the guide remarked it was a good thing we had waited until he was on our side of the river.

Downstream from the big silent form the water turned a dull red, but it was no matter. The bull would never have lived another winter. It was beginning to look a little like snow.

5.
In a subtly differing range of
habitats—from fecund grainfields
to blistered hills at the
desert's edge—prairie birds abound.

The sound is meager and elusive, coming with a gentle breeze. It is a thread of sound, resembling the faint squeak of a wire fence that is moved slightly through its staples by the wind. The moon rises cold and blue as the quick evening chill arrives.

In early morning the Hungarian partridge fed on wide grassy slopes where weed and grass seeds were thick; near midday they rested near the small creeks in familiar spots. Then, as evening approached, they moved off again in the late search for gravel and food.

The soft squeak is the call of a Hun lost from its covey and it is answered by other birds, separated from their friends by hawk or gunner. The birds are scattered over a ridge, somewhere near a fringe of buffalo grass, where a little patch of shale fans down from miniature rimrock outcroppings. Juniper clumps near the crest of the slope are black in the moonlight, more compact in outline than the buffalo berry bushes and the occasional sage.

Scattered birds may be quiet until sundown, but with the approach of darkness they become anxious for companionship. Their calls, somewhat ventriloquial, are hard for a predator to trace, but the birds are not widely separated, for the Hungarian tends to re-use his landing sites. Flushed from a familiar area, the individuals are likely to land again at a predetermined spot, even though they may be widely separated during flight.

In Europe, where a gunner stands in tweeds at a numbered butt and fires at hundreds of driven partridge, the wispy assembly call in evening is never heard by the sportsman. He shoots, but often does not hunt and does not know what becomes of the birds once they have passed the firing point. Hun habits are often surprising to American biologists, who only now are beginning to study them in the home they have made for half a century far from their ancestral fields.

The Hun is larger than the quail, with subdued colors which appear drab in flight. At close range it shows a short rufous tail (a prominent feature when the bird is flying nearby), a chestnut-barred gray breast, a dark, U-shaped blotch on the belly, and a rusty face. Males and females are hard to tell apart.

Perhaps the truest name of the Hun is the "European gray partridge," although it has been especially plentiful on the grainfields of Hungary, where some of the more successful American plantings have originated. The earliest serious attempts to establish the bird in this country were around 1900, some of the more successful occurring in Washington and Oregon, and in Alberta. Since then the Huns have spread through the grainfields, occupied the western sage slopes and even some of the high mountains, and there is no way to tell just which plantings were successful and which failed. But for some reason the birds that take so well to grain and grass in the West have not multiplied in the same latitudes farther east. In several midwestern and eastern states, only remnants are available for hunting, and these behave differently from the traveling ghosts of rimrock and benchland stubble, holding slavishly to small, easily hunted areas.

In northern states where seasons open in September, some of the birds are too young to be real game, for nesting may continue as late as August. A large clutch may contain sixteen olive-colored eggs. In grazing country the nests are frequently about thirty yards from a creek, preferably set on a well-drained slope, usually in a small clump of vegetation. So consistent is the location that an expert student with a careful dog can sometimes find a large percentage of the nests, even in vast rolling pastures that seem to offer a variety of attractive nesting sites. As the season opens, adults are easily distinguished from birds of the year; and since the early covey is generally a family group, the remaining birds are likely to become flustered if the adults fall. Youngsters often scatter and hold tightly, in contradiction to the Hun's reputation for flushing wildly.

There are, of course, Hun coveys that fly when shooters are hundreds of yards away, but veteran hunters believe the average flush is near fifteen yards from the gun—about the distance of the standard trapshooting rise. The Hun is very likely to swing near the shooters, even after a fairly wild flush.

Hard-pressed, a tired and frightened covey may plunge into thick cover, but for the most part the birds prefer lighter stuff, and even when resting near shade and water at midday they are likely to be at the edge of brush rather than in it. At midday they are likely to be in narrow ravines. When flushed near the bottom of a draw the birds often fly to their feeding grounds, no matter what the time of day.

It is often said that the Hun simply will not hold, but a given covey may flush wild and out of range several times, then hold for a close rise; it may even scatter to give shooting at singles. More likely than not, the fourth or fifth flush will bring them near the original starting point, the series of flights taking a circular route. The straggler is regularly encountered among Huns. Sometimes it fails to go with the covey, sometimes it drops out in midflight, and sometimes it simply walks away from the whole business.

It is on the ground that the Hun is most baffling. A full covey of fifteen birds may flush wild when frightened and sail over a knob. Thirty minutes later they may have walked back to their starting point by a circuitous route. Occasionally they make an identical flight when startled the second time.

Large, compact, well-marked coveys can fly into scantily grassed hillsides and disappear. The Hun has a habit of alighting near the top of a grassy hill, walking unseen over the brow, and then stopping high on the opposite slope, concealed in cover that seems far too sparse for so large a bird. Sometimes they will deliberately separate and walk back toward the spot from which they originally flushed, slipping past whatever may be following them.

This happens most often in sage and thick grass, where a partridge can easily sneak along the ground without being seen. In wheat or barley stubble, the Hun easily walks faster than a man, traveling with its head as low as necessary to remain unnoticed by a pursuer. Sudden appearance of an enemy will sometimes cause birds to freeze in stubble and some pointing dogs accomplish this if they crash-stop on catching body scent. Ground-trailing is less likely to hold the birds from flight since the dog goes more slowly. A covey that is headed off while running may squat in confusion.

A flushing covey often jumps almost straight up in whirring, chirping haste, heads turned to inspect the enemy as they slant to one side. Then the group bends suddenly as if in response to a single control. They drive briefly in their chosen direction, set their wings and glide. The sound is much like that of a flushing ruffed grouse, but multiplied by fifteen.

It is the hardiness of the Hun that has kept it thriving far north of the Canadian border; coveys have been known to select patches of snow for resting when dry ground was only a few yards away. Their enemies include several of the hawks and the golden eagle, as well as the coyote and fox. A hawk, patiently circling over a field, may be hunting almost any kind of small prey, but the field is likely to contain a Hun covey. A sharpshin will drive a flock from the air and into confused landings in willow bottoms or juniper clumps. A strangely scattered covey may be the result of a pair of coyotes systematically searching the partridges' hillside range, with occasional side trips for mice.

In early fall of a good year, the typical Hun covey will have ten to sixteen birds, a family group, but coveys are likely to combine later, going their separate ways only if hard pressed. At such times, families head for familiar refuges.

1

Habitat: Hungarian partridge feeds in wheat stubble (1)—and tunnels into it for safety (3)—but also favors rocky, sparsely covered slopes (2), a choice which surprised biologists when bird was introduced to U.S. Hardy ring-necked pheasant (4) sometimes displaces native birds on own range. Right: Abandoned, weed-grown homesteads are haunts of Huns and sharp-tailed grouse.

2

3

4

The Hun huddles, completely covered by snow in severe weather and during heavy storms, and an entire covey will plunge into a drift when frightened. A few moments later heads emerge to inspect the intruder and the birds can take off with their usual speed, unhampered by the snow as they beat with fast, rounded wings. They can roost in snow, but in mild weather they prefer sheltered, grassy areas. The abandoned roosting spot is marked by a patch of droppings nine to twelve inches across, located on the ground in grass or weeds.

At times the Hun seems to prefer the mountain cold to the valley feeding grounds, even in late fall. The evening feeding period during one peak-cycle year found flocks gliding down for two thousand feet to alight in wheat stubble. Called "displaced populations" by biologists, numerous bevies have been found at eight thousand feet, four thousand feet above the nearest valley. Those birds appeared to be satisfied with mountain grass seeds, while some Hun authorities stubbornly insisted they were birds of the grainfields.

The Hungarian partridge is a usurper on the plains, as are the Asiatic chukar and pheasant. There are still those who recall the heath hen, now extinct because the species was unable to live with agriculture and repeating shotguns, and it is a step into the past to hear a contemporary tell of the heath hen and its vanished race. It was the eastern version of the prairie chicken.

Huns and sharp-tailed grouse often live in the same habitat, although the sharp-tails make more use of trees and are more nomadic. The diets are almost the same. The chukar cares less for grain and water, although it will live with Huns and sharp-tails in a few locations—if it has rugged canyons nearby. Its beloved cheatgrass is a sign of overgrazing or impoverished soil.

The ring-necked pheasant is sometimes a neighbor of these species, following brushy creeks up into chukar country. In some places it has displaced the few surviving native prairie birds;

many believe it to be a more desirable game. It is true that the evil-tempered Chinese cock will chase a grouse from its range occasionally, but the over-all replacement is largely a matter of habitat, the pheasant accepting partitioned farmland and brush bottoms that defeat native birds.

The true prairie chicken, or pinnated grouse (*Tympanuchus cupido*), very nearly followed the heath hen but has been saved in scattered colonies, and is subject to hunting now in Nebraska, South Dakota, Oklahoma, Kansas, and Texas. It is the same bird that flushed in rolling waves ahead of market hunters and sportsmen until the world of grass was turned by the plow. Then it adapted to the grainfields, but the pressures of civilization almost destroyed it. At present, the longest seasons are in Nebraska, South Dakota, and some parts of Canada.

A more adaptable relative, the sharp-tailed grouse (*Pedioecetes phasianellus*), is holding on, perhaps increasing in some areas, although not so plentiful as some years ago. It is near the size of the true prairie chicken and carries that name (or sometimes "pintail") in most of its range. A quickly noted difference is that the true prairie chicken has a barred breast while the sharp-tail's is flecked. The sharp-tail will roost in trees and will take advantage of heavy cover, although the dozen or so olive brown eggs are laid in a ground nest. In flight the short, pointed tail shows considerable white. Like the true prairie chicken and the sage hen, the sharp-tail conducts a ceremonious mating dance. This plains species prospers sufficiently on farm and ranch land, so that a dozen states have open seasons.

On the Canadian prairies, sharp-tail range is interrupted by abandoned farmhouses, standing among stark skeletons of old farm machinery. Each implement stands in its patch of weeds and bushes, some undisturbed for half a century. Even where only twisted remains of buildings still stand, most of the shelterbelts have prospered. Rows of trees and bushes at each abandoned

Worried prairie chicken, or pinnated grouse, (left) calls to rest of flock. Near extinction at one time, bird is now subject to limited hunting. Hungarian partridge (below) was imported from Europe, has adapted successfully to western U.S. and Canada.

home still hold off the prairie blizzards, and provide valuable protection for game although no longer needed by homesteaders. At dawn the sandhill cranes pass in noisy, weaving lines, along with Canada geese.

In early October of a mild fall, the sharp-tailed grouse (the natives call them "chickens") follow a warm-weather pattern. In early morning they feed, either in stubble fields or among the rosebushes. They are partial to snowberry, silverberry, buckbrush, and rose.

A perfect spot for sharp-tail is a broken area of bushes, thick enough for secure cover in some places and interspersed with open patches of grass. In warm days of early fall, any movement will set up a sprinkle of grasshoppers. Near midday the birds fly to shady spots to rest until cool evening, their crops filled with rose hips,

*Prairie hunters (1)
move carefully around
dilapidated farm. Birds
are there, but ground
cover makes them hard to
see and to flush.
Sharp-tail (2) has broken
cover and skims away
in low-level flight. He
will not be easily
hit. On strutting ground
(3), sharp-tail performs
one of nature's more
spectacular shows.
Pronghorns (4) are curious
about sharp-tail hunter
patrolling their range.
After big-game season
opens, they will be warier
and inclined to flee
at sight of intruders.*

Vista: The rolling hills of the Great Plains (5) support many species of upland game birds. Hunter may work them with or without dogs. Food: Crested wheat grass (6), juniper berries (7), rose hips (8) are common bird fare in season. Dense and tangled juniper bushes also provide emergency cover for many creatures. Coyote (9) crosses bare wash. Remorselessly hunted, it actually is an ally in battle against rodents and rabbits. Its predation on game birds is slight.

5

7

8

9

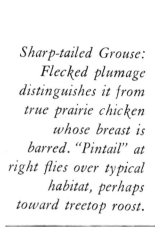

Sharp-tailed Grouse: Flecked plumage distinguishes it from true prairie chicken whose breast is barred. "Pintail" at right flies over typical habitat, perhaps toward treetop roost.

berries, seeds, and hoppers. Other sharp-tails feed in the open stubble, easily seen but difficult to approach as each covey is marked by at least two or three stretching necks and observant eyes.

In early morning or late evening, birds may be approached by walking through the clinging rosebushes and surprising them in small open areas surrounded by three-foot growth which masks a man's approach. On such flushes a cluster of sharp-tails will leave in a steep climb, their wings muttering into the wind, and the birds giving their monotone *cuk, cuk, cuk*. When a covey has leveled its course, thirty feet in the air, a straggler may drive off only three feet from the ground, swinging between bushes for fifty yards before climbing.

In the morning chill, coyotes drift between rosebush clumps and both whitetail and mule deer slip from the bottoms at any disturbance. Ducks are thick on the small potholes. A prairie falcon, certainly not noted as a duck hawk, will sometimes menace a scaup that changes waterholes.

In summer when young sharp-tailed grouse lie perfectly for a dog, Saskatchewan, Manitoba, and Alberta become favorite locations for southern dog trainers. But when the birds mature they tend to flush wild, and when the training season ends in September the trainers and their trucks of dogs head back for bobwhite quail cover.

During early morning, the birds generally flush at long range—or out of range—but as the day warms they move to the tiny aspen-poplar groves that dot the region. There might be only a dozen trees, but they are surrounded by a ring of brush much higher than that found farther from moisture. If the water has dried up, the ground within the circle of bushes will be bare and a flock of birds might be seen resting in the shade. Or, arriving by air, they might flutter down on the bare area and walk into the thick brush.

The approach is not simple and one gunner should stay well in the open while the other squirms through the brushy perimeter. In such areas a dog is confused by the operation and of little help. When the birds fly, it is likely that either the "inside" or the "outside" gunner will have a chance.

There is no land quite like the Canadian prairies; it should be hospitable to sharp-tailed grouse for years to come.

From the other side of the world, Asia's chukar came to America, scorned the proffered grainfields of the Midwest, faded from the humid cover of the Southeast, and accepted the cheatgrass hills and the blistered, jagged canyons of the near-deserts, prospering in a land that man finds uncongenial.

Such a ground is eastern Oregon, except for a few fertile valleys where grain, sugar beets, potatoes, and cattle provide pretty farms and busy towns.

The chukar has been entrenched in the United States only since the early nineteen-fifties and its dispersion through the arid West has been gratifying to game managers who observed the failures of a long series of exotic introductions, brightened only by records of the ring-necked pheasant and the tenacious little Hun.

Although the chukar prefers even more remote range than the Hungarian, it is, paradoxically, more easily reared in captivity and has been a favorite of game-preserve managers, behaving much like bobwhite quail in put-and-take operations. Hopefully released on midwestern farmlands, the bird appeared lost and reluctant to fly. It was the upended arid land of talus slopes, sheer cliffs, searing heat, and whistling storms that it finally chose.

The chukar lays eight to fifteen buffy, spotted eggs under a bush in a small hollow. Coveys are not restricted to family groups and become very large in the fall. Considerably larger than the Hun, the chukar has the silhouette of an outsized bobwhite quail. It has bright red legs and bill. Its sides are sharply barred, and the back is gray with considerable iridescence.

Chukar hunters (1) cover a
desert flat in eastern Oregon.
Bird prefers cheatgrass
hills and rugged canyons to lush
midwestern grainfields.
Scrambling pursuit (2) leads
through wash; hunters hope
to head off game, which
always "runs up." Chukar (3)
sometimes shares range
with valley quail (4). Rabbit
brush and sage (5) are
principal plants to be found
in chukar territory.

5

In dry weather, chukars are likely to be in a narrow Oregon canyon where a bumpy and sometimes faint trail follows the course of a tiny stream. Most of the creek bed is dry, the rounded stones providing the smoothest part of the immediate landscape. There are a few willows, and in a few places there may be tiny ponds, no more than two or three feet across. Chukars may rest among scattered clumps of sage and weeds along the route, but also group on the borders of the little bowls of water. A single plain track at the edge of one puddle where higher water has produced a patch of mud is strong indication of a regular watering spot. The bird's mark is almost as large as a pheasant's.

A disturbed flock will move from the stream bed proper and take to the gentle slopes that lead up to the vertical cliffs of reddish rock. The slopes will be patched with sage and weeds, but there are open places where there is little or no dry grass, a hot, midday sun glancing off varicolored pebbles and boulders. Chukars on a slope show as a series of flickering shadows that silently leave one sage clump and cross to another a little higher up. It is the shadows that are visible, dark against the crisp grass, for the chukar's gray-and-tan back fits the colors of sage and ground. The shadows move swiftly and unheard, always upward, for the chukar has a rule—run up and fly down. Once started up, it seldom takes to the air until the canyon wall is scaled.

When the covey stops on the upper cliffs, a single partridge stands atop a great boulder like a uniformed guardsman in a striped tunic and iridescent gray coat. The sentinel watches the toiling hunter and his wide-eyed dog, and as they approach he squats slightly in preparation for flight. Beside the boulder on the canyon's edge there is a shallow dip filled with sage and grass, and the hunter hopes there are unseen birds present, relying on the single watcher to warn them.

So he charges at top speed, feeling foolish as he runs, and the dog goes with him, pointing instincts forgotten and off for a lark of whirring birds and wild shooting. The sentry plunges over the canyon wall, driving hard until halfway down, and then swerving in a sloping glide to go a quarter mile down the canyon; several other chukars follow, making a little clucking noise as they go. More birds roar from the little sage swale. The hunter's best chance is with the laggards.

On an October night there is a gentle rain on the desert, hardly enough to be measured but enough to change the entire picture of chukar hunting. The tactics for the next day must be revised. The higher mountains have a patchy layer of snow and there is enough moisture for thousands of little rock indentations to have collected tiny pools. There is no need for the birds to go near the creek beds. The hunter trudges on higher ground and through wider valleys, some of them floored with alkali flats growing greasewood. Always there is the big sage, in some places living up to its name by standing higher than a man's head.

The land is nearly desert but it teems with life, and another chukar hunter, the golden eagle, feels for thermal drafts over the canyons. Sometimes he can catch a chukar, but the hunter has seen him in ignominious failure, plummeting at a covey only to miss his target and land in the sage, a great, disheveled wad of feathers and frustration, while the partridges duck and scurry to a safer place.

There are plentiful mule deer, generally sighted as they bounce from the heads of draws, but occasionally surprised on the sides of steep canyons. On an earlier trip the hunter, walking upwind, nearly stepped on a bedded muley; it leaped down the steep canyon wall in its fright, losing its footing and rolling and sliding almost to the bottom before it could recover. There are pronghorns in chukar country, and California valley quail, which may appear as a surprise on a sage flat or in thick cover along the creeks. The male California quail has a forward-turned feather plume on the top of his head. He has a black face, is about the size of a large bobwhite, and his belly has sharply outlined feathers reminiscent of the scaled quail. Otherwise he looks much like the Gambel's quail found in southwestern deserts. Even the female with her modified plume and muted colors is a strikingly beautiful bird.

The dog becomes excited and the hunter sees small forms darting among the bushes; the quail's feet move so fast that it appears the body is invisibly suspended but scooting about as if on a track. Thinking he can flush the birds, the hunter rushes at them. Some disappear, but several fly up for two or three feet, only to drop before he can fire. Finally, the covey is thoroughly scattered and the dog is able to point a few close-holding singles that must be literally kicked from the sage.

The chukar hunter knows that their crops are often found to contain mainly cheatgrass seed and sage berries; but those plants are everywhere, and so he looks for other signs. He finds a number of bowl-shaped holes in the shade of a bush, evidently a communal dusting ground, and he is sure when he finds chukar feathers.

Then several flocks fly from more than a hundred yards away, all disappearing into canyons, and he is positive it is a good area. He sees birds on the ground near the head of a draw, standing fairly close together. All of their heads are high and they are obviously watching him, but he approaches them anyway, hoping they may scatter and give his dog a chance. Some of the birds take off out of range and fly down into the draw, but he doubts that all of them have left. His dog agrees, quartering on up toward the top of a round hill. The hunter follows as closely as possible, hoping one of the running birds may fly back over him in observation of the chukar's rule of flying downhill, but they continue to travel unseen and well ahead. Finally he reaches the top of the knob, the dog points, and a single bird flies. The rest have vanished.

But now a new phase in the search for chukar begins. The hunter is among a series of narrow canyons and he knows the flock has scattered, so he stands quietly to take advantage of the chukar's weakness—instant loneliness. The calling begins within five minutes, vague as to distance and direction, but coming from several different birds. Some say that the chukar simply calls its name, *chuk-ar, chuk-ar,* when trying to assemble with other birds. At any rate, the call is like the guinea hen's but much softer.

Some of the calls come from a canyon, about eighty feet deep and edged with eroded rocks like ruined monuments. There are crevices and notches in which the cheatgrass extends down toward the canyon floor. The cheatgrass and sage are supplemented by white stalks of dead mustard weed, and rabbit brush is thick near the canyon's bottom.

He works his dog along the edge of the canyon, staying near the top, going straight toward a persistently calling bird. The calling stops. He knows he is very near, although he could not tell much by the sound. The dog fails to make a find, however, and he is disgusted to hear the calling resume, this time behind him. He has passed the bird and it is calling for its friends again. Then the dog points at the base of a bush, hardly five feet from its nose, and a bird flushes, an easy shot.

He hunts the calling birds for most of the day, and when he can find no more of them he starts in search of a new covey. He works the edge of a bluff over a very deep gorge with a clear river at the bottom, and he can make out ducks on the surface, each the apex of a tiny, shiny V. Then from the other side of a tumble of rock, a flock of chukars whirrs off into space and he cannot locate them until it is too late.

They plunge downward on set wings for hundreds of feet, disappearing in shadows of the canyon. They veer, catching the rays of a low sun on their wings, and go out of sight for good around a precipice a quarter of a mile away. It is too late to follow them, but it has been a good day.

6.

Once the sun is up, the geese
appear—migrants in midpassage,
gabbling and gleaning grain
before the V's beat south again.

Almost a hundred snow geese came as a gently weaving line, formed so that each bird except the leader used the draft of the bird ahead to ease its passage. From time to time, a leader would drop back to allow another mature bird to head the column, the direction of flight unchanged. The geese had flown for many hours, and earlier in the day they had been very high in the proper snow goose pattern, but a storm was building and clouds had forced them lower.

Part of the time they had been in the shape of an irregular V and sometimes it was actually two V's. For brief periods they had flown in a single diagonal line. But through all of these formations the wing beats had been steady, changes made with little commotion.

They traveled about forty miles an hour, air speed, and they had changed altitude several times to take advantage of light winds. Now the worsening weather caused them to be slightly more noisy than usual and their voices were high-pitched, although still musical. At a distance their sounds have been described as bell-like or resembling a gently touched harp, but there is more than a little of the sound of hounds baying far away, as if the coarser tones had been strained out, leaving only the pure bugle notes.

The flight aimed unerringly up a great river toward a mountain pass, but at dusk the narrowing valley filled with heavy gray clouds, ragged streamers reaching almost to the ground, and the view of the earth was broken by blown masses of vapor. Earlier in the day the ground had been a patchwork of yellow stubble fields, sections of alfalfa with the squared dark stacks of baled hay, and wide expanses of pasture specked with livestock. From the birds' height, the highways had been dark streaks. Much of the traffic on them moved faster than the geese. The geese had left Canada and entered the United States early that morning.

Now the route ahead was closing completely. Below the flight, lights came on in a town, and lamp lights near a park lake reflected from tempting flat water. Its illumination diffused and dulled by a fine mist, the entire town appeared as a light area below, its wet streets showing as canals or rivers, and its street lamps confusing to birds that are said to depend partly on stars for their courses.

The pass ahead was narrow, with cliffs on either side, and it was invisible to the snow geese. They made a turn and curved back over the town. An hour after sundown they were still swinging in a three-mile circle and other flocks had joined them, their calls plain above all but the loudest traffic. Their white wings, carrying only tips of black, were visible from below, enough of the town's light being reflected upward to show the lines of birds dimly. With binoculars, individual birds could be picked out easily.

By 10 P.M., the flocks had become more than a thousand birds, circling haphazardly but unwilling to leave the town. Sometimes they formed in lines of hundreds and met at slightly different heights to swing and join and separate again, their wings seemingly tireless.

Snow was falling now on high mountains to either side of the wheeling birds. Late at night there was a small opening in the clouds to the south and the birds changed their calls, steadied their columns, and disappeared through the pass to the south, wing beats slightly faster in a new cadence. Hunters who had been stepping outside every few minutes to hear the confused calling suddenly found no trace of geese. Some gunners scoured the area the following day, but the flight of snows was gone and the most experienced hunters knew that it was not a regular stopping place for them. Hunting was a waste of time. Such episodes occur dozens of times each fall in mountain passes, as waterfowl navigation fails in poor visibility.

Thus far man has had little effect upon the breeding grounds of snow geese and their near relatives, the blue geese, for they spend their summers so far north (above the Arctic Circle) that outland hunters seldom follow them, and civilization thus far has had no need for their bleak land. They have been hunted by Eskimos and Indians through generations, but this has had no great effect on their population.

The lesser snows winter on a strip of California and a portion of the Gulf Coast that includes parts of Texas, Mississippi, Alabama, and Louisiana. The greater snow, a larger bird of almost exactly the same coloration, winters along the eastern U.S. coast. It also comes from afar, and both species do most of their nesting north of Hudson Bay.

Observers say the fall snow goose migration starts as a co-ordinated journey, preceded by an interruption of regular feeding during which the birds retire to rest near saltwater beaches and adjust their feathers for a day or so. Thereafter, with the first favorable wind, they leave en masse. The route goes over brown-green tundra, crosses the rough and conifer-forested lands of northern Canada, then falters over the Canadian grainfields. There, part of the snows, together with other goose species, rest on rivers and lakes and make regular flights to the grainfields until cold weather forces them to continue their migration. It is believed that some snows and blue geese fly nonstop from Hudson Bay to the Gulf of Mexico.

The blue goose, mixing freely with the snows in Louisiana and Texas marshes during the winter, was for many years the most mysterious of all! It was late in the nineteen twenties before the breeding grounds were found on Baffin Island, on Southampton Island in the northern part of Hudson Bay, and on the northern shores of the Northwest Territories. Some authorities believe there is frequent interbreeding of snows and blues.

The common Canada goose nests in northern Canada, but also far down into the United States, as far as southern Utah. Romantic feelings about the great gray goose and his travels might be applied even more appropriately to the blues and snows, but none of them has the stentorian voice and huge silhouette of the common Canada, which averages almost ten pounds in weight and may reach thirteen. The honker traditionally mates for life, but there is evidence that if a mate dies the survivor will find another, and there is some evidence of exceptions to the rule of lifelong partnership.

The common Canadas, fairly typical of the several Canada species, nest as far north as Hudson Bay and Alaska. Their population holds steady because a poor season in part of their enormous nesting range is usually offset by a good season in another section. They are dark, gray-brown geese with glossy black necks and heads except for an oval patch of white on cheek and throat. Young birds have somewhat duller colors than their elders, sometimes flecked with brown, and this difference can be seen by a gunner if the light is very good.

All varieties of Canada geese have legs set well forward, and they are able to walk well on land, where much of their food is grazed or gleaned. They are among the first of the waterfowl to migrate northward, and their nesting occurs from March to June, depending upon the latitude. The five or six white eggs are generally laid in a natural depression with a lining of down and grass, although abandoned nests of other birds are sometimes appropriated. The eggs hatch in twenty-eight to thirty days. Only the goose sits on the eggs. Both gander and goose guard the goslings.

Predators of the youngsters are gulls, hawks, eagles, foxes, coyotes, and pike. One of the greatest losses of young common Canadas occurred in 1961 in the Far North when a booming population of lemmings suddenly disappeared. The fox population, which had grown with that of the lemmings, then turned to the goslings for food.

In the summer the adult birds moult and

82 *Flights of geese (1) may include several species. Blues and snows are frequent traveling companions. Once feeding site (2) is chosen, generations of geese will use it. Hunter's underside view of snow goose (3). Pair of lordly Canadas (4). Snows (5) walk as capably as they swim.*

2

4

5

are unable to fly for a time, remaining well concealed in water growth with their young. Then both young and adult birds are ready to fly southward at about the same time.

There is southerly movement among the geese in early September when hunting seasons open in Canada and Alaska, but the shooter who hunts at this time is generally after resident birds. In southern Alberta we were on a round hill at dawn, a hill our host had used each fall for thirty years. It commanded a view of perhaps two hundred square miles of the prairie country. From his post he could identify all features—the most distant glimmers of water, the row of trees that marked a farmhouse. He knew the locations of old, overgrown shelterbelts, their houses long gone, and now appearing incongruous in otherwise treeless sections. Plainly seen from our hill, such landmarks could be found by road or path only through intimate knowledge, for once we left the hill our perspective was gone.

The prairies were a map, studied by sections with binoculars, almost as if they had been gridded by a mapmaker, and our veteran could give the mileages from this point to that, even though the view was foreshortened by optical magnification.

It was a little chilly that early in the day, but it would be warm later and already the sun's edge showed red on the horizon. It followed the dawn streaks that had silhouetted a few quick wedges of early ducks going to feed. Most geese do not move until the sun is well up, and for a while it appeared that none would be seen.

They arrived first as a dark raveling in the haze, curling lazily quite near the ground, invisible to the naked eye, faint to the binoculars, but close when viewed through a twenty-power spotting scope. Through the scope they seemed close enough that their silence was strange. They had left a river, the host explained, and would not go far to feed since they had not gained much height. He followed them with his glasses as they made one fishhook turn and glided down beyond a low rise. A few minutes later another undulating file appeared, this one giving off tiny flecks of light—a flock of snow geese heading for the same feeding spot. When a third flight had been watched in the same pattern, the veteran said we might as well leave and plan our hunt. He took us for fifteen miles, turning into a country lane that ended with abandoned farm buildings and the inevitable brushy shelterbelt.

We stopped our car and went on afoot for a short distance to where the veteran glassed a rolling section of stubble and plowed ground. The geese were invisible at first, but now and then a head would show above a gentle rise, and the feeding gabble was plainly audible. It was midmorning or later when the geese began to take off in flocks, heading straight to the river for the day's resting. They might dredge a little for mollusks, or prune marsh vegetation, but most of the day would be spent in loafing.

The hunt was planned over coffee at a nearby farmhouse. The farmer who owned the wheatfield that attracted the geese had planned to shoot them himself, but the project evolved into a co-operative one and we dug the three pits that afternoon. The ground was hard from drought, and crowbars were used to cut through. We went deep enough for the pits to conceal sitting men, and the earth from the holes was carefully scattered over the stubble and covered with a few armfuls of loose straw. The dusty ground was densely patterned with the triangular footprints of geese that had moved constantly as they gleaned the field. Our pits were located at the edge of the feeding area rather than in the center, so that we would not be in a section already picked over.

Geese walk as much as they swim. Their beaks, with toothy strainers, are made for dry as well as aquatic forage, and they collect grasses and seeds by snaky reaches and quick, twisting movements of their heads. Their favorite har-

Blue goose (below) has typical grazer's beak, which is more pointed than most ducks'. Brant (right), a small coastal goose, spends little time on land. Bird made remarkable adaptation to other food when eelgrass died out.

vested fields are usually wheat and barley, where they collect waste grain, and they also feed in ripe corn.

From land, their takeoff is made with a short run, and agile gunners who have stalked as far as possible on feeding geese and are still not quite close enough to shoot can gain considerably on the heavy birds by running at them as they slowly gain flying speed. Few geese are killed in that manner in prairie country, however. They generally feed at safe distance from anything that might conceal a man or a coyote.

The goose is most vulnerable just as his broad feet reach for water or land. His flying speed has been killed for the landing and his momentum is downward. The gunner who finds such a bird within easy range has, for the moment, a stationary target, and one which cannot acquire flying speed quickly. Once a goose is actually flying again, however, he is not addicted to the towering habits of some dabbling ducks which ascend at a steep angle, gaining altitude first and horizontal distance second. Instead, a goose will fly off by the quickest route.

In the dusty wheatfield, we dug our pits to take advantage of prevailing morning breezes.

We used hinged pit covers made of chicken wire and pipe, which bulged upward only slightly. Straw was thatched into the wire, so that at a few yards the entire pit would be only a gentle bulge in the stubble. There were gaps in the thatching to permit easy viewing of the surroundings, and the whole concealment could be thrown back instantly at the veteran's command.

The decoys, meticulous inflated birds complete with natural-looking feet, would not be placed until the following dawn. Evening feeding began at five o'clock, and two of us camped at the abandoned farmhouse to watch the reaction to our pits. We lay on the top of the old barn and heard the distant clamor that meant geese were about to leave the river, then watched a series of flocks of Canadas, lesser Canadas, and snow geese weave in ragged lines to the feeding grounds where they fed until dusk, returning then to the river. Only the snow geese had appeared hesitant about landing near the pits and had made repeated low sweeps of the field—although that is a snow goose characteristic, even when no suspicion is involved. We were satisfied.

Here, among abandoned buildings with scattered grains left over from years of harvest

1

2

Although generally welcome, huge flocks of geese descending on grainfield (opposite) can be hardship to farmer. White-fronted goose (1) is California favorite. Canadas (2) are known for size, range, and honking. Pit blind and decoys (3) in Alberta. Resting area (4), from which geese fly twice a day to feeding site. Goose diet includes wild oats (5).

4

and planting, the protection of corrals and fences, and the ever-present shelterbelt of trees and bushes, our camp intruded upon established residents. A flock of sharp-tailed grouse and a covey of Hungarian partridge lived in harmony on the premises. The sharp-tails flushed from somewhere on the ground and alighted in a row on the barn roof, reluctant to leave. Finally they flew a short distance and disappeared in rosebushes along the shelterbelt. The Huns scurried along parallel to the outer windbreak, chirping frenetically, but did not fly. It was not yet open season on those birds.

In half-light the following morning we placed the decoys under the veteran's supervision. Since it was an established feeding site, he felt a dozen would be sufficient. More would increase the chance for error in placement. Forgoing the sport, I crouched in my pit with a camera, only to learn that I was carelessly faced directly into a rising sun. Worse than the mud, which commonly lines goose pits, the ash-dry soil crumbled in cascades of dust, penetrating equipment and clothing.

Shortly after sunup the distant gabble of geese on the river increased to pandemonium, the hoarse bawls of the big Canadas mixed with lighter calls of snow geese and the lesser Canadas. An indescribable change in the tone signaled a takeoff and about fifty Canadas came first. I tried to photograph the line of birds through the stubble, then ducked low and listened to the conversational tones of the calling and the incredibly loud swish of wings as the flock neared and wheeled into the breeze. The even swish changed to a sustained hiss as a hundred wings braked against the air—but the absent-minded sounds of birds picking exact landing spots changed to confused calls, the slither of midair contact was followed by the brisk bugle of a re-formed flight, and the sounds faded while the veteran hunter left his pit and hurried about the set.

There was nothing serious, he said. He thought my camera lens had caught a splash of sunlight, and I contritely stayed down for the next flight—four big birds that swung once and then alighted a hundred yards from the gunning pits. The wind was from the back of the shooters, the pits planned so that the geese would come into the decoys to land against the breeze and facing the gunners, but the four nonconformists had been too high as they made their approach and they landed behind the pits. The veteran opened his pit cover and shouted them away lest they provide out-of-range competition for our decoys.

Ten minutes later a great sweep of Canadas came from the resting water half a mile away and the heavily loaded guns boomed while big wings hammered the air. Then came the snows. By midmorning the shooting stopped with birds still gliding to the set, encouraged by an expertly operated goose call, used sparingly. Established feeding grounds, which birds have found safe through days of use, are excellent locations for gunners. Even on bluebird days, the birds can be counted on at such stands. Foul weather with high winds will drive geese from their resting waters and make for shooting in a wide variety of locations, but clear, warm weather demands careful observations. The true hunting is in the preparation, such as that made by our host, a true student of geese.

The very scope of the wild goose's range has brought about a varied approach to the hunt, experienced gunners of one area becoming confused with the change of method a few miles away.

In California's Sacramento Valley, cramped hunters lie in a shallow ditch, taking up their positions at daybreak. They do not use decoys, but a mile away white-fronted geese swarm over a field of rice that has already suffered from their onslaught. A light plane may dip over the field to move the busy birds, raising thousands in a roar of wings and a clatter of calls as they reluctantly leave the rice in tattered files and pods. A few hundred yards from the crop they form flocks at different heights and one group makes a line, beating low toward the hunters' ditch, and so the long wait ends.

Farther north, still in California, the season opens with ducks and geese rising like curling smoke from Tule Lake. Hunters stand in knee-deep water behind scanty cover and hope for a shred of the high flocks to peel off. Other gunners are hidden in the rocks of surrounding hills to catch birds laboring for altitude as they fly up the slope.

In the Midwest, river hunters spend a snowy day in white clothing and use their binoculars on long stretches of river to find resting flocks; then they make elaborate and grueling stalks through cockle burrs, ragweed, and finally willows. Fifty years ago in that country, my school was dismissed temporarily because a flock of big, gray Canadas had landed on a pond a quarter mile away and we were allowed to watch hunters sneak behind the earthen dam.

Traditions of waterfowling come from the eastern seaboard, where birds are found in heavy concentrations and hunting methods are sophisticated. The little American brant found there is truly a saltwater goose, spending his winters from New Hampshire to North Carolina. Like the other wild geese, he winters far in the north on shores of Canada and Greenland and he cruises the coastal marshes and open bays in low lines. His opposite number on the West Coast is the black brant. On New Jersey's Barnegat Bay, home of the Barnegat sneakbox, the brant is hunted on a landscape whose barrenness is broken by low islands, grounded houseboats, and weathered old clubhouses, some of them used more than half a century ago by famous leaders of industry and politics.

The sneakbox is often beautifully hand-fashioned for generations of use, a specialized craft that permits a prone gunner to scull silently. In early season its deck may be grassed up with

sedge, in cold weather it may be iced over, and a Barnegat guide I know uses a shotgun painted olive drab—to resist the inroads of salt spray and give no traitorous flashes in the sun. But the Barnegat Bay sneakbox is only the best known of a dozen locally preferred designs along the Atlantic Coast, and as the gunner takes his low view of the oncoming brant, almost at water level, he sees the game as a hundred years of gunners have seen it on the eastern shore.

The history of the American brant is one of adaptation. The little goose is a true aquatic resident, seldom grazing on land as do most of the other species. Eelgrass was the brant's staple through his known history—a diet that made the birds first choice of the gourmet. Then in the thirties disease struck the eelgrass of the Atlantic Coast, and with the eelgrass went the brant, falling from his traditional plenty to a skeletal population of some 30,000 birds. Gunning seasons were closed and extinction seemed likely.

But the brant turned to other foods, especially sea lettuce, a plant that had seldom appeared in brant crops before. The geese also increased their intake of widgeon grass—and began the road back. Some of the new diet damaged the taste of the birds at the table, and veteran hunters say that no brant with a greenish abdomen is fit to eat. By 1970 the population was at a nearly normal 200,000 birds, most of which wintered along the New Jersey coast. The eelgrass was coming back by that time, but the brant had proved it could live without it—a triumph of adaptation. On the West Coast, where eelgrass had never suffered, the black brant had continued to prosper.

If there is game the nonhunter knows, or believes he knows, it is the wild goose, for he has heard the far-carrying calls and seen the haze-dimmed threads of birds in spring and fall. The wild goose may well be the hunter's most valuable liaison with the nonhunting world, which does not understand him and his sport but whose help must be had for the future of all wildlife.

7.

Under a wide sky, where
purple hills shimmer in midday heat,
pronghorn and sage grouse watch
for alder clumps that promise water.

A wasteland wanderer and the fastest of hoofed animals, the pronghorn is finally re-established as a permanent resident of the West—after being pushed to the edge of extinction. Both the pronghorn and his plains have been abused and misunderstood. He has been hunted unfairly and executed in the alfalfa he has trampled. An exciting target for the trophy hunter who brings down a buck after a grueling stalk, the pronghorn is too often taken the easy way—chased by motor vehicles and butchered by strafing fire.

The pronghorn, adapted as he is to his world of great distances, is no master of unusual situations. Capable of seeing danger for miles, he is completely befuddled when it somehow appears at close range, and the stalker who gets near through luck and management may, surprisingly, have ample shooting time while being regarded with uncomprehending amazement.

The shock of encountering a stranger nearby is nearly always defeating for creatures that rely on eyesight for defense. I once made a very long stalk in a dry creek bed, heading for a single buck antelope I had seen grazing with a doe. I knew they were near the creek and I laboriously followed its meanderings for much of a day, only to be seen by the buck when he moved to a small knoll, and lose him as he left the area without communicating with the doe. For the moment the doe was not visible, grazing somewhere about the creek bed, and I continued my sneak, hoping there might be other bucks ahead. Finally, keeping to the dry ditch, I saw the back of the feeding animal and decided she was alone, but by that time I was so near I wanted to learn how close I could get, working upwind. Eventually, I crawled to a lump of black earth left by erosion and found I was near enough to touch the doe with one quick step. My ambition to "catch" a wild antelope with my bare hands was tempered by mental pictures of coyotes and rattlesnakes carved to death or launched into limping flight by tiny, stabbing pronghorn hooves, and I finally decided against even so much as counting coup by slapping the animal's tawny flank.

She grazed rather noisily and I said, "Hey, Sis!" The munching stopped and the doe stood, head still down, and with the big eye on my side turned instantly back toward me. When I hissed again, she leaped to one side and faced me, but she did not leave for almost a minute. A stationary man at a range of five feet was beyond her experience and her defense was not programmed for it.

Two days before a season opened in Wyoming, my wife and I drove a wallowing truck slowly across sagebrush hills to camp at a sheepshearing headquarters, long abandoned and scarred with the roughly carved initials and Spanish names of herders who had worked there almost half a century ago. On the great dry slopes of grass and sage a forgotten building is a gathering place for opportunists of the wild; in taking advantage of ready shelter, they establish a concentrated community of predators and quarry.

A quick appraisal of the old living quarters disclosed a clutch of wood rat collections, heaped treasures in every cranny, ranging from twine to broken spoons. We promptly decided to sleep in the truck, knowing nightfall would bring noisy traffic through the paintless wreckage. We found damp earth and dug to fresh water in the nearby arroyo, an operation observed critically by a knot of pronghorns on the crest of a small rise. They were does and fawns, but a big buck watched from another knoll a few yards away from them. With binoculars we saw pronghorns on several other slopes, grazing well into the cool night. No sooner had we gone to bed than there was a scratching, tinkling sound of wood rats trying to climb into the truck, arguing excitedly and falling with thumps from precarious perches beneath us.

Then something made a great clatter among some pans we had stacked on piled rocks and we gave up all attempts at sleep to turn a flashlight on a bushy-tailed wood rat, squirrel-like

Opening pages: Pronghorn antelope,
the fastest of North American hoofed game,
can run over fifty miles per hour.
Open mouth is characteristic. Running
requires vast drafts of air.

and only momentarily puzzled by the light. This was high plains country, suitable for the bushy-tail, although he is better known in the mountains. Not afraid of rats but reluctant to have them tour our sleeping bags, we lay awake until certain they could not enter the truck, and we had hardly dozed before we seemed to hear some sheepherder from the past begin to tidy up the entire living quarters. He seemed to sweep energetically while the rats squalled in confusion, and once I thought I heard a death squeal. Finally, the eerie sounds stopped and I slept. At dawn, I faced the sweeper, no ghost at all but a great horned owl sitting in disturbed dignity on a paneless window sash and glaring at the truck twenty feet away. Even *his* muffled wings had made sound as they brushed the old building's interior.

A big buck pronghorn, feeding on the opposite edge of the big draw, watched us at daylight and we marked him as a trophy, hoping he would return the next morning when the season opened. All day we had pronghorn visitors—not trophy animals, but mostly curious youngsters. One of them, a young doe, rushed to within thirty yards of our camp and gave a soft squeal, followed by the peculiar pronghorn wheeze that sounds like a deformed bullet ricocheting. After this she raced away at a speed to put a big head-slogging buck to shame. If there are sixty-mile-an-hour pronghorns they must be the young does, who go with a whistling run, barely skimming the sage tops, their heads almost steady, and with placid expressions, the actual wind of their passing audible between light hoofbeats and flailing grass. Other runners may bob and leap; the pronghorn is a ground racer without waste motion, stretching for the earth with slender legs and shock-absorbing hooves. The young does run lightly; the big, trophy bucks with more drive and effort, but both can go for miles and few people have actually seen them at top speed.

A pronghorn that already appears to be racing can accelerate startlingly if inspired by a close shot. At speed, the pronghorn feels for the ground and scorns high leaps, even stopping headlong flight to crawl under a fence. Unless wounded, fleeing pronghorns seek running room. Injured, a buck may head for brushy bottoms.

The next day, a fine September morning, our Wyoming season opened, and there was the big buck grazing across the draw, accompanied by two does. They were a bit too far away for a certain shot, so my wife hurriedly mapped a stalk through a series of draws that would take her within range. She disappeared into a nearby wash, and although I did not see her again for a long while, her progress was marked. Within ten minutes, a skunk appeared on her hidden course, moving out of a draw like an animated black and white plume in the first streaks of daylight. He came to our camp and disappeared beneath the old building without more than a casual glance upward where I crouched behind a spotting scope to watch the hunter's objective. The old building was his home and he had returned from his nightly hunt a little early.

A little later a ground squirrel appeared far out on the other side of the ravine, scurrying for his hole in a tantrum of haste, and a red-tailed hawk bounced from his steady glide, seeing both creeping hunter and alarmed rodent. A tiny speck of bird, probably a horned lark, then flitted from a draw that went within a short distance of the grazing antelope, and I knew the stalker was in range—if she could but locate her target after an hour of searching for a hidden passage in the haphazard ravines.

Something in the sequence of events had drawn the pronghorns' attention; they stopped feeding and looked toward the unseen stalker. Perhaps she had shown a tip of rifle barrel or an inch of cap somewhere along the route, or the bird and ground squirrel behavior had been too hurried. The antelope's rump hairs rose in white rosettes of excitement and they milled with quick, false starts. Finally, a doe pranced straight to the

Big sage (*1*) and buffalo berry (*2*) provide food and cover in pronghorn-sage grouse country. Horned owl (*3*) and prairie dogs (*4*) are other plains residents. Pronghorn buck (*5*) grazes on sparse prairie vegetation. A weed eater, he does not compete with domestic stock for grass. Scattered trees (*6*) line little draws of typical plains environment. Band of antelope takes off (*7*), with rump hairs standing in white rosettes. Big buck at left runs in typical rear position of herd master.

1

3

2

4

6

7

*Young plains badger
with traditional prey—a ground
squirrel. A strong and resourceful
hunter, he is also
scourge of prairie-dog towns.*

brink of the dangerous draw, looked down, then rushed back to the buck and the other doe. Both does returned together to look, swept into a curve of speed, throwing tiny dust trails, and from my distance I could imagine their excited blowing, but they arced back to the big buck, who pranced nervously.

Still nothing showed in the hunter's draw and I expected no more wildlife to appear from it, for she must have been inching about for a view of her trophy. She may as well have stayed motionless, for pronghorn curiosity can be overwhelming. The big buck pranced and made several little runs toward the depression, knowing better but fighting a losing battle with the curiosity of his kind—curiosity that makes it possible to attract unhunted pronghorns by waving a big hat from a ridge a mile away.

At last the big buck rushed to the draw's edge and stood stock still, staring down into it. The crash of the rifle was an easily predicted ending.

More properly classified as a goat than an antelope, the pronghorn is purely American. The pioneers encountered pronghorns in untold thousands among the buffalo, and hunted them nearly to extinction. They recovered, however, as cattle replaced the buffalo and crowded the plains. Grazed-over land brings the weeds the pronghorn loves. They compete little with cattle on open range, but anger the rancher by bedding in his alfalfa fields. An oddity among game animals, the pronghorn sheds the shells of his true horns each year. A doe conceals her one or two fawns, sometimes having difficulty returning to the exact spot, and the leggy youngsters are so odorless that hunting dogs may rest within a few feet of them and smell nothing. Within a few days the fawns can run for short distances. As young adults they can travel at a speed which reliable estimates place at nearly sixty miles an hour. The cheetah is faster in a sprint and actually has caught pronghorns in tests, but the pronghorn is a distance runner and can maintain a pace of thirty-five miles an hour for great distances.

The old Indian hunting game of flagging antelope will still work on young animals, and I have sat in plain sight and signaled a foursome of wild yearling bucks to within fifteen yards, coming downwind. A brief circle to catch my scent and they retired for two hundred yards for a snorting, jittery conference. But if they have been hunted for a few days, pronghorns will sometimes flush when a hunter is sighted at a true mile. In a land of distances the pronghorn's eyesight is famous. While dressing a kill I have had one appear as a pearl of dust a mile away, had him approach at high speed to within a hundred yards to see what I was doing, then lost him again as he wheezed and lit out for the horizon.

Some of the finest antelope country lies in transitional zones, where scattered pines and stark rimrock outcroppings lend beauty to the wide skies, the endless grass, and soft-toned sage. In these semiarid lands the pronghorn needs the small creeks and the certain running water marked by alders. The alder must have water constantly, although neighboring willows and cottonwoods can do without it for considerable periods. The creek bottoms may have gooseberries, wheat grass, rosebushes, and buffalo berry bush. In summer, pale blue lupines and wild geraniums show brightly. In hunting season the scene becomes more drab and the hibernating marmots disappear from their rock notches, where they have whistled all summer, just above the pronghorn's home. The prairie falcon, red-tailed hawk, and the wider-ranging golden eagle keep hungry watch on the ground squirrels, which will soon disappear to hibernate, perhaps on a prairie dog city—an animal metropolis with miles of linking underground passages.

If the weather is warm, rattlesnakes may still be in the dog town streets even as antelope season opens. Rattlers often inhabit dog towns while the rodents go on living there, apparently not terribly concerned by the presence of snakes, even though the rattlers probe the tunnels to eat the young of their builders. The spindle-legged little burrowing owl lives in abandoned tunnels. Sometimes one will be seen standing on the rim of a hole doing regular dipping exercises as if gravity had overcome its delicate, top-heavy balance.

Much of a pronghorn hunter's time is spent in actual stalking, failing with one herd, and going on to another group in good country. After an hour of inspecting sage roots and anthills a few inches from his nose, he must judge shooting distances of hundreds of yards, but some of the plains residents may be met at surprisingly close range. Eye-to-eye confrontation with a belligerent badger is disconcerting if the hunter must stay on all fours. If the badger is merely surveying from his burrow, he is likely to go through a series of jack-in-the-box appearances, undecided whether to retire or not, but reassured each time he ducks inside his familiar home, and therefore putting his bandit's face above the rim again.

It is when caught or cornered in the open that the badger turns fighter with tremendous hisses and choking snarls. Crossing a rocky area in antelope range, we met a crusty old male who disputed the right of way with our three-quarter-ton, four-wheel-drive truck. He retreated inches at a time, feeling furtively for a soft place to dig, and finally disappeared in some broken rock. He

hunts rodents and snakes in the plains country, accepting semiarid grass and bush lands as well as the fence rows of farm country. Once enraged, he will follow a retreating man in a move that would be considered a charge if conducted by a big-game animal. No mammal seems capable of more abandoned fury when battle is joined.

Much of pronghorn country is sage grouse country as well, the spectacular birds sometimes weighing nearly eight pounds. My first experience with sage hens was a heavy thumping of wings which foiled a careful stalk on pronghorns. A mainstay of pioneer diet and a game bird under the right circumstances, the sage hen is almost too unpredictable for biologists because of unexplained groupings and short migrations, but he joins the pronghorn in many things, even in love for tender alfalfa. Sage grouse feed on big sage, fringe sage, and gumweed. The latter contains a sticky substance that sometimes causes the birds' breast feathers to become gummy. Although the grouse are found on greasewood flats, biologists report they do not eat that plant. They are often seen in grain stubble, but do not glean grain. They consume several leafy plants that grow between the rows, especially wild lettuce.

Many a casual student of wildlife has seen only the mating-season pictures of sage grouse, which show the cock in strutting form with fanned tail and enormously puffed chest—actually an inflated esophagus—with which he produces his incredible booming call. The cock is then working himself into a booming frenzy and competing with other exhibitionists for flocks of admiring hens. (It is his ceremonial bowing to the points of the compass that may have inspired strutting Indian dances.) Dawn is an established time for booming, and after a long exhibition a whole party of show-offs may suddenly deflate and fly away from the arena.

In fall, sage grouse group in immense, loose flocks, disperse almost overnight, and migrate mysteriously, even over mountain ranges nearly

Sage grouse hunter (opposite) examines plains flora. This slope is covered with rabbit brush and sage, and borders alfalfa field at rear. Sage grouse cock (1) in course of ceremonial mating dance. Gumweed (2) is common grouse food. Flying grouse (3) have great stamina, cover long distances. Hens have a distinctive swerve to their flight. Head of female (4) blends with habitat. Where cover is thin, birds (5) flush at long range.

10,000 feet in height, with intermittent fluttering and gliding flights. In flight it is the hen which twists erratically. On the ground she walks evenly, while the cock waddles.

In the sage the grouse are able to travel swiftly on foot. On one sage grouse hunt, I marked down a single, sure he would flap up like a condor when I approached. Although I had located his landing site within a dozen feet, even a pointing dog was unable to find him, but went off on what I thought was a silly journey, followed faithfully by my hunting companion.

I saw them top a sage ridge a mile away while I stubbornly searched for the original bird. At dusk they returned, and my friend reported the dog had been following moving grouse the whole time. Several had finally flushed wild after nearly two miles on the ground, probably with my original quarry somewhere among them. This is common procedure with sage grouse, a bird falling out of the march at intervals until only one or two remain to storm upward at the end of the retreat. But the sage hen's low repute comes from the gunner who finds them clumsily taking off and flying loudly in all directions.

Once under way and driving down a sage slope, the grouse are swift and may travel for a mile before putting down. Leaf eaters with a digestive apparatus that operates inefficiently on seeds, they dote on alfalfa. The rim of an alfalfa field, surrounded by sage, bears close inspection. Or find an isolated stock pond in sagebrush country; a radius of half a mile is likely to contain large patches of mottled droppings, the sign of a grouse roost. For the meticulous student, even matted grass where individual birds have sat may be a clue, or big, chicken-like tracks in patches of bare sand. Tracks are the best indicators of all, for it would take a chemist to date the durable droppings.

Twice I have walked literally into miles of sage grouse in pronghorn country, the birds clustered in little bands of five or six and seemingly disorganized about their escape routes, sometimes flying almost into the gun, while a befuddled dog pointed in all directions with bulging eyes and nervously dripping tongue. Such flocks, obviously amalgamations of family groups, seem without leadership or purpose, and lack the tricky ground maneuvers of small bunches. Perhaps it is crude hunting, but I have forsaken my rifle and gone for the shotgun in the sheer excitement of big threshing wings in the sage tops and the utter unpredictability of random flights. A year later at the same point, hunting may be fruitless; the birds may be only a few miles away, but somehow they are never found.

When sage is sprayed for the questionable purpose of pasture improvement, the sage grouse may disappear. Its requirements are specialized and it cannot accommodate to other habitat. The pronghorn may still hold forth, even though more nutritious graze has given way to cheatgrass before the onslaught of munching sheep and cattle. Management officials confide that the pronghorn's numbers could be greatly increased with the approval of land users, and efforts at paid hunting programs have showed some progress, as ranchers learn that the white-and-tan specks on distant hills can be as harvestable as mutton or beef.

Subject to a reasonable hunting fee, we followed a rancher's Land Rover for miles into an enormous, rolling plain, broken by the little cottonwood and willow draws and miniature rimrock bluffs, patched by shadows of drifting clouds and an occasional abandoned homestead with a broken windmill. Some of the old houses have stood for almost a hundred years, settling slowly to rubble but resisting dusty winds and splitting cold, aided by the preserving dryness of pronghorn country.

Our host showed us a camping spot near water, pointed to a skylined watcher on a distant ridge, and jokingly asked us to keep that one for him since the old resident had become a fixture. The glass showed the sentry to be a shouldery buck with jutting horns, motionless and intent upon outstaring the 20-power spotting scope.

We set up our little tent, and at dusk two jackrabbits played tag briefly not far away. Almost as if from some over-dramatic script, a coyote broke his series of crisp yelps with one long yowl and got his answer from another rabbit hunter on some other ridge. Such wasted breath soon gave way to serious foraging, however, and the only sound then was gentle wind in the sage. Later, there was a faint murmur of high and distant geese. Evidently it concerned navigational matters only. They had no thought of landing.

We moved for the big buck at dawn, sighting him near where he had been the night before. A long, roundabout hike brought us to what appeared to be the final ridge. Two mesmerized Richardson's ground squirrels sat staring by their holes and forgot to squeak. We knew our quarry was no yearling to be hypnotized by a waved bandanna, and I spent five minutes raising my bare head by sweaty degrees until I could peer over into a little basin to find myself intently studied by several does and a little buck with seven-inch beginnings of horns. The big buck had left and was possibly studying our strange behavior from miles away.

Days later, as our hunt neared its end, I was ready to settle for a smaller trophy. I had a working knowledge of our area, aided by the ever-present sheepherders' monuments—neat pyramids of stone set on the higher points of grazing country, partly as landmarks, partly to relieve the monotony of months alone, partly as a lonely man's permanent ciphers in a gigantic world of sky and sage. Occasionally, chipmunks live in the neatly laid stones; I have seen a red-tailed hawk perched on top of a monument, and I have crowded hard against one of the little stone spires in a futile effort at camouflage, while pronghorns gave a wide berth to a familiar landmark with an unfamiliar bulge.

With only one day to hunt, I stalked a herd of pronghorns which sighted me and moved easily for half a mile to another slope. Behind them galloped three domestic sheep, abandoned when the rest of their band had been moved from the area. For our entire stay, they had furnished comic relief, firmly believing they were pronghorns and obviously puzzled that their considerable speed could not keep them abreast of their grazing companions.

I followed the pronghorns. Each time I peered over a new ridge they were watching, but they gradually became just a little curious and twice I could have shot a straggling doe at close range. There were two fair bucks which stayed close to the herd, and after a long and dogged pursuit I herded the bunch into an area of broken erosion along a big draw. For the twentieth time, I inched one eye around a steep mound and saw a white rump disappear into a notch two hundred yards away. This time I did not move closer. The plodding pattern of pursuit had been set and I waited for a rear-guard appraisal, my rifle rested carefully and my prone position comfortable.

It was ten minutes later that two black specks appeared in a notch of low ridge. They became two horns. An alert head followed. Two long minutes later a buck's neck and chest came into view almost where the scope's cross hairs intersected. I moved the ready rifle only a fraction of an inch before I fired.

A buzzard banked above me as I dressed my game. It had been a little chillier that day. The next morning the sky was dull and a distant Denver radio station promised snow. Loading cooled game into the truck, we heard a ragged, musical chant and saw great swinging lines of sandhill cranes, moving south in thousands, their firm wing strokes and short glides taking them from where we had left them a few days before in Alberta's sand hills. The Gulf of Mexico was their destination. By now they had only a few hundred miles more to go.

8.
Sounds of a tawny autumn
forest: a whirr of grouse, a muley's
lightfooted progress, and
the domineering bugle of an elk.

The challenge of the bull elk is one of the unforgettable sounds of the American wild, loved as much as the cries of hunting wolves and the wavering signals of migrating geese. The rutting bull not only accepts battle but seeks it under the goad of his desire. Only the piercing whistle is heard at great distance. The concluding grunts of passion are buried in the shadows of a timbered canyon or brushed by mountain winds from a rocky point.

In much of the elk range, hunters never hear the call, as the season may open after the sounds of rage have subsided. The sound itself is an oddity, the whistling presumably coming through teeth shaped for the purpose and sounding something like a boatswain's pipe. The tone is deeper and rounder, however, the beginning harsh and wheezing, then rising to a pure bugle tone which concludes with a shriek and is followed by a short series of guttural, profane grunts. After you have watched a herd bull issue his war cry, you cannot hear the sound, even in the distance, without visualizing its author, red-eyed and maniacal, his antlers jutting over his herd of cows, as he goads himself into slobbering rage. Or perhaps he has been dispossessed by another bull and wants revenge. I admit I am afraid of a rutting bull elk.

Fascinated by the sound, and hoping to see the ritual of rage that accompanies it, I went into Yellowstone National Park to observe more closely than was possible in hunting country. The park wapiti, part wild, part tame, were accessible enough and I trudged off the road after sighting a good bull with a pair of cows. He had bugled several times, but half-heartedly, then nibbled grass, and I could see he was in relatively good humor. It was a small grassy valley, bordered by firs, and the animals were grazing near a big windfall at the forest's edge. After watching with binoculars for a time, I essayed a rather clumsy call since I had no bugle with me.

The response was immediate. The bull strode back and forth and worked himself into a tantrum of resentment. He raised his head until his antlers lay along his back and emitted a noble blast. I answered, and he repeated his call. In a frenzy, he made a stamping, hooking charge at the crown of the big windfall, then turned again toward me, tatters of branches and grass hanging from his tines and foam showing at his mouth. Before I could fumble another call, it dawned upon me that he knew I was no elk—that he could see me, perhaps scent me, and was challenging a man who had somehow invaded an elk valley with awkward imitations of elk noises. Suddenly I felt alone. I lost my interest in nature study and withdrew with forced nonchalance, repressing a desire to run.

Even the vocal spleen of a raging park elk lacks the impact of a challenge from some wild and unseen stag in high mountain country, hunting season or not. Grouse gunners in the Rockies may catch the rutting season at its height, walking the ridges before elk hunting is legal, and may meet elk or bear when armed only with bird shot. Two of us climbed to a rocky crest through wheat grass, foxtail, and old firs, looking for blue (dusky) grouse, a bird nearly always associated with elk hunting, prized as camp fare and a dilemma when sitting stolidly on a limb. An elk hunter, faced by a perched grouse, must decide whether to risk losing a chance at big game by a reverberating shot. If he weakens and snips the bird's neck with a rifle bullet, he never knows whether he will be congratulated by his friends or berated for driving elk out of the watershed. But on a deliberate grouse hunt we had no such qualms and would have shot any grouse that showed itself. We moved a few mule deer, first seen as hesitantly moving legs far ahead; then heard as loud thuds as they bounced away. From the thuds we tried to estimate numbers and sizes—a sage observation in such circumstances being impossible to disprove.

After we topped the ridge crest, we were

Opening pages: *Among the most thrilling of wild sounds is early fall bugle of bull elk challenging rivals to battle. Formerly plains animals, elk now live in remotest North American wilderness.*

105

fairly quiet, looking for grouse tracks in a trace of snow that was melting fast and would soon be useless. A distant elk bugle brought us to a grinning stop, looking foolishly at each other in complete enjoyment of our remote surroundings. A second call from the other side of the ridge caused us to turn abruptly and look down the timbered slope, and a third bugle from the ridge top ahead was close enough to bring us to the hunter's automatic crouch. We dropped to our knees and listened to a round-robin exchange of elk insults and dares. We guessed at the bulls' size by the pitch of their whistles, and chuckled at the efforts of one adolescent who gave forth broken toots and cracked grunts, undoubtedly well separated from any herd of cows and intending to keep his distance. At any rate, we were in disputed territory and surrounded by some half dozen bulls.

It was a natural thing to essay a bugle myself and walk toward the nearest answer—straight ahead somewhere in fairly open timber that sloped both ways from the ridge peak. There were some down trees, lumpy rock ledges, and clumps of juniper. As usual, I had misjudged the bull's distance; this time he was closer than I had suspected, his call muffled by very heavy timber and a slight indentation of the mountain's side. After a pause, a full challenge came, startlingly near, and we stopped at the edge of a tiny grassy park, an opening in the forest. A minute later we heard a branch crack ahead, and not trusting my elk rhetoric at such close range, I simply snorted and broke a small stick. After that there was no stealth in the sounds ahead, only brisk cracklings and a muttering grunt.

I hissed, "Here he comes!", an unnecessary bit of news, and the bull brought up short from a trot at the far edge of the little park. He lifted his head and stared at us from thirty yards, his harem of cows visible in timber behind him in uncertain dabs of brown, creamy patches of rump, and sharply outlined ears.

It was no frosty-coated giant, just a proddy five-pointer hunting a reputation, but he was close enough. We waved our arms and yelled as humanly as possible, willing to end the confrontation. He and his cows dissolved into the forest and he declined to answer a questioning bleat from the youngster down the slope. After our outcry, all except the juvenile suspended buglings, and he was answered only by a red-tailed hawk over the canyon. Perhaps the youngster thought he had finally gotten the hang of it and had shamed the other bulls into trembling silence.

Unless wounded or tormented, elk can hardly be classified as dangerous game, but the capacity is there and heavy stags have thrown packhorses from disputed ledges and driven domestic bulls from haystacks. Elk fights sometimes result in death and a swift cow can kill a dog or coyote with thrusting, front-footed blows, even while chasing the victim.

Adult elk have little to fear from carnivores in most of their range, although the biggest bull may be helpless in deep and crusted snow. He can then be a victim of wolves or coyotes, but the situation is unusual since he can march through a snow depth that would confine even large mule deer to a yard. An adult cougar can kill elk, but cat predation has been a minor factor in recent years.

Elk have distinctly reddish-brown summer pelage. It is fall when they begin to show the gray backs and grow manes. In winter wear, lightest colored of all are the older bulls, some of them appearing almost white. Early September is mating time in most mountain elk country. The elk calves, spotted like most young of the deer family, are born in May or June, some eight and a half months after the mating season. The awkward calves are almost scentless recluses at first, but run with their mothers in a week or so.

A trophy bull should have at least six points on each side and should have heavy beams. Six points on each side makes him a "royal"; seven

1

2

3

4

In highest Rockies (1),
elk are sighted in small
meadows near timber
at dawn and dusk. Bulls (2)
fight for possession
of harem; loser usually
leaves area. Cow elk
and calf (3) in security of
deep forest. Solitary
bull (4) beds down in snow.

7

*Elk (5) prefer grazing to
browsing. Grassy slopes near
timber are favored
feeding places. Mule deer
(6) may share site with
elk, but will browse rather
than graze. An elk herd
(7) usually travels in line,
holding formation even
when frightened in open.*

make him an "imperial." White or "ivory" tips add to the desirability of the head.

Although the bulls stay apart much of the time after the rut, it is not a fast rule, for they are also found as part of herds that may number more than a hundred animals of all ages. Some distance apart from any cows or calves, bands of bulls are seen skylined on high ridges or moving single file across grassy parks to disappear in high forests. A trophy hunter may glass cows and small bulls for days, grumble across his campfire that there are no big animals in his entire area, and then see them all at once, creamy-coated giants with great dark manes, usually as they stride in close-ordered, formal dignity along another mountain. Then his party must match strength and time against the vagaries of elk wanderings. A veteran hunter may wait another day and glass the route at dawn and dusk. With a second sighting of big bulls, possibly so far away that their scooping antlers may be only a fuzzy aura above them, the hunt may be planned. Better yet, if the patriarchs are sighted grazing on an open knob it will be worthwhile to approach it at first light. Evening shooting involves the problem of caring for a downed animal in darkness when the hunter may be a long and intricate distance from camp.

An elk kill, especially a big bull, must be dressed immediately and the deep shoulder section must be split to prevent spoilage, even in cold weather. A herd bull may weigh a thousand pounds; the Roosevelt strain of Washington and Oregon may be even heavier.

The elk adapts well. He is a creature of different habits than his ancestors. A plains animal at least part of the time, the elk was seen on grassy prairies by pioneers. Probably even then the hot weather was spent in the mountains, for an elk herd is swift to migrate. At any rate, the pattern later was to graze the high pastures in summer, use the wind-cleared grass ridges through early snows, and then march down through the heavy drifts to valley grasslands for the winter. Soft snow of a foot or two is no trouble to the animals and long-range inspection of high parks will show the snow ploughed and tossed in heaps and furrows by feeding elk.

Fences and cattle gradually blocked the historical routes to the valleys. The herds were confined more and more to the mountains and heavy forests. In mild winters elk can make do in high country. In the occasional winter of steady cold and deep snow, the herds move down through necessity on whatever routes they can find, smashing fences, driving off domestic cattle, and rending the neat alfalfa stacks. Then comes the confrontation of rancher and sportsman, game management biologist and fuming farmer. The loser is the elk.

But in some areas the elk adapts to year-round living in heavy forest, broken only by small parks and burns. There are such colonies in almost all of the elk states. Although Idaho, Montana, Wyoming, and Colorado may be discussed most frequently by traveling hunters, there are thirteen states with some sort of elk season, and western Canada also has sizable herds.

Most elk are in rugged country, although not necessarily distant in miles from civilization. Many a wild herd beds on an overlook within sight of taxis and within hearing of truck engines and police sirens. Elk can do without high mountains if civilization permits, and many live today in low hills with brushy canyons. At one time their range covered almost the entire United States.

The elk prefers grass but is both a grazer and a browser, feeding on a wide variety of trees and shrubs. He eats willow, pine, and snowbush, especially in winter and spring, and his favorite grasses include wheat grass, brome grass, fescue grass, and needle grass. He also feeds on sedges. In winter, when he must turn to browse, the "elk line" on trees may go up to nine feet, and all wood below that height is stripped bare; surprisingly

Bugling royal bull (left) in British Columbia has full, white-tipped antlers valued by trophy hunter. Sportsman below hopes to provoke argument with rutting bull by blasts on "elk bugle."

Bugling royal bull (left) in British Columbia has full, white-tipped antlers valued by trophy hunter. Sportsman below hopes to provoke argument with rutting bull by blasts on "elk bugle."

large branches are eaten. Under these conditions the elk can feed while deer starve, unable to reach the browse.

The best elk range with the most constant population is likely to include an expanse of grassy hillsides and heavy forests for normal living, and an almost impossibly dense tangle of canyons, precipices, and down timber with colorful names bestowed by exhausted hunters. (I have no idea just how many "Hellroaring" canyons there are.) At any rate, if there is no other escape the elk vanish into these canyons after the first few days of hunting, coming out only when forced by weather or enticed by reduced hunting pressure. Because of his great size an elk in thick timber is one of the most unusual quarries of the American hunter. He is capable of rabbit-like concealment and his great rack of antlers can be hard to see against brush. The elk sometimes slips away at close range while his pursuer is looking much too far ahead.

The hunter must move as silently as possible, upwind. Although he is sure to make noise,

he must keep it to a minimum and wait for a while if he should break a branch. Since I am ordinarily much noisier in the woods, I am frequently startled on such quiet elk hunts when I find myself in close proximity to easily frightened residents. In most elk country I have found snowshoe rabbits very tame if I move slowly, and they appear foolish if nature has turned them white when there is no early snow to match. A snowshoe rabbit (or varying hare) will simply stop his nibbling of grass or twigs to inspect the hunter, then hop off for a few feet or possibly disappear into a crevice of loose rock. If there is no snow and the hare decides to crouch for concealment, the effort is a travesty of camouflage and many an elk hunter, tired of canned and dehydrated food, has used a stick to good advantage, or even closed his day's hunt with a rifle shot.

But the truly delicate subject for the elk hunter in thick lodgepole or Douglas fir is the ruffed grouse. He will be hunting in country remote enough that no shotgunner or setter will have visited it, and the ruffed grouse will have an

Ruffed grouse (1) often are killed by elk hunters for meat. Large hoofprint (2)—note comparison with rifle shell—shows characteristic rounded elk toe. Moose marks are more splayed, more pointed. Snowshoe rabbit in winter pelage (3) is year-round resident of western mountains. Noisy chatter of pine (or red) squirrel (4) may herald approach of either hunter or his game.

1

2

4

3

Pack train (7) transports elk hunters to mountain camp. Many move into area early to be on scene when shooting season starts. Foxtail grass (5) is prevalent in mountain meadows. Willow leaves (6) are browse for both elk and moose. Aspen and Douglas fir (8) are numerous in elk forests. Blue grouse (9) makes reverse migration: fall in high country, summer near canyon streams.

7

8

9

entirely different outlook from that of the fugitive eastern bird who hurtles furiously from his perch, startling even the veteran gunner into occasional wild firing. Told of the behavior of the backwoods ruffs of elk country, the eastern grouse man will first argue that it must be a different species, and then go and sulk with his English shotgun.

I have stopped to listen for movements ahead and finally realized that I was within ten or fifteen feet of a ruffed grouse. Generally, he will watch briefly and then fly off as silently as possible, feeling the situation calls for stealth instead of thundering wings. Once I found three of them walking ahead of me on a game trail along a rather steep slope. When I walked faster, they went faster. Finally I crowded them so hard that they spread their wings halfway in an effort at better balance, stretched their heads out ahead and ran, at last turning off the trail and into a thicket of buffalo berry, still stubbornly refusing to flush.

The elk, even a bull weighing almost a thousand pounds, can be surprisingly quiet in heavy timber. His antlers lie back on his withers, and there is no explaining the way he can carry a dozen tines through the thick branches roofing the narrow trails. If there is snow, a hunter can trail a trophy bull all day in a small patch of timber, but once the elk knows he is being followed, the chances of the trailer getting a shot are rather dim. An associate willing to take a stand and hold it may get a shot when the bull is circling to scrutinize his back trail.

From a great distance I once watched a big bull go into a patch of lodgepole pine, no more than three hundred yards in diameter and isolated from other timber on a gently rounded hill. I reached his entry point and for some time I crept along his trail in the fresh snow, but saw nothing of him except a fading shadow. I heard a red squirrel (locally, a pine squirrel), busybody informer of the high forests, belaboring the slinking bull with a clatter of abuse somewhere up ahead and I quickly learned just how far I was behind the game, for when I reached the squirrel's domain I also received his denunciation.

After I had followed the bull for some time, he suddenly made a break out of the timber for another and larger section of cover and I heard his hoofbeats fade away, all of his stealth suspended while he made his run. Although the elk can move in surprising silence, he will suddenly abandon caution, and I have had a herd move down upon me with crashing and banging that nearly made me step behind a tree for protection. They were probably hurrying from some other hunter, but were not really bolting; simply going without caution.

For short distances elk can run swiftly, but their top speed is lost quickly and I have seen them heaving hard and lolling their tongues after a short sprint in warm weather. But the elk's long trot will bring him to a new forest at a speed faster than most mountain horses can manage.

Elk movements are on a large scale when hunters enter their range on opening day or just before, and simply watching a cross-country game trail has resulted in the collection of many trophies. The threadbare story of the camp cook who finds a royal bull staring at him from a few yards away is repeated every year—the displaced animal traveling into unfamiliar country, and pausing in fatal confusion before a hunter's tent, which is logically near a main trail.

The mountain game trails are a network as efficient as anything produced by highway engineers, and by studying a contour map the careful hunter can make educated guesses as to evacuation routes that will be used once the first shots are heard. Where the map shows a narrow strip of timber joining two large forest areas at high altitude there is a logical crossing. Any narrow strip of timber that leads from heavy forest to an open area of grass is a good route for animals frightened from their grazing area, and requires special study in early morning. Elk take advantage of forest edges, even when they do not actually

enter the timber. A narrow ridge joining two major mountains may be traveled, even though it exposes the game to full view.

Two of us guessed right in Montana's Gravelly Range one year, and followed a hard-used path that ran near the top of a ridge, the trail winding to take advantage of screening by fir patches and aspen groves, passing just beneath some small rimrock ledges.

We saw a band of elk coming at their space-eating walk, actually jostling each other for precedence on the trail. My single shot scattered them instantly. The animal I had chosen was lost in the melee as tons of elk smashed through the brush and rolling rocks of the hillside—completely disappearing through some instinctive choice of escape routes. The sound died in a few seconds. Under such conditions, headlong flight quickly changes to silent, guarded sneaking, and it is questionable whether the little band reunited

that day—or ever, for that matter.

Shaken by the possibility that I could have missed at such range, I went to the trail. There was no snow and a minute hands-and-knees study at first showed no blood on the rocks or pine needles, only deep toe gouges where my bull had made his first leap after the shot. He had turned uphill and I checked his digging tracks where he had heaved upward in some soft earth and through a few rosebushes. I finally found a single dot of blood on a triangle of shale rock; then I caught a movement ahead in some mountain maple—a big shadow that seemed to break apart and disappear in a clump of aspen. Just ahead of me was a pool of blood where he had gone down. If I had waited a few more minutes he might have been unable to rise, but this second time we did wait and the two of us then went on slowly. I lost the trail on more rock, appalled that I could not follow an animal bleeding so badly.

Some time later I saw something shiny protruding at an odd angle. It was an antler tip. My bull was dead where he had fallen, within a hundred yards of where he had first gone down. With lungs virtually destroyed by a large-caliber bullet, the elk had moved until he died on his feet, demonstration of the driving vitality of an essentially high-strung creature. In this he is comparable to the whitetail, the mule deer, and the mountain sheep. The heavier moose is more phlegmatic and more easily stopped.

Most elk appear as dark shadows in the forest. I once ate lunch by an old pine windfall, its crumpled top entertaining some vine growth—a tiny jungle, suitable for ruffed grouse. After ten minutes of lunch stop, a spike bull elk leaped noisily from within the fallen treetop only thirty feet away, giving a shrill squeal and startling me into momentary paralysis. I ran uselessly around the tree, teeth clenching my sandwich, and rifle in

Royal bull (below) has earned designation from six points on each antler. Hunters opposite break their silhouettes with vegetation while glassing timber edges and grassy parks for elk.

hand, but the forest was quiet again and all I had really seen was the two swordlike black spikes as they bounced above the brush on the first lunge. The young bull's nerves had finally cracked and broken his earlier resolve to remain hidden.

Generally, though, the "timbered up" elk can withstand the pressure of nearby danger without acting rashly, and a rifleman in the deep woods is sometimes unnerved to find himself in the midst of a silent herd, making out ear fringes and eyes or possibly a few long legs and seemingly unattached rump patches. Eventually, in such a situation, someone must move.

The deadliest elk spy I know is Don Williams, a Montana guide and hunter, who travels thousands of miles each year on highways adjacent to elk range, learning individual herd habits from a distance with a spotting scope. The questing glass may show mountain goats, even bighorn sheep, and hundreds of mule deer. The art is not only knowing where to look, but what to look for.

The hunt begins for Williams in late winter, after shooting season is over, and the watcher notes what is left over from the fall hunt, counting and recounting the bunches, so he can recognize them in other parts of the mountain range if they move; thus he is less likely to score the same band twice and count too many.

A month before the next season opens, Williams will say that there is a really big bull on such-and-such a mountain and another on a mountain the map shows to be thirty miles away from the first. Several times he has taken me hunting, amused at my obsession with getting a really big trophy bull, after having turned down many chances in ten years of abstinence. As each season ended I settled for a freezer full of venison, and he was positively gleeful when I turned away from two bedded bulls he had pointed out across a canyon, but which didn't quite measure up. On that day, he showed me one hundred and two elk and I am not sure I would have seen any of them had I been alone, so great is his proficiency at studying terrain and discerning its wildlife.

The perfect elk mountain has both timber and grassland. When the animals are undisturbed Williams sights scattered herds on broad, open hillsides and sometimes a considerable distance from timber. This occurs at dawn and dusk. While the light is good, he checks very close to timber edges. Such finds are usually made at very long range, and the game appears as dark specks against the lighter grass. When the background is the edge of the timber itself he looks for the frosty capes of the older bulls against the dark forests. He studies the same area for a long period, hoping to discern a slight rearrangement of apparent bushes or rocks. At that distance the observer may not see movement, but is conscious that something has changed since he started watching. Broadside on a slope, both deer and elk show as rectangular patches, their legs invisible at great distances. First looks are a matter of elimination—the rejection of objects he is sure are not elk. The watcher endeavors to establish a size reference. He will guess that a bush is probably juniper and knows about what height it will reach in a given area. He guesses the height of the mature trees and tries to apply that measurement to his search. The beginner may be looking for an object the size of a locomotive because he has not established distance or reference.

After hunting pressure increases, the elk will enter heavy cover earlier in the morning and come out later in the evening. Williams will then pay extra attention to very small grass areas well surrounded by woods and concentrate on areas only a few feet from cover. Hardest of all is the discovery of bedded elk, but it can be regularly done if there is snow. The rule here is that the animals want to be concealed and yet have a good view of their surroundings, especially the lower levels. Cross-canyon spying is a good method, since a bedded bull may lie in a small opening, invisible from above or below on the same slope. The animal lies facing downward and is best approached by a roundabout route from above.

Williams took me into elk country before daylight on a one-day hunt. We drove some miles from the highway, then scaled a forested mountain in the snow by a series of switchbacks. In one spot we had a clear view of several huge snow flats and studied them for a long while, paying special attention to the edges where elk might graze out from timber.

We began to walk upward and Williams approached a series of small parks with care. Finally we found what we wanted, a narrow band of elk tracks along the edge of a park, made only a short while before. The snow edges of the tracks had crumbled only slightly, and where the animals had crossed a small seep no new ice had formed after they had broken through. The track bottoms were muddy and crushed sedge had not straightened. We were in a fold of the mountains, visibility restricted to only one or two slopes at a time. The tracks were mostly the smaller prints of cows and calves, but apparently there were two bulls. The snow had been nosed away for grazing. Elk prints are cowlike and a stray Hereford or black Angus has embarrassed many an elk tracker in ranch country. Cattle tracks become more elk-like if the toes are worn round, not an uncommon situation in rough country.

We found three parks where the little band had eaten and then we trailed it into a pine forest. The elk went in a loose group, not in the tight march of fast-traveling animals, and Williams pointed silently to a set of large tracks a little to one side, obviously a bull's. The feeding had been near dawn and the next procedure would be morning bedding, we assumed, probably not too far from the grazing spots.

An hour later the apparently aimless wanderings ended at seven "smoking" beds, abandoned only shortly before. On hands and knees, we made close examination and found the unpleasant, sweetish, musty smell of elk still there. We checked the tracks that left the beds and de-

cided there had been no hurry; simply a change of resting area. Two of the beds, as we had hoped, were bigger than the others. The elk rests with legs doubled under him and size of the legs is a helpful indication, easily read by deep marks they make in the snow, especially the front knees, which generally protrude ahead of the brisket.

The temperature was only slightly below freezing, a condition in which mountain elk actually prefer shade and snow. The trail went on, crossing a small creek, and was undoubtedly very fresh, for the prints there held a little muddy water, only beginning to take a gauze of ice. The tracks moved close-spaced through some four inches of soft snow and into an area where the old snow had melted before the new fell. We went with little sound, viewed only by a porcupine who paused in his chore of girdling a sapling and tried sluggishly to interpret the visitation of two men with rifles and pack frames.

Then we caught the full, heavy odor of the elk on the still air, smiled at each other and crouched a little. I slipped off my right glove and defeated an impulse to ease back the bolt and see if there really was a cartridge in the chamber.

"Here they are!" whispered Williams.

We were closer than seemed possible and a cow stood up only thirty yards away and stared stupidly, her calf getting up in boredom, wondering why he had to move. Then I saw a picket of uneven antler tines. It was a poor head—rag horns. I had the rifle up, but put it down again. The elk left rapidly, but not in complete panic. Last to go was an unseen one to the right who seemed to leave at a different angle from the rest.

"The other bull," said Williams. "Hear his horns hit the brush?"

We giggled boyishly and jabbered about the stalk. Williams seemed just as happy as if I had shot a record head. It had been a complete hunt, except that we had never sighted the one bull, and there was still the anticipation of the trophy I would kill on some other day.

9.
Mule deer bed down on forested hillsides with good sight lines, where early warning is a better defense than concealment against the predator's approach.

The illusion fades when he turns a little, but head-on—his gray muzzle shaped like the upper part of a funnel and his black nose adding to an expression of blank surprise—a mule deer looks like a poor job of taxidermy.

His most loyal followers will confess that he sometimes presents just such a view to a hunter when he should be bouncing away, but mule deer are individuals, sometimes capable of large-scale strategy; and some heavy-headed old males have lived to a ripe age among swarming hunters.

The individual mule deer covers more territory than his sophisticated white-tailed cousin, being less tolerant of civilization, and often hard for the hunter to reach. The muley's wilder country dwindles while the whitetail adapts to apple orchards and unwatched lettuce patches. The larger muley bucks may spend their resting hours in rimrock notches or abrupt, open-forested hillsides giving clear downhill views; they rely more on early warning than complete concealment. This is a westerner with western views about space, and while he may not slide into brush like a slipping whitetail, he can fade across a high ridge, blend with the vertical lines of snow-bound spruce, and become a bush of sage.

Around 1900, with the West just about settled, a single mule deer track might be followed all day. Fifty years of hungry pioneers and nonexistent conservation measures left game thinly spread. If that was the low point for mule deer, the period shortly after World War II must have been the high mark, a time when game managers pleaded with sportsmen to harvest does, and westerners shot winter's meat from highways.

Deer died in areas where worthwhile browse had been destroyed as high as the biggest buck could reach, and hunters who reveled in the fall crowding were indoors during the heavy winter kills and refused to believe them. The deer died, generally with their stomachs deceptively full of materials of little nutritional value, growth they would not touch in normal times. The self-destroying population surge came partly from lack of predators and hunters, partly from the program of new growth in logged or burned areas, and partly from the twin-bearing habit of mature does, which is maintained until forage finally fails.

Normally, few deer will stay in mature stands of timber. They rely on fires or logging for new growth, live in the edge areas between timber and prairie, or become sage dwellers.

Nothing in wildlife was more neatly matched than the cougar's hunger and the deer's rate of propagation, and the fanged shadow has been both deadly enemy and essential neighbor. It was the cougar, bobcat, and coyote that adjusted the balance between distended herds and dwindling range, but hunters who dream of fat venison unmolested by slinking villains have repeatedly encouraged management practices leading to habitat destruction through overcrowding.

The tragic case of Arizona's Kaibab Forest is sadly recited whenever predator destruction is discussed, an instance in which a healthy deer herd, largely controlled by cougars, grew to disastrous numbers when the lions were hunted out. Then came range destruction and starvation.

So secretive are the cougar's kills that biologists argue about their frequency, the actual count probably being dependent upon the prevalence of other prey. A full-grown cougar may kill a deer every week or oftener. He is capable of downing the largest buck and some observers feel he kills the two extremes—the largest and the smallest, because the weakling is easy to catch from a herd, and the biggest buck is apt to be a loner and more easily stalked.

Weighing more than one hundred pounds, the soft-footed cougar seldom shows animosity toward man and often retreats from the lowliest mongrel, but he has been destroyed for damage to livestock, which is his second choice to venison. No animal of his size is so hard to view in the wild, and individual cats have lived out their lives well known by men who have never seen them,

*Opening pages: Mule deer buck
of trophy size leads retinue to safety of
mountainside timber. Although often
found in open, experienced muleys
are adept at evasive action.*

but who have watched their trails and found their kills. Packs of hounds coupled with reckless horsemanship or strong legs make cat hunting; left to his own devices, a man sees a cougar only by chance. The cat can drift away in cover unlikely to hide a rabbit.

The very size and capability of a cat are enough to make any novice cautious, although the few attacks on humans have invariably occurred under unusual circumstances. Nevertheless, a lion-chasing friend of mine returned to camp somewhat shaken. A good tracker, he knew of a particular cat in the Colorado Rockies and had several times amused himself with wilderness hide-and-seek. When he entered the lion's territory, it frequently followed him. He would double back, circle briefly, and strike its trail. After tracing the lion for a while, he would leave its track, circle again, and find it was again following him —all of this going on within a rather small area, no more than a square mile.

As he ate his chocolate bar and jerky on that particular day, he was watched by his old but never-seen acquaintance. That, too, was nothing new, although he found the snow imprint of the crouched lion behind a nearer boulder than usual. But what caused my friend to give up the game forever was a detail of the snow-mould left a few minutes before he found it. As the cat had watched, the tip of its tail had switched gently, the sign of a hunting feline whose prey is near.

There are stories of unpleasant cougars in the south Florida swamps, their last eastern stronghold, where settlers in clearings of the mangrove-sawgrass areas have told me of cats that resented interference with their nocturnal prowling for stray livestock. Those panthers were said to snarl and hiss and stand their ground, but I have heard of no real attack.

A half-eaten wolverine that I found surrounded by cat tracks in the North Woods indicated that the lion does not always flee from those with fighting reputations. He has the power to pull down a big deer, or even a horse, if hunger is strong enough, but his kill signs show he seldom dives from tree limbs in the style favored by magazine artists.

In most of his range the mule deer can move far enough into rough country so that few hunters will follow, and the easy harvest desired by most sportsmen is a result of overcrowding, harsh weather, or the early season naïveté of animals that have been undisturbed all summer.

In tan summer pelage, the muley is seldom seen during the heat of the day, but appears for early morning and late evening feeding. With forage plentiful, muleys take up semipermanent residence and ranchers become acquainted with individual animals through weeks of observation. They retire to more difficult country when the season starts.

Wilderness hunting of mule deer is best of all, anyway. Most of the real prizes never come too near the valley ranch houses. In mountain hunting the early season stalker must get high and find the north slopes during warm weather. One Montana mountain carries a mature forest so located as to provide early season bedding and adjoining steep parks for feeding, with help from neither logging nor recent fire—a textbook habitat formed by the mountain's shape and by strategic rock formations. I climb it in early morning, staying to the southeast face to avoid the game I expect to find bedded on the northwest side as the sun ascends.

The altitude is about 8,000 feet and climbing is slow, but there is no hurry. This kind of hunting does not depend on game movement. In fact, it may be most effective when the deer are at rest and a little off guard. The sun is well up as I cross a series of open parks trimmed with patches of juniper and crowded with other vegetation showing effects of early frosts, but still standing lush and inviting for either deer or elk. There is sagebrush, scattered mountain mahogany and buffalo berry, and a small patch of raspberries. In

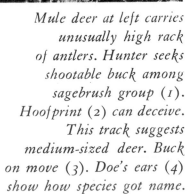

Mule deer at left carries unusually high rack of antlers. Hunter seeks shootable buck among sagebrush group (1). Hoofprint (2) can deceive. This track suggests medium-sized deer. Buck on move (3). Doe's ears (4) show how species got name.

3

4

many places on the open slopes, there are loose mounds formed by pocket gophers, some of them scattered by the feet of feeding deer. It is hard to trace any specific track, but the gophers' earthworks reveal an occasional clear print, generally that of a doe or fawn. Some are large tracks, probably those of good bucks or very large does. Browsing has clipped the tips of some bushes but nothing is trimmed clean, a sure sign food is plentiful.

At that time of morning it is a little chilly, the kind of weather that brings out the clown in ravens. One of them, obviously looking for deviltry, croaks, does a tentative bank and turn, then glides steeply downhill and pulls up as if testing his controls. Near the top of the mountain, I begin moving around toward the north slope, using caution as I am approaching bedding territory. I am high enough to look down into several hazy canyons, and relieved as a little breeze appears. I check its exact drift with a trickled powder of crumbled leaf. I can cope with the breeze, for its direction is determined. It is the thermal drafts of a still day that can give away a hunter's scent, no matter how learnedly he may decide just how they should travel. A firm breeze is more honest.

The wool shirt that was so good at dawn is now unbuttoned and I feel the sweat start along my back—possibly a chilling nuisance on the way downhill, for I am now finished with climbing. Abruptly I am in the shade of both mountain and forest, among mature Douglas firs. The north slope is very steep and is terraced by years of horizontal game trails, some of them worn into paths but covered with matted grass and fir needles. It is a busy community, although at first all that can be heard is the wind. A Canada jay appears on a low limb and I hear a soft, overhead *whoo, whoo* from the flight of a Clark's nutcracker; generally the sound is credited to the jay.

The ideal bedding spot on this slope is just above a big tree's base. The tree forms a platform of earth, needles, twigs, and cones, and the animal can lie on the level, his outline broken by the tree, and still get a perfect downhill view by peering around the trunk. From above, the deer is more vulnerable, but by now the tawny summer coat has changed to a smoky gray that blends with bark and shaded ground, and scattered windfalls are utilized by the more cautious deer as added concealment. It is slow hunting, but the hard work is over. For the rest of the day, I shall slip slowly down the mountain, zigzagging, checking the wind, and studying hundreds of potential beds.

But disappointment comes early in the game. Already I have checked several old beds. Now I feel one that is still warm, evidence that I have frightened my game. I resolve to move more slowly and watch more carefully. Worst of all, I find four black gouges set close together in a mat of spruce needles. Not only has my deer left, he has left in a bouncing, thumping hurry. The muley runs in a series of overdone bounds, going up and down like a carousel deer, with built-in problems for the rifleman, who bobs his sight in ridiculous rhythm and tries to shoot at the peak or bottom of a leap. The deer lands with all four feet nearly together and kicks all of them at once, doing more than twenty feet on level ground with each bound.

A few minutes later I hear measured thuds somewhere below me and sit down in frustration, knowing another deer is leaving. In half an hour I move again, looking for a flicked tail, twitched ear, or a blocky, dark outline at a tree base. Suddenly I see four deer watching me from below, already out of their beds but not yet ready to run. I sit down slowly and stare back at them: an adult doe, her two fawns of the year, and a fat, fork-horned buck. The little buck and the fawns wait for the doe's decision, and she decides to try my scent, somehow fading out of view in circling. Ten minutes later she snorts very near me and I jump, although I had expected just such a performance. I turn and see her plainly and she leads a brisk withdrawal of all four. It is much too early for the rut and my hope for meeting a larger buck in the neighborhood of the doe was a forlorn one.

(The snort was a familiar sound, a signal of danger for the doe's followers, and a similar blast passes for rage or indignation. Camped on a postage stamp of an island in California's Lake Shasta when it was a new impoundment, I became almost afraid of a doe that spent an hour snorting around my boat and sleeping bag one night. It was summer and she may have had a fawn nearby, but I never found out. The snort and a reedy bleat are important doe language. Fawns make squeaky complaints when looking for their mothers. Bucks have deep, grunting sounds of rage and softer, throaty remarks when in good humor.)

I need venison for the freezer and I stop trophy hunting in midafternoon, planning to look for meat as well as antlers. I am more than halfway down the slope when I see a small buck a hundred yards farther along and bedded tightly against a tree trunk. As I slip quietly into sitting position, he gets to his feet and looks about—whether because of a foreign sound, a raveling of man scent, or pure coincidence, I do not know, but I hurry the shot and he rolls downhill. After a ten-minute search I find where he has gone under a down tree.

I should have shot a doe; not enough are taken, but I confess to a reluctance to do so, in a bow to public opinion. I recall how my wife was treated coolly by an entire hunting party when she shot a doe fawn, which she had rightly judged as an exceptional piece of camp meat. Born a little apart from the herd in spring, the fawn is sometimes overwhelmingly curious when hunting season opens in fall, and not too difficult to collect. In hunting season a trace of spots may still remain. Generally born in twos in good years, the fawns are fairly helpless and almost scentless for a while, but acquire strength quickly, nourished on what is recognized as highly nutritious milk.

The big bucks are easier to come by in November, their caution blunted by the rut and their range lowered by high mountain snow pack.

At that time they gather harems of does, fight off lesser competitors, and tolerate only does, fawns, and naïve forkhorns and spikes in their entourages. The herd gatherings are fluid, however. A buck may lose his collection one way or another and then strike out for more romance and war. In rutting season, the big racks are often seen moving steadily and purposefully from one watershed to another, a time when they are especially vulnerable. By October, they have a feeling of restlessness; thereafter they bow to the urge.

The big buck dominates a herd, a mature doe leads it. Most of the fights between males are simply a matter of assertion by a larger, heavier buck, and flattened ears and a couple of vicious hooks at the air generally will discourage a smaller swain, although more furtive romancers frequently infiltrate the harem while the herd buck, bullnecked and red-eyed, uses up his summer fat in angry charges at more obvious usurpers. When well-matched bucks meet, the fight is a thrusting, grinding business with dug-in hooves, and the fighters may be shoved to their knees, but most males get through the season with minor scratches.

I remember an occasion in Montana when a light, fresh snow gave me perfect tracking across the steep draws running down from a high spine called Bangtail Ridge, and I picked up what I thought was a good track. Its maker had splayed his toes with his extra weight, and the hoof tips had brushed the snow slightly in what I interpreted as the surly gait of a trouble-hunting male.

There are all sorts of foolproof recipes for trophy-buck tracks. First, the hoofprint must be large, and a splayed mark indicates weight, as does a strong imprint of dewclaws. The toes are supposed to drag, and if other deer are on the same trail, the big buck should be last to pass. Most doe and fawn tracks are neatly heart-shaped, but after long, hard trailing I have found numerous "big buck" tracks with overweight does standing in them. Nevertheless, I considered the Bang-

Clue to mule deer is mountain mahogany (*1*), a prime food. Aspen groves (*2*) provide concealment as well as browse. Deer are so habituated they use groves even after leaves have fallen. Bobcats may kill young mule deer but generally prefer rabbits. Ravens destroy some young birds and eggs, but are useful as scavengers. Bald eagle, a threatened species, ranges from wetlands to high peaks.

1

2

Cougar (1), seldom seen by hunters, but ever-present in much of high country, is stabilizing factor in maintenance of mule deer herds. Sign: Mule deer droppings (2) are small pellets, sometimes little larger than those of jackrabbit. Game passed this way: After snow comes, routes through upland pasture (3) will be widened and deepened into trenches through constant use by traveling herds.

2

tail mark worth following and its steady gait was encouraging.

After a quarter mile I came upon real encouragement. At one side of the trail was a little fir with freshly shredded branches and all of the new snow knocked off—a sure sign of antler polishing. I hurried along. There appeared to be more snow on the way and it was already mid-afternoon. I had little hope of trotting up behind a traveling buck, but looked far ahead as I topped each sloping ridge, expecting to see my quarry rounding up does or circling a ready-made harem with a disgruntled former master sulking in the wings. I finally saw a single doe standing on a small bench across a wide basin, and I sat down by a little pine to watch her, encouraged when she looked back at the dark timber from which she evidently had emerged for evening feeding. Another doe came out, and behind her came my heavy-antlered buck, for the moment interested only in the does. It was a long shot but I saw no way of getting closer, so I fired from a tree rest after estimating the distance through spitting snow and failing daylight. Even as I started to climb across the big basin to my kill, I saw the does join a smaller buck on its upper rim.

The mountain muleys move up and down with changeable fall weather, and a sage observation that the deer are "high" can be completely untrue tomorrow, for a mountain deer can go from high to low in an hour or less. Some years ago, we laid an ambush for hundreds of deer along the Madison Range, near Ennis, Montana. There had been heavy snow, forcing them to feed on the benchland pastures, but they fed there at night, only to return to mountain forest shortly after sunup.

Our plan was to walk through the herds of

Hunter glassing mule deer country must expect some long-range shots. Fine rack on buck below has four main tines and brow tine on each side. Pair has "stuffed deer" look which falsely suggests stupidity.

129

deer in darkness, take up our stands before dawn, and select our game as the animals returned to the mountains at daylight. As we crossed the pasture land, silently as possible, we moved bands of deer, dark blobs against snowy slopes, and occasionally confronted the specter of a Hereford steer, head-on in the darkness, his white face, chest, and legs making a very credible ghost. We stumbled in badger holes and broke through a frozen ditch, but reached the wire pasture boundary well before light. Deer movement back toward the high ground began with earliest daylight, the barbed fence twanging regularly as deer crawled through it (when startled they jump a stock fence off-handedly). Sitting silently with our silhouettes broken by small sage bushes, we watched a nearby parade of deer, our party of six selecting and shooting four trophies. The firing was done in moments, after which the other game disappeared.

As with most game, there are mule deer "rules," frequently broken but essential for anyone who hunts on his own in strange country. Alarmed muleys generally move upward in mountain country, and hunters traveling on the lower levels play beaters for those farther up. A few thrown pebbles or rolled rocks may start a buck toward the head of his gulch, stopping frequently to see what caused the noise.

Tossed pebbles may bring out other residents of a canyon—few of them as easily seen as deer. An occasional bobcat is sighted, always longer-legged than expected, and filtering soundlessly through bushes. He is less likely to top out than is the deer, and more inclined to fade into the caves and crevices of canyon walls. In many ways, he is a smaller edition of the cougar, but I find him easier to see despite his smaller stature. His favorite foods are rabbits and rodents, al-

*Magnificent panorama at
left is mule deer range. Muley
travels over much wider
area than whitetail. Top: Deer
feeding on steep slope will
disappear instantly
into brushy cover in
background if frightened.
Above: Primarily a browser,
mule deer eats a variety
of vegetation and
will move snow to get at it.*

though he has raided domestic flocks and sometimes kills the young of livestock. His consumption of mule deer is generally confined to the young, but he is nearly always in attendance in good deer country, a special hazard if a kill must be left out overnight.

When a hunter must leave a kill hanging or lying overnight, he suddenly finds himself taking account of all the other predators who enjoy venison. On such an occasion, I have mentally listed bobcats, foxes, coyotes, vultures, magpies, hawks, owls, bears, and assorted rodents as my temporary competitors. A bobcat will take a large piece if he can. Coyotes usually are foiled if the game is hung high.

There are endless schemes for protecting meat that must be exposed for a considerable period. Sometimes the discarded viscera can be left in a way that will draw attention for a while. Hanging game in thick branches may sometimes discourage birds, but the success of such a cache depends largely on how hungry the area is.

I have had success with an undershirt, draped over hanging game, the impregnated man scent being readily caught by most animals. Other hunters swear by burned matches. Nothing seems to discourage the magpie, whose perception must outdo that of more romantic birds of prey. He watches ceaselessly and can gather a crowd of fellow pirates in a few minutes. Even when I left a dressed mulcy for two hours in deep snow, magpies made a costly raid. I had cleverly covered the heart and liver with snow and shielded the deer with brush, since there was no convenient place to hang him. But when I came back with help and a 4 X truck, the liver was completely eaten, the heart was half gone, and the glossy thieves were beginning on the buck's ham. The snow was beaten as level as a street. All of these, however, are accepted hazards of mountain hunting.

Canyon hunting is a marksman's game, the shots likely to be long and difficult. It is well done by horsemen if the terrain is not too rugged.

Given an entire season in the same country, an observant hunter can learn the habits of certain deer and generally locate their escape routes, especially before the rut. They come and go in a definite pattern and by moving them with no thought of a shot a hunter can learn what they consider the shortest route to safety. On a later occasion he can take advantage of their habits.

Big old bucks may be lucky at first; in later years they stretch their lives through sagacity. I have seen an old-timer creeping in whitetail fashion. When a big buck is killed it is likely that his territory will be occupied by a similar prize the next year.

Like all of his close relatives, the mule deer relies strongly on his nose and his big ears. He sees monochromatically and is seldom alarmed by objects which are poorly defined and motionless. An unmoving object, even in the open, may be paid long attention, but then be forgotten.

Moving only when their heads were down in feeding and helped by favorable wind and a glaring sun at my back, I once sneaked to within thirty yards of a good buck and his crowd of does and fawns. The procedure took only an hour from the time I first sighted them from a ridge a mile away. The sage was about three feet high and I stooped only slightly, but stopped each time a head came up.

As with any game, a wounded mule deer is a crushing experience for a serious hunter. He may tell himself that the most painful of deaths is more charitable than the slow starvation encountered in nature. He may try to hide his unpardonable mistake in game-management statistics. But the plight of the single, suffering deer is temporarily more important than all of these unseen thousands of casualties. Whatever the cause—misjudgment of distance, poor marksmanship, or even bad luck—*he* is responsible. If he feels otherwise, he should not be a hunter.

In November we came upon a perfect setting, an old burn coming into its own as a deer feeding ground. Fast-growing plants were binding the soil along the ravines and a border of heavy timber and rough cliffs was perfect for bedding. New plant succession had already brought back a few young conifers, and dead trunks remaining from fires of years ago were making their contribution of fertilization. There was some mountain maple, and the remains of last summer's wildflowers were holding patches of fall snow among thimbleberry clumps on the gully shoulders. Rosebushes and serviceberry were recognizable in the old burn and a patch of quaking aspens, their gaudy leaves fallen, broke the pattern of conifers at the burn's edge.

As we kept to the edge of the burn, we saw a single doe moving slowly along a draw, not far from the timber, and half a mile away we made out a big buck, unerringly heading her way with his head thrust forward, moving almost entirely in the open, although close to timber. Certain the two would meet, we found a position in range of the buck's projected course and waited. When he walked rapidly past a chosen spot, my companion fired a single, poorly judged shot.

The buck flinched and jumped awkwardly into the timber. Sure at first that it had been a lung shot, we followed him in and found a blood patch where he had gone down almost immediately, but there was no sign of lung tissue in the faint blood spray at the place where he had been struck, and my friend acknowledged that he might have hit too far back.

We were very tired. It was afternoon of a day that had begun hours before light, and the prospects of a long track were grim. We began to follow the light blood trail, the other hunter sticking to the track, while I tried to stay just a little ahead of him, working along a timbered and brushy slope a hundred yards to one side—an ancient method which depends upon the game's concentration on the man trailing him, and his fatal exposure to the rifleman on the flank.

A half dozen times the deer bedded, only to move on when my friend approached. Twice I saw a sliding shadow, but nothing to fire at. Once a pair of magpies sailed upward, marking the route of the unseen fugitive. The bedded spots showed a decreasing amount of blood, but the tactic of giving the deer half an hour to stiffen did not work. Toward nightfall he began to seem stronger and as I was about to give out completely, his trail suddenly turned upward (where a wounded deer is not supposed to go) and over a crest. Both of us floundered after him in knee-deep snow. The other man started to circle and I made a stumbling run across a sage flat only to see our quarry laboring up another slope across a canyon he had managed with his renewed vitality. I sat down hard in the snow, and somehow held my wheezing breath long enough to press off a single, perfect shot. The big buck plunged forward on his nose, the last thrust from his injured hindquarters taking him three more feet up the steep slope. It was a long trail back to familiar territory and two days before I was rested enough to hunt again.

I reflect one evening in camp that mule deer season may be closed by nature's edict, rather than man's law. It is now winter. The big wall tent is dirty white canvas, and with the gasoline lantern inside it throws an eerie light on a great space of snow along the slope, lumpy with snow-buried sage bushes. The camp is now too cold to be really comfortable. The tent is set in a declivity, and the little creek that trickles through it down from the higher mountains is now almost frozen solid and barely moving.

Before we go to bed on our last night in camp there is a wild sound that seems to surround us, the bugling honk of Canada geese, and we finally realize that they are confused and circling our lighted area. We step outside but cannot make them out. After half an hour they are gone, apparently having found a pass to the south.

For us, mule deer season is over.

10.
Spring-fed creeks resist the creeping chill, harboring flights of ducks as the year wanes —and anglers try a final cast.

A successful duck year begins in southern Canada with good winter snows and abundant spring rains. This region and much of the northern United States comprise an area which has been christened the "duck factory" by conservationists, for it is the nesting ground of most of the puddle ducks and many of the divers. Through study of the pothole country experts can make a prediction of the entire waterfowl population.

Both the puddle ducks (those that tip up to feed in shallow water) and the divers (those that can dive to considerable depth for their food) are subject to extreme fluctuations in numbers. Most of them nest in freshwater areas, highly dependent on the annual precipitation. Their populations change more rapidly than those of geese, since their habitat changes more from year to year. Most of the geese have nesting areas in coastal marshes of the Far North, where conditions do not change so drastically, and some breed over such a wide range that famine in one region is offset by plenty in another.

For many years groups with conflicting interests have spent large funds in the pothole country of southern Canada and the northern United States; government funds have been used to drain marshes, while sportsmen's dollars have gone to building new ones. Prairie potholes, most of them located in farming country, are the most important factor in duck propagation. If the potholes are drained, or become dry for want of rain, northward migrating ducks will either continue on to less desirable nesting areas or will simply fail to nest. In some bad years drought has struck the entire three hundred thousand square miles of Canadian and American pothole country. Then the northbound flocks that pass over the dry country may continue to northern tundra for their nesting. Such nests are not so productive as those farther south in a good year, but they are enough to maintain a skeletal population which can build back strongly when the rains come.

The common mallard, best-known and most sought of the dabbling ducks, has a pattern which with minor variations fits most of the hunted ducks, and it is a leader of the northward migration in spring. Mallards begin moving from all of the southern states in late February, dawdling along their route, emigrants mixing with residential birds. Migration and seasonal residence are confusing, for the winter home is most of the United States south of Nebraska. In some areas, there are year-round populations, wintering populations that spend only the cold months, and migratory birds; these ducks, all of the same species, are distinguished from each other only by subtle differences in actions and, occasionally, by minor variations in coloration and weight. Individual birds head for the same nesting areas in which they were reared, and if conditions are satisfactory the nesting begins promptly.

In early summer begins a complex, little-understood series of changes in the mallard's life. Once the female is busy with incubation, the drake begins a nearly complete moult, even losing his wing feathers, so that for a time he is unable to fly. His summer feathers come in almost exactly the same as the hen's, and a new moult begins almost immediately afterward, as he is changing into his brilliant prenuptial winter plumage; few Canadian hunters ever collect ducks in full winter color. During winter and spring, the adult female undergoes a gradual moult, her feathers replaced without loss of flight capability, but a second, summertime moult brings a flightless period. It is completed in August or September. Almost all puddle ducks have a similar routine; it is somewhat modified in the diving breeds.

Mallards nest at the edge of grassy ponds, and sometimes well out into open prairie, and occasionally in the unused tree nests of hawks. Hatched in about twenty-six days, the ducklings are cared for completely by their mother, while drakes are sulking about, moulting. The youngsters are masters of camouflage and vanish into the scantiest water growth when their mother gives the alarm. As a frustrated wildlife photographer, I have watched a brood of half-grown mallards disappear against what I thought was a reasonably clear pond bank. Such tactics work well when foxes or coyotes approach the family, but the submarine approach of a northern pike is almost impossible to avoid. Fortunately the very young ducklings usually operate in water too shallow for such attacks.

In September, when the Canadian hunting season opens, the colors of a speeding mallard drake will appear somewhat dim at a distance, for fall plumage is not yet complete and streaks of brown summer feathers blur what will soon be sharp outlines. To find the time and place for shooting, a serious hunter must spend considerable effort watching for ducks on their feeding trips. A high vantage point near grainfields and prairie ponds will serve the purpose.

The duck flock seeking a grainfield is an uncertain form in the distance, grouping and regrouping constantly, very different from the formation of those on a long flight, even though the birds may be as high as migrating flocks.

Once the ducks have neared the feeding area there will be false maneuvers by uncertain younger birds. Little groups will drop out and then hurry to catch up with the leaders. Invariably, a few break away to form their own little pod, and drop in ahead of the main flock.

These are the things the scout watches for from his high-ground viewpoint. The first flock may not pinpoint its landing spot for him, but it will bring him fairly close, and the next group is likely to show him the exact location. He pays little attention to firm formations; these obviously are bound for distant points. He locates specific stubble fields from highways and back roads, often with the help of binoculars. General routes may be established by watching birds leave from midday resting places on lakes or ponds—the larger the resting flocks, the easier their movements are to follow.

Ducks generally prefer to land near the center of a field, safely distant from its margins where predators might be hidden in weeds or brush. Decoys seldom tempt birds to the edges, and hunters sited there may be forced to satisfy themselves with pass shooting. The alternative is to find a midfield ditch or dig a pit blind.

In a harvested grainfield, each newly arrived flock endeavors to overshoot its predecessors a little in order to find new ground not yet depleted of seed. When those at the rear find the gleaning sparse, they flutter ahead of the crowd, an action which always sets off a disapproving gabble. Gunners have sometimes taken advantage of this competitive leap-frogging, and by keeping quiet in an irrigation ditch or swale have found the vanguard bearing into range in pigeon-toed haste, craning necks and chuckling smugly.

Birds using the same fields for long periods will alight in the same general area day after day. In Illinois, where fields are smaller than on the Canadian prairies, they may trade back and forth, evidently feeling that the scattered grain will be more plentiful beyond the next fence. Even that far south, teal may be careless of a stationary gunner and drop into a field quickly without so much as an investigative turn.

At the season's beginning in southern Canada, most of the ducks are young birds and far different from those that have dodged hunters for a thousand miles down the flyways. On windy days with promised rain, I have seen Canadian mallards, pintails, and baldpates decoyed to triangular pieces of black cloth, ceremoniously removed from a paper bag and placed by a native obviously pleased by the skepticism of his guests from the States. With a car parked only a hundred yards from the "decoys," three of us sat on the ground one afternoon in the middle of a great prairie grainfield with the wind to our backs, and I felt like a juvenile who had been taken on a clandestine snipe hunt with lantern and burlap sack—although I know that, in dry years espe-

Atlantic Coast hunter (above) bags black duck on wide marsh. Pintails (1) live in tiny prairie pools, become wary running flyway gantlet. Redhead drake (2) is among speediest of diving ducks. Blue-winged teal (3) migrates in early fall and is elusive target. Goldeneyes (4) are inured to coldest weather. Widgeon (5), puddlers themselves, will steal tidbits from divers.

1

2

4

5

cially, a shiny sheet of clear plastic with decoys scattered over it can simulate a small pothole.

For five minutes the only bird we saw was a hovering sparrow hawk. But after that came the ducks. It was a mixture of mallards and pintails that appeared high, bunching and spreading, and then came teetering down upon our black rags with a sustained hiss of braking against the wind. There was no interest in the three men with shiny shotguns, sitting bolt upright thirty yards away. The rags were simply a hint of mallard heads, accepted by birds who expected to see mallard heads and were thinking of food. When we refrained from firing and allowed them to land, they first were puzzled by the rags, then conscious of our motionless presence, and they took off once more to land noisily only a short distance away. Occasionally an old bird stretched his neck and looked back at us as if he did not approve of the site but had been outvoted. I contemplated the fact that a few weeks later I would shiver in a sleet-battered blind for one chance at a mallard.

As migration time nears, the Canadian ducks bunch into feeding flocks, although seldom appearing in the geometric formations of south-bound travelers. Hunters finding busy grass ponds can do nearly as well there as we did in barley stubble, and if there is suitable cover for a stalk midday is as good a time as any to find birds resting on water or supplementing their grain diet with aquatic plants and the seeds of marginal weeds. The time after morning feeding is good for watching the birds slide back into the ponds.

Stalking ponds in pastureland is simpler because of the presence of livestock, a routine, constantly moving part of the ducks' view. The entire route of approach should be mapped and each declivity memorized, so that the stalker can remain low. A single gooseberry bush can be important, if strategically approached to make the most of its cover. If only clumps of grass and weeds are present, the hunter may protect his gun in an old guncase and drag it behind him with a length of rope as he crawls—hoping weather has been cool enough to send the rattlesnakes into hibernation.

Almost invariably, the birds first seen by the stalking hunter are not those nearest to him on the pond, and he must be doubly careful not to startle those he has not located; it helps if he knows the water's shape from earlier experience.

Even when he is finally sighted by lookouts, the ducks may have a moment of indecision, for a man on all fours, or on his stomach, might be any number of harmless things. If he is in range when he feels he has been discovered, he can simply stand up and shoot; if he has only a short distance to get within range, he may gain a little by making a quick run toward the pond. If he can see the flock while stalking, he must stop and stay completely quiet whenever even one neck is stretched. Birds that stop feeding or sleeping and bunch tightly before he is in range probably are lost opportunities.

If he gets quite close before the flush, he is more likely to fire too soon than too late. It takes some little time for feeding ducks to take off, and they often get up raggedly. Most likely some will have their heads under water when the alarm is given. A bunched and suspicious flock, of course, can leave instantly. In any event, there is likely to be considerable noise and the temptation is to fire too soon, especially with a second shot, which is best saved until the shooter is sure of his target bird's flight direction.

Most hunters have a built-in preference for the "northern" or migrating ducks, as if they were a distinct race of bigger and tastier birds. "Northerns" for the Texas shooter may have come down from Nebraska. For the Nebraska shooter, they may be fresh from the Dakota potholes. For the Dakota hunter, a "northern" is from the Saskatchewan prairie ponds.

In Canada and the northern United States, there is a period of slow shooting which comes after the local ducks have learned to be wary and before the migratory birds move in, unaware of the established blind-locations. In southern Canada, migration may be touched off by a sudden hard freeze, causing ducks to abandon their grassy ponds and potholes. But it will not necessarily be a general migration. Many ducks may remain to prospect for open water, and when the cold wave subsides, the first flight may be found casually working back northward.

Most duck water is shallow, however, and at some point in the fall a sudden freeze is certain. A thousand resting places will turn to ice, and prairie-pond gunning will be finished for the time being. Any open water is a sure attraction then, and gunners who know a spring hole or two study the weather reports, trying to learn just how far south the ponds are freezing. If it becomes really cold, the warmer spring-fed ponds and creeks will be at a premium. Those that have held native ducks before migration is in full swing are most likely to attract traveling birds.

As the season advances and the cold becomes more constant, ducks assemble at the sources of spring creeks and seepy areas, wallowing in the banks of watercress and enjoying water not yet chilled by passage through subfreezing valleys. Many a late-season pheasant hunter has been startled by a mallard leaping from a wet patch of green marked by a willow or two.

One spring-fed creek in the western mountains lies in a valley that enjoys a belt of somewhat milder weather. It is subject to the white cold of its latitude, but warming chinook winds somehow find it more readily than other valleys.

The spring creek is a fishing stream in summer and well into the fall, the seasons overlapping so that a duck hunter may find a fly caster busy at a point where he would like to put his decoys. Blind-building is an easy matter, for the stream is lined with rosebushes, willows, cottonwoods, and small pines. Anything the hunter builds is likely to be accepted as a natural part of the landscape, and in some places the natural vegetation itself serves as a blind.

In early fall, I take an axe to the creek to make a blind on an overgrown point where a clear-water slough forks off the stream. It is a little more trouble to set up the decoys there, but it is a natural landing spot for mallards. The slough is trimmed by a few cattails and assorted bushes, and there is a wide band of watercress along its shore. It is a spot any careful hunter would choose, for the vegetation is near the surface and easily available to tipping ducks. Strips of the plants are swallowed whole and there is a harvest of underwater life that clings to the growth. In such an area decoys are simply reassurance for the ducks, since they are already looking for a spot to alight when they arrive.

While I cut a few branches to fashion a blind between two big cottonwood logs, several muskrats pass the site, industriously hauling a collection of greenery. Part of the time they are submerged, and are plainly visible under water, scooting expertly along light green avenues of waving milfoil and pondweed. In front of the blind, where the milfoil is matted on the surface in several places, they sit on top and munch choice leaves and stems. Ducks often perch on the matted areas which are partly made up of muskrat collections. Sometimes the muskrats take delight in submerging, then popping to the surface and throwing a spatter of water in the face of a startled duck, possibly feeling the duck is a competitor for food.

As I finish my work, a water ouzel makes his improbable reconnaissance along the opposite shore, walking, swimming, and diving. It is evening when I wade back across the creek to my vehicle, and the two mallards take off again from almost the same spot.

For the moment, I have forgotten the beaver who has left drag trails in the willows near my blind, and whose engineering has considerable bearing on the creek's duck hunting. He scares me for an instant with a tremendous warning crack

142

So Near Yet So Far:
Clouds of waterfowl (1)
rise from marsh, but
skill is needed to bring
them within range.
Cold, camouflaged hunter
(2) waits for mallards.
Jump shooter (3)
scans ditches for resting
puddlers. Southern
gunner (4) seeks wood
duck or teal in cypress
swamp. Reeds give
natural cover to hunter
(5). Shooter among potholes
scans sky for mallards.

of his tail at short range.

The beaver, a builder of quiet ponds, is an ally in creek hunting, changing small stream courses from year to year, and making deep resting areas that are slow to freeze at times when more shallow ponds ice over. Ducks and geese use beaver lodges as resting areas and occasionally nest there. Where stream flow is delayed by a beaver dam, a pool forms that is receptive to algae, desirable for both ducks and fish. As he builds his dams the beaver cuts down the large trees along the streams, leading to a crop of willows and weeds, much more desirable for wildlife than the mature forest. Ducks use the willows and other marginal growth as cover, and feed on pondweed and bulrush, as well as on the insects that gather in the shoreline plants.

The scene has changed when I come back to the spring creek.

The weather reports had told of a Canadian storm. In Alberta and Saskatchewan the small ponds should be frozen hard. The snow comes first in big, soft flakes, then in smaller, icy ones. The whistling wind dies when the cold strikes. In the small hours of the second morning, I rise in the dark and head for the creek, the tires of my four-wheel drive crunching loudly as I leave town by a deserted street.

At the point where I shall wade the creek, I get stiffly to the ground, hampered by insulated underwear, uncounted woolen shirts, and chest-high waders. The dozen decoys are stuffed in a bag lashed to a pack frame, my shells are in a canvas belt hung around my neck for dry storage and easy reach. I struggle into the pack straps, then hang an enormous thing over the frame. It is an inflated inner tube, covered with canvas and with a seat inside the doughnut shape; I will use it to recover kills in the deep water near the blind. I stalk toward the creek, an apparition of meaningless shape.

The stars are brilliant in the clear cold and the white mountains seem bigger and nearer than usual. The spring creek is a great wall of dead white, its steam rising straight up for forty feet before dispersing. The treetops visible above it are coated with ice. The water, although it gurgles in friendly tones, is a black abyss to be waded with special care, and I hold the shotgun high. There are restless duck sounds about me now, the questioning squawk of a mallard hen, the lighter quack of teal, a pintail's gentle whistle. My beaver does not appear.

As I gain the other bank and start across the solid ground, walking gets difficult. The wet has frozen on my waders and their soles have picked up rounded cakes of snow and ice. The first section of slough is frozen and I break through it with some effort. The water is not moving much and the warming influence of the creek is not enough to keep it open. I make a mental note that the birds will not land there.

As I put out my decoys, there is more agitated duck discourse around me, and what appears to be a little bunch of mallards takes off, one bird coming within a few feet of my head, showing vaguely in the sea of white. I hear its wings plainly. I expect the birds to leave, but I know they are likely to return when the commotion ceases.

In the little blind I hear takeoffs and landings, and as daylight approaches, a pair of pert green-winged teal splat into the decoys, look around with quickly jerking heads, then take off and land again a few yards away. There are plenty of birds about me and I wonder how many of them have been there before, beating ahead of other storms in other years.

With shooting time comes some air movement and the steam blanket grows ragged. None of the sitting birds is within range now, and I get out of the blind to start them moving, hoping for a shot when they return. A few minutes later, a scattered bunch of mallards comes back, wings set and dropping fast. I kill one. Overhead is the whistle of a band of goldeneyes making a quick sweep. Far behind me a flock of Canada geese passes, following the main river. A lonely mallard hen drops in, salutes the decoys, and is offended by their stolid silence. She flies off a few yards and is allowed to remain as an auxiliary attraction, providing better duck talk than I can manage with my call.

I allow lesser ducks to pass, waiting for mallards. A streamlined merganser, his woodpecker's head splitting the cold air, elects to make three strafing runs at the decoys. He passes over them at twenty feet, each time pulling up to a considerable height half a mile away, and then whistling in at incredible speed, wings driving even as he nears the bottom of his plunge. (The merganser is equally graceful under water scooting like a sleek, feathered arrow over the bottom gravel in pursuit of small fish.)

It is midmorning when I end my hunt. I have looked to the north and seen a faint dotted line that turns into a streak of mallards, treetop high and closing fast. They are part of the Canadian contingent and are ready to pitch into any satisfactory water. The line splits into small bunches, one pod heading straight for the decoys, swinging off a little, and then banking in, slipping sidewise just a little and bent on landing. I give a feeding chuckle on my call and am helped by the stray mallard hen which issues a brazen invitation. It is an easy shot, even for a tired croucher, cramped with cold.

As I pick up the decoys, the lines freezing in my hands, a muskrat impudently passes my knees in the clear water, two feet below the surface, but somehow in another world and unafraid of my bulky and slow-moving waders. Walking out, I startle half a dozen jacksnipe that have been feeding with great ceremony where a little water trickling through an old dam keeps a small mud patch from freezing. They leave in their darting, disorganized flight; already they may have come a long way from their summer grounds above the Arctic Circle. Now the jacksnipe dally as long as they can find spots of soft earth for their exploring beaks.

Half a mile away is the main river, which generally runs clear at this time of year. Ducks rest on its rocky bars, well away from the main brushy shoreline. At midday many of them will have their heads under their wings, trusting to the watchfulness of a few sentries. Stalking them here is hard, especially as the season wears on and the birds become more wary of intruders. A hunter may be given away by a startled deer, or a flushing merganser.

More than two thousand miles from where the storm-pushed pintails seek out the spring creeks, others of their kind flock happily into brackish mangrove pockets to feed on widgeon and turtle grass. Here again the first requirement is that the water be shallow enough for feeding. A school of frightened mullet, darting about near the surface, indicates shallow water; the fish can't submerge far enough to hide their wakes.

We go to the lower west coast of Florida, where even a slight frost is a rare thing. At evening, wading birds soar into the rookeries in noisy droves and the big wood storks appear at great height in sweeping turns. They might never be noticed by duck hunters, except that when the sun catches their upper wings it appears that a cluster of bright lights has suddenly turned on in the blue sky. The same effect is achieved by circling white pelicans. The curved upper surfaces of the wings reflect the light only when the birds turn at the proper angle; then there is an instant reflection from the entire flock. The osprey and the bald eagle are generally circling much lower.

No part of the hunter's world is in more jeopardy than the Everglades. Since the great rookeries were riddled by plume hunters half a century ago, wildlife there has had to struggle constantly against new menaces. Latest of the endangered species is the alligator, whose skin is of sufficient commercial value to encourage poachers to decimate the species. The Glades are so

3 1 2

*Opposite: Coot
is clownish companion
of ducks. Coot decoys
will lull ducks' suspicions.
Alligator, an endangered
species, is ecologically
important builder of southern
ponds. Duck boats vary;
Tennessee sportsman placing
decoys uses canoe.
This page, from top: Ospreys
live over waterfowl habitat.
Snapping turtle hopes
to seize dangling waterfowl
leg. Coyote also has
taste for ducklings. Industrious
beaver forms acres of
resting water by construction
of dams. Retriever recovers
winged bird from shallows.*

4

5

6

7

8

large that complete policing is impossible.

Many of the high-ground hammocks have grown from a single alligator nest. The female covers the eggs with a mound of vegetation, and heat generated from the decaying plants hatches the popeyed young. The mound becomes earth of a sort and a succession of plants begins, building an island in the sawgrass sea. It is the alligator which forms the sawgrass-bordered ponds where water and ducks hold during drought, when much of the remainder of the Everglades burns, with a choking smoke drifting offshore in clouds.

The Everglades, known as the "river of grass," is truly a flowing stream that moves gently southward across most of southern Florida in normal weather. In some places the slope is only an inch to the mile. It is the slow-moving fresh water that attracts coastal wildlife to the shores of the peninsula's tip, and its mixture with salt water brings about the enormous "incubator" environment of the mangrove coasts—a nursery for millions of fishes and other aquatic forms, and a winter home for ducks and wading birds.

A short distance inland from the mangrove bays and rivers is the sawgrass of the true Everglades, the transition from twisted roots to grass coming abruptly at the line between salt and fresh water. The line pushes inland year by year, however, for man has channeled off much of the fresh water, and the mangrove takes over gradually from sawgrass as water becomes salty enough to support it. Especially in dry weather, sawgrass ponds are often located by the circling of wading birds—or by the ducks themselves. A stork is an easily seen indicator, planing down from great height to a shallow pond. Coots on such a pond are a good sign, since their feeding requirements are much the same as those of dabbling ducks.

In some sectors of the sawgrass country, there is almost too much noise at night. Camped on a dry hammock, the hunter listens to thousands of frogs, an occasional alligator, and a variety of bird squawks and croaks, often subordinated to the depressing complaints of the limpkin. It takes an experienced naturalist to separate the sounds, although there is little mistaking the occasional raccoon riot which breaks out near shore. Depending upon the maturity of the litigants, a raccoon argument may sound shrilly furious or snarlingly ominous, and it is a surprise to find no blood or mangled bodies in the morning. Whether the debate concerns an especially fat clam or a doomed frog, it may be continued into the treetops, and I have hurled missiles into the darkness in hope of a little peace. In the meantime, man's contribution to the din may be the rising and falling roar of airboats, miles away in the Glades, as their operators look for shining frog's eyes with their headlights gleaming across the tines of murderous gigs.

A mangrove gunner may get to his private observatory with considerable effort. I have often spent much of a night boating through the mangrove creeks to reach a particular pocket the pintails or baldpates were known to be using. For very short runs the boater could follow a shoreline with occasional use of a flashlight. If he expects to go a long distance in a short time, he must learn to navigate by the treetops against the sky. The method is impossible unless he has an excellent idea of the contours of the streams and bays he must follow. He does not look for specific trees as landmarks, rather he goes by those that appear to be of even height. Thus the watercourses are rimmed by dark tree outlines which recede in the distance. A long way off the trees may appear as a single dark bank; approached closer they will have notches and gaps. On clear nights star reflections distinguish water from shore. The boater carefully studies a chart before attempting a night trip, and the use of a light is a hindrance, since it reflects from the trees and ruins his night vision. After ten miles of swamp travel most hunters are glad to reach their blind.

Before daylight the mangrove blind is occupied, the decoys are out only a short distance away, and everything is as natural as possible. These pintails are not the trusting youngsters who spilled into black rags in a barley field. Now it is Christmas week and they are snaky-necked veterans of the flyways, unlikely to decoy if they once examine the stool, and likely to twist their heads for endless angles of view as they continue to another spot. Baldpates may be less suspicious than pintails while flying, although more restless when on the water; scaups will plunk in without a second look.

The water is only nine inches deep at low tide, and the boat we came with is carefully covered a quarter mile away in a channel. We have poled to the mangrove blind in a flat-bottomed johnboat.

We have surprise on our side. Even a veteran pintail group leader does not expect to find shotguns this far from civilization, and the dawn flight is almost sure to be productive, at least one or two bunches coming straight in with their feet down. That is the best of the shooting. Later on the birds may stick to more open water and fly higher, or they may flare from our boat, even when it seems perfectly hidden in the channel.

One friend believes firmly in shooting from a tree, ten feet from the water, feeling sure the ducks will be studying the decoys as they swing in and will ignore the gunner, and he goes to great pains to build an unobtrusive blind on the mangrove limbs. On the larger mangrove bays we are careful to have the wind at our backs; in the small holes it makes no difference.

Bald eagles live a long while, and perhaps the one that used to oversee my duck hunting had watched a generation of gunners come and go. As soon as it was light, I could see his white head and hackles in a treetop a quarter mile away. Just how he knew the hunt was on, I never learned, but he would patiently wait for a shot and then come for the blind at top speed in a race for the downed birds. Screamed insults and vile

names had no effect on the old thief and the only solution was to pole or wade rapidly toward the game, firing a shotgun at intervals. Once the bird was noisily retrieved by either eagle or human, it would be some time before any duck would come near the area.

If hunting was poor, our Everglades eagle might leave his perch and scout for fishing ospreys. I have watched him dive several times on one; despite evasive action he could usually force the smaller bird to drop its mullet, which he then fielded in midair in classic eagle fashion. I always enjoyed his successes, for it meant he would not be duck hunting for a while.

Everglades coots are excellent adjuncts to the decoys, reassuring suspicious ducks. A flock can muddy an acre of water where eelgrass is plentiful, and individuals will fight and screech endlessly over a piece of grass that looks to the non-coot like any other piece of grass. I have often seen a single coot disappear amid a flock of its fellows, slowly sinking with loud squalls and frantic flapping. Although I have heard otters, small alligators, gars, and snapping turtles blamed, I am convinced the turtle is the coot taker most of the time. At any rate, the only time I have left a blind and grabbed a submerging coot, I found a sizable snapping turtle hanging to one foot, waiting for its quarry to drown. Undoubtedly an occasional duck is a victim of the snapper.

Duck-hunting areas have shrunk, partly because of human development, partly because of necessary preserve areas where shooting has been shut off. Other game in the Everglades is principally whitetail deer and turkey in the hammocks and bobwhite quail on the larger sections of high ground.

Alligator poacher and deer jacklighter are still enemies of wildlife, but it is the housing development, the stretching airplane runways, the creeping suburbs, and man's insatiable demand for water that could mean an eventual end to the river of grass and its border of mangroves.

11.
The cruising owl observes
the rabbits' games on moonlit snow;
forgetful squirrels bury
nuts that help renew the woods.

Rabbits are lifelong fugitives, among the lowest animals in the order of predatory relationships, along with many of the rodents they closely resemble. Their protection is speed, camouflage, and fecundity. There is no doubt that rabbits are the most popular American game, both as subjects of the most elemental pursuit and as training for hunting more glamorous trophies. Rabbits are defenders of fawns and upland game birds—which is to say that foxes, coyotes, bobcats, and other carnivores are regular rabbit eaters and turn to other foods only when rabbits are scarce.

Rabbit cycles, which seem to be renewed about every ten years, may reach a low point as a result of an easily isolated disease, although at other times the population declines for reasons the biologists cannot learn. Tularemia has been the greatest killer of the rabbit, but in recent years there has been talk of agricultural chemicals adding to the toll.

Cottontails are the most plentiful of rabbits, most widely hunted, and among the most rapidly reproductive. A doe may have four or more litters a year. In good times, with the cycle near its peak, there may be as many as seven young at a time; when the cycle is near a low point the litter may be no more than three. Four is about average. A cottontail nest is a depression several inches deep, lined with fur and usually located in thick grass or weeds. The mother covers it lightly when she leaves, using scraps of vegetation and fur. When she wishes to move her young she picks them up as a female cat carries kittens.

The widest area is held by the eastern cottontail, which populates most of the United States, while the mountain cottontail inhabits the West. The West Coast has the brush rabbit, and the Southwest the desert cottontail. There is the marsh rabbit in the Southeast and the swamp rabbit in the South Central states. All of them are similar in appearance, all of them have some special physical characteristic to fit them to their specific habitat, and all behave much the same when pursued by predators. All of them are good swimmers; the marsh and swamp rabbits take to water readily. Even the eastern cottontail, which does not like the water and is generally thought to be a strictly terrestrial animal, will sometimes swim a stream or pond when hotly pressed by a pursuer. In addition, spring floods will occasionally force cottontails to swim to higher ground. Some animals seem to sense the approach of a flood in time to escape it on foot, but evidently this is not true of rabbits.

Cottontails are sufficiently active at night to be called nocturnal, but they are generally classified as crepuscular since their busiest periods are at dusk and dawn. Although the individual rabbit may not have a wide range, he knows an intricate network of paths—perhaps miles of them—the trails of one rabbit running into the home territory of another. Within his range the bunny is a steady traveler; a few hours after a fresh snow there will be beaten trails—sometimes formed by the repeated passage of only one or two animals but giving the impression of a veritable rabbit horde in the vicinity. The travel is partly a matter of play. Games of tag continue even during periods of feeding, the participants stopping headlong chases to nibble grass or bark. The habit of following communal trails is strong in all American rabbits and hares. Even in desert country it is possible to detect faint traceries through scanty grass, trails that will become firm-bottomed trenches in the snows of a hard winter. Anyone who waits long enough near one of these trails will find that, eventually, the rabbits will come to him in their endless rambling.

Most of his enemies hope to catch the cottontail with a short sprint or a single leap before he can reach safety, usually a den made by some other animal, or a hollow log, preferably with two entrances. The common house cat is among the most efficient of rabbit hunters, dozing away the daylight hours and becoming an impla-

Opening pages: Cottontail rabbit is
Number One game animal of North America.
A vegetarian, with only strong legs for protection,
it is near bottom of predation scale. This
rabbit knows a small living area extremely well.

cable predator at night. The duck hunter, concealed in his blind at dawn, often sees farm cats slipping back to their daytime homes, after all-night forays. In addition to the domestic cat, the bobcat, the fox, and the coyote, there are several other important predators. Weasels and great horned owls will kill a full-grown cottontail. Raccoons will sometimes prey on young rabbits in the nest; the young are also endangered by snakes—particularly the pilot blacksnake.

Most of the cottontail bag goes to shotgunners who either kick up the game or shoot ahead of dogs. Among the truly skillful rabbit hunters is the rifleman who sights the bunny in his squat, or form, and then shoots him before he leaves. I learned this hunting as a boy in the Midwest.

Without snow, it takes an expert to make out sitting cottontails. In one of the most exacting kinds of still-hunting, the expert with a .22 rifle walks slowly along a tiny creek sighting the crouched rabbits along the bank, generally in a damp place with grass or weeds covering all but the entrances to their squats. Some of them make their forms for close-coupled squatting; others are almost fully extended—and much easier to see.

It is a matter of perception rather than sharp eyesight. My father, who collected many rabbits in a lifetime on the farm, was able to point out squatting bunnies to me even after his eyes were too poor to use the rifle sights; and more embarrassing, it was often impossible for me to make out the animal after he pointed to it. He would patiently describe the parts he could see, and I have actually killed rabbits by aiming at a point in the grass and willows, carefully described by my father, without actually seeing the target.

Generally, a rabbit appears dark against either live or dead foliage. When he is hidden in briers or weeds the trick is to look *through* the cover for the broken outlines behind it (or for the round, dark eye which betrays him most frequently). It is the act of looking through the

153

brush, as my father told me, that locates the game. I remember looking, many years later, through the distracting vertical lines of an aspen grove to see a great mule deer bedded, his antlers flat against his withers, like a cottontail with his ears laid back.

The midwestern still-hunt usually begins soon after a new snowstorm. For a time there are no tracks at all. The cottontails hold tightly to their forms, the old trails are covered, and the blackberry patches appear as softly contoured white mounds over dark openings. A rabbit will sit in a compact ball under his chosen tussock of dead grass, perhaps sheltered further by briers, willows, or a snow-clogged tumbleweed. His ears are back and the ground is damp from his body heat, although he gets some protection from the matted grass beneath him.

Cottontails are surprisingly sensitive to cold weather. A Michigan game biologist once used ferrets to explore abandoned animal burrows in which cottontails were taking refuge on frigid winter days. When the temperature was between twelve and thirty-two degrees, he found that fourteen per cent of these dens were occupied, but when it dropped to between eight and twelve degrees, forty-two per cent of the dens were occupied. It would seem that when the temperature is too cold for a winter-clad hunter to be comfortable moving about outdoors, it is also too cold for the rabbits to be out, and hunting is likely to be poor.

During a storm a rabbit moves only in emergency; probably he is invisible, and using an air hole if the snow is deep. But after the snow stops he will hop out to feed, rooting to grass if there is no crusted snow. If the snow is badly frozen, he leaves his marks where he has gnawed willow bases or young catalpas, for the cottontail accepts as wide a variety of food as any American mammal.

In spring and summer, bluegrass is probably preferred over all other foods, but the cotton-

*Bramble patch with network of
tunnels (1) is good cottontail cover. Beagle
vs. rabbit (2) is big hunt on small
scale. Peering cottontail (3) will squat if
approached. Litter (4) huddles in typical nest.*

155

tail also loves timothy, wild rye, goldenrod, alfalfa, clover, truck crops, and most other green plants. In berry patches, which are favorite feeding sites, the cottontail is more likely to nibble the new green shoots than the woody stalks or even the fruit. Both used and abandoned apple and peach orchards are as appealing to rabbits as to whitetail deer. But when such crops are gone and the first fall frosts spread over the grasses, cottontails move into brush patches, fencerows, windbreaks, and woodlands.

A brush pile offers shelter and concealment as well as food. For the same reason, honeysuckle tangles, multiflora rose, grape vines, and sumac patches are frequently sought. Because sumac has a high fat content in its bark, it is a favorite winter food. A rabbit's forepaws are incapable of grasping, but the pliable cleft lip can pull in even tiny bits of greenery, and the animal can tilt its head to gnaw efficiently at bark and twigs in winter when other food is scarce.

On sunny winter days, rabbits can sometimes be spotted basking on hillsides, but in bad weather they will retreat to the brambles and heavy brush or will stay underground. They can go for a week without eating when forced to do so by shortages or cold temperatures, but afterward they are likely to go on an eating spree which will considerably lengthen their dawn and dusk periods of peak activity.

The first night after a snow the rabbit and his friends leave a maze of tracks in an orgy of racing and jumping games. The ideal hunting time is the day following a snowfall that ended late at night. Only early-morning tracks will show.

The hunter goes to a small pasture creek, only a step across and not yet frozen solid, and he watches the rabbit trails along the bank, perhaps two or three feet above the water which trickles under a shield of ice. He is especially attentive when he nears a sharp bend in the little stream, a U-shaped haven, safe from wind, where the snow settles gently. At that point a rabbit track runs

over the edge of the bank and he sees no return trail. He withdraws a little and steps to the opposite side of the creek, his boots silent in the new snow. From the other side he inspects the track, which goes down over the little bank and disappears under a small overhang. For a few moments the hunter sees only a dark hole, but then he picks up the reflection from a rabbit's shiny eye. His hunt has succeeded. Slowly he raises his little rifle. The distance is only a dozen feet.

The world of the cottontail is small, which is the key to hunting him with beagles. He either bounces into some familiar hideout or circles back toward his starting place, unwilling to chance the protection of strange bramble patches or unfamiliar hollow logs. Dog users find a good vantage point when the race begins, expecting the rabbits to stay well ahead of the trailing hounds, and they wait for the inevitable circling maneuver that keeps a cottontail in familiar territory. If the hunter can find a visible rabbit trail, so much the better, for the chase is likely to cover that route eventually.

The snowshoe rabbit, or varying hare, shows less tendency to seek cover under pressure. He sometimes weighs as much as four pounds and travels well on top of soft snow because of cushioned, widespreading feet. The snowshoe lives over much of Canada and parts of the northern United States, often in wilderness areas, although sharing the garden-raiding habits of the cottontail. He is dark brown in summer and white in winter; occasionally his camouflage is out of phase with the season, as in snowless falls when he is a ghostly presence in brown and green timberlands. Second-growth scrub and brush in heavy timber provides ample food and cover. The snowshoe is often killed for camp meat by backwoods travelers, although few serious hunting expeditions are aimed at him. He is excellent food. Like the cottontail, the snowshoe is subject to tremendous fluctuations of population over something like a ten-year period. Since the varying

Black-tailed jackrabbit
(left) can outrun almost any
pursuer but greyhound.
Desert cottontail (below) is
prey of coyote. Bottom:
Camouflage of snowshoe
rabbit is sometimes
out of phase with season,
making animal
likelier victim of predators.

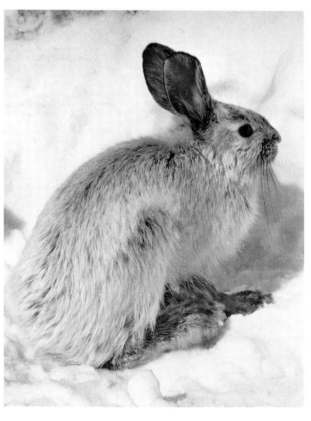

hare is an important staple of the northern bob-cat's diet, the bobcat population tends to rise and dip with the snowshoe rabbit population.

Even larger are the jackrabbits, all of which have much longer ears than the cottontails. Among all of America's game animals, they rate second only to the pronghorn in ground speed, but they can be run down by greyhounds. They are often hunted by riflemen who practice shoot-ing at them while they run. But the practical time to shoot a jackrabbit with a rifle is after he has been frightened from his form, moves off, and then stops to inspect the intruder. This pause is very nearly certain unless he is pursued by a dog. Jacks—which belong to the hare and not the rabbit family—will browse on all the same greenery that provides fodder for cottontails and varying hares, but they also subsist in semiarid regions—together with the desert cottontail—where the chief vegetation consists of sage, tum-bleweeds, cactus, and the like.

The long, flexible, sensitive ears of all rabbits and hares can be swiveled in any direc-tion, and give early warning of danger. But in the open country where jacks abound, a rabbit is not likely to rely on stationary concealment when sounds of danger approach closely. Speed is the chief defense, and the pause to check on the enemy is the most frequent cause of a jackrabbit's downfall.

In many areas the coyote's fortunes rise and fall with the jackrabbit cycles, just as the bobcat's fortunes depend on the snowshoe rabbit. Although for a hundred years his name has been a synonym for cowardice, the coyote actually withstands pain in silence, recovers from terrible injuries that would kill more noble beasts, and when run to exhaustion by coursing hounds will die fighting the whole pack.

In the West the hunter can find coyote tracks on the alkali and greasewood flats, near rabbit trails that show faintly in the grass and become deep grooves after heavy snowfalls. The coyote, with a price on his head for generations, adapted to the small farms, and then to the large farms and the big cattle and sheep ranches. He has penetrated the East, the South, and even the Far North, ranging from Alaska to Puerto Rico. In the big picture he is part of the prairie balance, but farmers and ranchers hate him for his oc-casional depredations of livestock and poultry. I remember looking as a sleepy child through a steamy kitchen window at dawn to see a prairie wolf clear a hog fence, catch a squawking leghorn five feet from the ground in a precision leap, and sail back over the fence to race for the safety of a willowed draw.

A real danger to lambs, or even adult sheep in hungry times, the coyote has stunned farmers in territory where his presence was not even suspected. On a southern deer stand, watch-ing a burn just recovering with tender green plants, I listened to hounds working distant sand pines and saw a familiar outline, moving low and swiftly through and over the new growth. It was far away, but there was the flowing tail and the energy-saving lope. The apparition disappeared in timber and I hurried to where it had crossed a sand road, but there was such a spatter of dog tracks that I was never sure which prints belonged to my ghost. My story drew covert smiles, but a few years later sheep flocks were raided in that vicinity and biologists were called to examine some small pups caught by a rancher. Identifica-tion was positive.

In settled areas the coyote's falsetto wail and choppy bark are sometimes the only signs the human residents have of his presence. As a boy in southeastern Kansas, where the rolling plains tip upward to the Missouri Ozarks, I lived among coyotes but seldom saw them except dur-ing organized drives. It was thirty years later that a boyhood friend showed me what real coyote hunting is like. He has gone to a precision varmint rifle and uses methods unthought of when we were boys. His best sport comes with

1

Busy rabbits leave sign of their presence after each snowfall (1). Tracks entering at right are fox's. Purposeful red fox (2) prowls rabbit country. Cottontail (3) would have ears farther back if he were at top speed. Gray squirrel (4) stays close to safe tree. Holes in tree trunk (5), some big enough for squirrel's nest, are work of pileated woodpecker. Jack (6) is browser, as well as grazer. Coyote (7) seeks winter meal.

2

3

5

6

Predators & Prey (from left): Slow-footed raccoon dines on rabbit carcass. Weasel is killer of many small animals and their young— among them the western prairie dog. Squirrels usually are hidden in nests during nocturnal hunts of great horned owl. Pilot blacksnake eats young of small game, but also wars on rodents.

fresh snow, and he locates coyote territory by tracks, then hunts the back roads.

It is, as my friend says, simply a matter of knowing what to look for. The binoculars may show a gray or tawny patch, possibly against a background of dead sunflower stalks, and then forward-thrust ears, and finally the entire coyote is suddenly quite plain. I am sure we passed a thousand such as youngsters, seeing only the occasional animal that moved. I see coyotes myself now, some of them high on rocky ridges in plain sight, but usually dead still, their ears pricked in interest, always watching me.

His success at camouflage can be the little wolf's undoing, for having watched man and his works for a few years without detection, he will sit, a composed victim of his curiosity, while a long-range rifleman gets warily into position.

It is in calling that coyote hunting reaches a peak. The hunter may use a call that imitates a rabbit's squeal of terror, or produce a howl to copy the coyote himself. The latter method is best left to true experts, but when it draws an answering cry from a sagebrush ridge or rocky

point the hunting area is greatly narrowed.

A domestic dog is fascinating to a coyote, especially in wilderness areas, and I have seen the two distant relatives studying each other at long range in silence, neither caring to move closer. Coyotes and dogs are generally considered mortal enemies, but there is the interbred "coydog" that shows up frequently, the cross being anything from a short-lived, stupid misfit to a leader of the clan, with extra size and some extra insight into the ways of man.

As the coyote has been called "small big game," the squirrel has been dubbed "the smallest big-game animal" because pursuit of him is a complex hunt in miniature. Some of the finest woodsmen have served their apprenticeship in an acre or two of woodlot, and some have felt it unnecessary to go farther for all the things that cause them to be hunters.

Squirrels have been creatures of the deep forest since white men first hunted in America and they were an important part of pioneer diet. Although they may live now in more narrow stands of timber in much of their range, their lives are keyed to trees—tall trees—for the squirrel's home, livelihood, and defense depend upon forests.

The eastern gray squirrel, best known of the tribes, occupies the eastern half of the United States. There are some in eastern Canada and the habitat reaches to the southern tip of Florida. The populations are not so great as they once were, but this is probably due to the axe and saw rather than the gun. At any rate, the supply is still plentiful.

There are times when all of the forest world seems to feed, play, and travel; at other times the only sounds are those of the wind and the outdoorsman's footsteps on the padding of leaves. Squirrels are barometers of forest life, among the first to dart into activity when a busy period begins, and among the first to disappear when the forest begins one of its periodic slumbers. I know of one grove of enormous laurel oaks where it is sometimes possible to see twenty gray squirrels from one stand, all at the same time. In the two acres of the highest trees there must be at least forty residents for part of some years, provided the acorn crop has been good.

But it is not so much the numbers of squirrels in the oaks that amazes the watcher as it is their frenzied activity—and disappearances. Dawn and dusk are logical feeding times for almost all game, and usually the squirrels are busy then—not always. Sometimes there are early morning periods with no squirrels moving. Frequently there are periods during midday when they are eating nuts, burying nuts, playing games of tag, attempting prodigious leaps in the upper branches, and making bouncing forays along the ground. At the same time on the following day they may be hidden and silent. Part of this is attributed to barometric changes; part of it may be caused by movements of sun and moon. The tide tables used by fishermen in learning feeding periods will work to some extent on squirrels, but they are not entirely reliable. The important thing is that the squirrel's activity or lack of it is an indication to the grouse seeker, the deer hunter, or any other student of wildlife. When the squirrel moves, it is likely that other game moves.

Gray squirrels seldom venture far from trees unless they are actually migrating to new territory. Their larger relatives, the fox squirrels,

Coyote (1) has adapted well to civilization despite severe hunting pressure, and has spread range over most of U.S. Hickory-nut hulls (2) tell hunter squirrel is nearby. Gray squirrel (3, 4) shows usual mixture of curiosity and caution. Smaller red squirrel (5) and larger fox squirrel (6) are varicolored.

2

1

4

5

6

are more likely to be caught in the open on a feeding tour. Grays are very difficult to cut off from their trees, as most squirrel dogs have learned, but they industriously bury nuts, only a small number of which are ever recovered. Forgotten nuts are an important part of forest propagation and renewal.

Mating occurs in early spring, when the males fight noisily and athletically on branches or on the ground. This is one of few times when the gray squirrel shows pugnacity; the evil-tempered little red squirrel, despite his smaller size, can usually thrash the gray at will. Although the two species share the same forests, the red is the unquestioned master. Squirrel romances are brief affairs, and the female is in complete charge of rearing young. The nests, which are used as shelter for adults as well as for the young, may be large, leafy bowers with waterproof roofs, or a hollow in a tree. The gestation period is about forty-four days and the usual litter is two to four young, born hairless and blind. It is about six weeks before young squirrels leave the nest. Two litters a year are common.

Anyone wishing to see squirrels in the wild can use four distinct methods. He can still-hunt, moving through squirrel territory as silently as possible; he can take a stand and keep as quiet as possible; he can take a stand and try to attract squirrels by calling or making sounds calculated to arouse their curiosity; he can use a dog which will find squirrels on the ground and tree them. Most good hunters combine two or more methods.

In still-hunting the ideal situation is for the squirrels to move enough to be sighted, yet not enough to escape completely. Picture-book views of wild squirrels are rare. In a tree crotch a gray squirrel is likely to appear as a shapeless lump, his color matching the bark almost perfectly. On a limb it is likely he will show only his head as he keeps one eye on the intruder. If he has been caught well out in small branches he may be sighted scrambling in a series of leaps and tumbles, using his plumed tail to balance and steer. If he falls, the gray squirrel seems to survive the longest plunge without harm, simply bouncing to the nearest tree trunk, even though he may have thudded down from fifty feet or more.

But the efficient tail, which helps him balance and steers his course through incredible leaps, is a traitor when the gray flattens on a limb to escape detection. Wise watchers will try to look against the light whenever possible. Light shining through the coarse tail hairs appears as a sort of aura; this is the giveaway, for then the rest of the squirrel becomes apparent.

Both fox and gray squirrels employ the same method of hiding when outside a nest. They simply move to keep a trunk or branch between them and a hunter, a ruse that will save them from even a hunting hawk or owl. The smaller the branch, the harder concealment becomes. A hunter looks for light shining through the tail, or for tiny knobs which may be the squirrel's feet as the animal keeps its body out of sight. He may see the top of the animal's head—down as far as the eye.

Two hunters may stand together for a while and then separate, one going around the tree and causing the squirrel to move into plain view for the other. A lone hunter can leave his coat on one side of the tree and slip quietly to the other. He can stand quietly and toss a branch or stone to the opposite side, causing his quarry to believe he has moved. Once the squirrel becomes confused he may move several times in rapid succession and be seen plainly.

The woodsman who decides to take a stand and wait, first looks for squirrel sign. Squirrels eating nuts on high limbs may scatter the cuttings widely and the shell particles may be found almost anywhere under the tree. On other occasions the squirrel may choose to dine repeatedly in one place and leave a considerable pile of shells under his perch. The little red squirrel, generally considered too small to be game, may do his nut cracking at the same spot for weeks, leaving a great heap of scraps, but the grays and fox squirrels are less consistent. Where game is thick there is usually sign of digging among leaves on the ground.

Once he has selected his stand the hunter does well to sit comfortably with his back to a tree and thus avoid movement. His red coat will attract no special notice from the color-blind squirrels. He should have several likely trees before him in easy view. It is often sound that first attracts his attention. A squirrel moving on the ground in dry leaves makes a great racket; even on wet leaves he makes a rustling sound. It is possible to hear a squirrel's teeth grinding on a nut from a surprising distance on a quiet day. The tiny patter of discarded nut particles comes through plainly to a practiced ear, especially when dropped from the crown of an eighty-foot oak.

A squirrel feeding in a tree is likely to be seen easily. Either he must sit up on a broad branch or he must hang head down by his rear feet, so that the nut can be held in his forepaws. The head-down pose is a practical one although unthinking observers may take it as a matter of useless gymnastics.

Sometimes a gray or fox squirrel will become excited and chatter at a quiet hunter, although this usually happens only where the hunting pressure is light. But the hunter who wants to attract squirrel attention when the animals seem to be in hiding can resort to several types of calls. Some of them actually imitate squirrel sounds. Others serve only to arouse curiosity.

Two stones knocked briskly together sounds a little like a squirrel's bark. At any rate it often works. By pressing his lips to the back of his hand and making an exaggerated kissing sound the hunter can produce a squirrel-like squeak. There are also efficient calls that work by striking carefully shaped pieces of wood together; the sound is a crisp bark. And there are accordion-pleated rubber calls that are compressed and released rapidly and repeatedly to sound like squirrel chatter.

In the South, hunting in oak hammocks, I have found that a palmetto frond can be brushed across the ground to create a sound much like a squirrel scrambling through small branches. It is likely to cause investigation by squirrels believing others to be on the move.

In the Midwest I have seen considerable squirrel traffic between groves of oak or black walnut and a nearby creek. When water is available, both grays and fox squirrels drink frequently. Hunters using dogs are especially likely to find game on the ground if they will stay near water. The best squirrel dogs, regardless of breed, are capable of finding a squirrel trail and then flushing the game into a tree. Frequently used routes to water are especially good for this approach.

Squirrels can adapt to other forest, even though they prefer the oaks and nut trees. In southeastern Kansas I have found fox squirrels plentiful among overgrown rows of Osage orange, originally planted as fences but now grown to large trees. In winter they will eat the Osage orange "hedge balls."

The fox squirrel, much larger than the gray, appears in a variety of colors. He is reddish gray over much of his range, but in the South he has a nearly black head with some nearly white parts. Most sportsmen believe he is easier to hunt than the gray.

City dwellers, who are accustomed to seeing tame, unhunted gray squirrels in manicured parks, are puzzled when they discover how elusive these animals become in a forest frequented by men with .22 rifles or shotguns. The species that will eat out of a child's hand in a city park becomes true game when hunting pressure is applied.

Squirrels, rabbits, and coyotes are hunted in much the same ways as larger and more remote game. They have been the tutors of a large share of America's best outdoorsmen.

12.
On farm and ranch land, alfalfa
perfectly covers the pheasant's nest
and draws hungry whitetails
from the forest's verge at evening.

The whitetail deer has many homes, from wilderness unmarked by man to surburban woodlots within earshot of human voices. In tightly settled America he prospers even more than he did when a gray squirrel could travel from New England to the Caribbean without leaving the trees.

He has accepted man as a cutter of timber—leaving new growth to feed generations of whitetails; and as a burner of woodlands—replacing open forest floors with brushy cover and endless browse. And he has accepted man as a restrained predator who harvests deer but worries about the supply. He has survived man's bungling efforts at conservation and prospered as the methods became more thoughtful. And through all of this he has adapted in size, temperament, habit, and requirements—appearing as a fifty-pound wraith among the palmettos of the Florida Keys and as a three-hundred-pound giant in the New England hills. In southeastern swamps he may live most of his life with wet feet; in Mexico his only drink may be dew and the water stored in desert plants.

A total of some thirty subspecies of the whitetail come very near to blanketing the entire United States, a much wider distribution than that of any other big-game animal. The "big game" classification is questioned by some who prefer to class deer as "medium" game, and perhaps it does seem illogical to put deer in the same category as elk or moose. But the whitetail has no competitor in popularity among animals larger than rabbits, and populations are found in all of the contiguous states, as well as in Canada and all of Central America.

Geographical distribution is less impressive than the variety of terrain. Hunting methods are fitted to the habitat, of course, and what is a clever maneuver by the Alabama hound-user would be considered unsportsmanlike in Pennsylvania. In New England the whitetail may be sought along logging roads, the hunters driving or still-hunting in small sectors of forest, expecting game at close range, while in the Southwest a rifleman may cover miles of high ridges in a day aboard a mountain horse, his long-range rifle booted under his leg for quick access if a bouncing flag appears on a cross-canyon slope. All of this is whitetail hunting, and perhaps no sportsman has tried it all. Volumes have been written about local deer hunting to the amazement of other whitetail lovers of other areas who never dreamed such methods existed.

Twins are frequent in whitetail families, most of the spotted fawns being born in late spring or early summer over much of the range. The doe seems to make little selection of the place of birth. The fawns' spots begin to disappear in about seventy days and late fall finds the young ones about the same color as their parents. Whitetails range from light tan to dark gray. The buck's tines emerge from two main beams, rather than from the forked beams of mule deer.

The whitetail may live out his life in little more than a square mile of territory, wisely learning every thicket and bog, and foolishly clinging to his home grounds even though the food supply may fail. His senses are tuned to the restraint of close quarters with red-coated enemies; he can sneak silently through cover hardly sufficient to hide a rabbit. His manner of moving puts a premium on the hunter's woodcraft. Trophy whitetails are hard to come by, if the hunter is satisfied to use hit-or-miss tracking methods.

The whitetail buck in the East is likely to bed down in high thickets or swamps, and feed in valleys or on the lower slopes of ridges and mountains. His route to and from his feeding grounds is generally similar from day to day. After watching the game and checking tracks the hunter has at least an approximate idea of the crossings—routes that may be concentrated into narrow runways where they are pinched by heavy undergrowth. A stand may be taken along the general route with a good field of view, but the obvious choice of an ambush where the traffic must be confined to a narrow trail may have the disadvantage of poor visibility. The bedding-feeding-traveling procedure is flexible, often completely disrupted by the presence of hunters, and a procedure carefully planned before opening day may be thwarted when other hunters change the deer's feeding locations. Under pressure he retires farther into areas of thick growth.

A hunt may logically start with the location of feeding grounds. Sometimes these are marked by old antler-polishing spots, or newer ones as the rut approaches. The buck will rub his weapons on almost any young tree but he seems to prefer conifers that are small enough to bend readily. One of about three or four feet in height is ideal and he often kills such a tree by persistent savagery. Eastern deer love apple orchards and maple browse; when acorns fall they become the preferred fare. Sumac, aspen, willows, blueberries, and blackberries also are attractive. The wise hunter knows the local preferences, which may vary widely for the indiscriminate whitetail. He is equally happy with rhododendron in North Carolina mountains and lespedeza in Missouri. But whatever the food, there is the flow of whitetail life the hunter must learn.

Before the rut, the trophy whitetail buck is a loner. His bed for the daylight hours is a matted, kidney-shaped or oval spot, unmarked by any hoof-gouging or other preparation, simply formed by his weight. It is likely to be softened by fallen leaves or matted grass and is further identified by tracks of the maker in the vicinity. There are likely to be droppings, generally small round pellets that may be little larger than those of a jackrabbit. Although the size of a bed will not surely indicate a buck, its carefully isolated location is strong evidence. The does are less choosey about bed selection, are likely to cluster in small groups, and often are accompanied by fawns, which make smaller beds.

The whitetail almost always feeds at dawn, even though he has foraged intermittently during most of the night. As light increases, the deer is noticeably restless, stopping his feeding for long inspections of the entire area. He is likely to move a little closer to what he considers an escape route, generally brush that leads toward his bedding area. Most of the deer tracks seen in wide-open fields have been made at night.

Once he starts toward his bedding area he pauses frequently to test the air and will freeze at the sound of a snapped twig on the slope ahead of him. The buck browses very little once he starts for his bed. Does and fawns do more nibbling on the way. As he nears the bedding ground the buck may take a fishhook route. He will place his bed so he can observe his own back trail, choosing a spot downwind from the trail. Few trackers seriously trail a deer to his bed unless there is snow to make the tracks visible. On his first visit the hunter probably will cause his quarry to slip away undetected, but even one bed used within the past few days indicates that the deer probably rests in the area regularly, though most of his nearby beds are undiscovered.

Selection of a deer stand is a complex matter, whether the hunter waits for a deer heading for a bedding area or expects other hunters to drive the game to him.

A deer watches most carefully at his own level. Since an adult has no fear of birds, he does not expect danger from above. Thus tree blinds and elaborately constructed metal stands become more popular. Not only is the elevated hunter out of the deer's area of inspection; he is in an excellent spot for observation. His scent seldom flows low enough to alarm the deer.

A traveling buck seldom crosses an open space without pausing to inspect the entire area, and he tends to skirt the edge of a large opening. A deer stand should command a view of the margins of cover as well as the open spots.

The deer is color-blind by human standards, but his eyes are extremely sensitive to movement and outline. Although he does not see a

Southeastern buck (*1*) walks
gingerly through cover,
staying close to edges of
timber and brush.
Western range (*2*) contains
both whitetail and
pheasant. Meandering trail
of buck seeking browse
in winter (*3*). Florida
whitetail (*4*), generally
smaller than northern
cousin, is at home in swamps.
Trophy whitetail runs
closer to ground than mule
deer. White flag is
not always carried erect.

1

2

3

4

*Whitetail neighbors: Gray fox (1),
unlike red, is adept at climbing trees. Plump
black bear (2) looks down from perch
in North Carolina woodland. Porcupine (3)
is slow-witted, clumsy bark eater.*

172 red or orange coat as a discordant color, he may catch a reflection from any shiny material. He is especially critical of an unusual object in familiar surroundings. He might pay little attention to a stationary hunter in strange territory, but he quickly notices anything new along his more frequently traveled trails.

Since other creatures also may use a game trail, the deer is especially attentive to the area straight ahead, and since his traditional enemies are trailers, he closely watches his back trail. Objects well to one side receive less scrutiny. A silhouette against the sky, an outline against a single large and well-lighted tree trunk, or a sharp image against a smooth boulder face will attract attention immediately. The moving buck who becomes suspicious is likely to take a roundabout route to avoid what has disturbed him; thus he frequently appears a considerable distance from an established trail.

The waiting hunter's position must be comfortable. He must be able to stay in one position for a long period without much movement, for the unseen deer may approach just as he shifts an aching leg or adjusts his jacket. He need not be hidden in the sense that he is obscured from view, but his outline should be broken by natural foliage and he should be able to see over as wide an area as possible without moving. His gun should be ready to aim with a minimum of motion. Some hunters allow themselves a small fire, saying that it does not frighten deer; others would not consider it.

A distracting natural sound may actually help the stander. A porcupine, methodically stripping bark nearby, for instance, covers slight noises that otherwise would be picked up instantly by game. The porcupine is seldom bothered much by human presence, and will go about his business within a few feet of a silent hunter. He is a paragon of stupidity, slow in movement and dedicated to his food, which can range from first choices of hemlock, maple, and beech to dis-

carded gloves (salty). In recent years his destruction of valuable trees has cost him his free pass as a savior of lost men (he can be killed with a club and for a long time was regarded as a sort of resident emergency ration).

In an indirect way the porcupine can be deadly to large animals. His quills are barbed in such a way that they work ever deeper into flesh as the victim moves, and sometimes they reach the vitals. In other cases they make wounds that become infected and can be fatal to all sorts of livestock. Hunting dogs are frequent victims of the porcupine's tail and its collection of loosely attached quills. Even a stray quill, long separated from its owner, can be picked up accidentally in a leg, as I once found out on a backpacking expedition. It was painful.

It is as a destroyer of trees, however, that the porky is most frequently condemned, since he often girdles trees in his bark-eating forays. At any rate, his presence in a nearby tree and the resultant showering shreds of outer bark are a helpful hunter's cover-up, as are the activities of any kind of woodpecker or squirrel—as long as the sound is not one of excitement or rage at the hunter. Many standers believe any busy wildlife is likely to allay deer suspicions. At least it does no harm, and a song sparrow or a chipmunk can relieve a watcher's boredom.

It is almost a rule that a deer never appears exactly where expected; and it happens quite frequently, especially during the rut, that the hunter carelessly frightens a deer he does not want, thus warning the game he is after. Generally, the quarry leaves without the hunter ever knowing of its presence. During the rut the buck usually follows the doe and fawns, and his large track will be found over theirs in runways. If a hunter can allow does and fawns to pass without suspicion, he will very likely find himself in a good position for a shot at a buck.

The slipping whitetail buck, known as the most elusive of all big game, can go almost sound-

1

2

3

lessly. In thick cover his progress is more likely to be revealed by other creatures than by his own footfalls or antler scraping. His muzzle is elevated to drop his rack on his neck, which makes for a lower silhouette and allows branches to slide silently along the curve of the antler's beam rather than catching in the forward-thrusting tines. The sneaking whitetail can walk unbelievably low, truly in a silent crawl with his legs supporting him in a constant crouch. When the deer is sneaking along, the white flag is down, tucked in. Once he breaks for safety, leaping smoothly and swiftly, he waves his flag gracefully. Sometimes he switches and snaps it as he drives for real speed, forgetting caution and quiet. Even at a restrained run, the deer can choose his landing spots so carefully that he makes virtually no noise.

On a quiet day in the woods, even the smallest resident can sound the alert. A cranky red squirrel may make a few remarks, or a blue jay may squall. Even a chickadee moving out of the way is an indication. The hunter's location also may be given away by observant animals—in the unlikely event that his game does not have him pinpointed already. The ruffed grouse, a hunter's prize on other days, can be a roaring catastrophe in whitetail country, especially in heavily hunted thickets. In remote, lightly hunted country, however, the grouse may leave as silently as a shadow.

The attempt to outmaneuver a whitetail is, above all, a stalk on a small scale. The whitetail buck can keep silence under pressure of pursuit that would cause many other animals to flee in noisy terror. Many a trophy buck has continued his slipping, even when within a few yards of the hunter, and many a prize has stayed bedded

*Opposite: Whitetail
tracks follow logging
road in Ontario.
Wilderness highways like
these are excellent
deer stands. Spotted fawn
(above) will learn
enough about whitetail
life to leave doe in
few months. Heavily
browsed maple sprouts
(left) may mean deer
have overpopulated area.*

176

*Birches (left) show marks
of antler rubbing. White flag
and indistinct, swift-moving
form are only view many hunters get
of elusive deer. Bobcat
(right) kills some fawns, but is
not hazard to deer populations.*

while hunters ate lunch within fifty feet. His hiding is a demonstration of steely composure.

During the rut the whitetail buck becomes more heedless of his safety. He seldom becomes as carelessly preoccupied as the muley who has acquired a harem, but he retains a fighting humor. The whitetail has a feudal attitude toward his territory, making hoof scrapes as a warning to bucks and an invitation to does. The scrape is a cleared area, generally about three feet across and is dampened with urine.

In the West, whitetail hunting more closely follows the methods of mule deer pursuit. The hunters cover a wider area, sometimes on horseback. In much of the West the two species have overlapping range, but the whitetail stays to the bottoms for the most part, while the muley prefers higher country. Where ground is disputed, the whitetail has a reputation for being able to outfight a muley buck.

True to his reputation for adaptability to new situations, the whitetail will take to unusual country. I have seen a big buck traveling far out in the grasslands, displaced from his chosen territory by hunters. He will leave the willows of the river breaks to take to sagebrush on nearby hills, which he will share with the mule deer.

In many northwestern sections, especially farm and ranch land, the whitetail lives in the valleys and wet bottoms where natural creeks or irrigation ditches leave patches of willows and streaks of cottonwoods with their attendant weed and berry patches. From these strongholds deer reach hayfields and grain at night, and may live there for long periods without detection even by the landowner.

Often it is a pheasant hunter in that country, walking the thick cover, who is startled to see a two-hundred-pound buck leap from a thicket where he expected to flush a gaudy bird. In such cover the pheasant moves much like the deer, even maintaining a similar feeding schedule, and I have seen a fan of cackling pheasants start deer moving far ahead of the hunters. The pheasant-hunting methods are different from those employed in the cornfields of Nebraska or the beet fields of Oregon. The organized drive is seldom employed along the draws. Generally the hunting party is made up of only two or three shooters. The pheasant, which is able to outrun

Fast-rising pheasant (opposite) is tracked by hurried gun. Hunters working farmland (above) may have a distracted dog if pheasants run instead of flushing. Nest (right) in field risks destruction by mower.

a man with ease, moves ahead of the hunters in many cases, and even after the cover runs out at the end of a ditch or fence line, he may hurry another hundred yards before taking to the air, knowing somehow that the shooting does not start while he is still on the ground.

Owners of fine bird dogs sometimes refuse to hunt the pheasant, since his running and sneaking tactics may unnerve a staunch pointer. The pheasant gunner who does not use a dog will employ a ruse which has worked many times for the whitetail and much other game: He walks briskly and then stops for a considerable period. The hiding bird feels it has been discovered and is so unnerved that it flies. The same ruse works for nearly every bird or animal that hides.

One of only a few imports that have added to America's sport, the pheasant has displaced some prairie birds and lives in harmony with others. There is no doubt that the cock is a vicious fighter and capable of withstanding severe weather, but the pheasant's reign in many areas is weakened by changing farming practices. Perhaps its worst enemy is alfalfa, a hazard it never learns. Alfalfa makes the perfect brood cover, but the hen is loyal to her nest and the mowing machine kills her where she sits, or takes her new brood before they are old enough to escape. Alfalfa also attracts (but does not harm) the whitetails, which can be seen on the field edges at late evening. Even when deer are impossible to approach, binocular study of such edges provides quick insight into the local population and its probable bedding areas.

In the South the whitetail season begins around Thanksgiving and runs well into January, and hunting is a co-operative affair. The deer camp is a permanent building, its comforts gathered through many years of use. Perhaps the current hunters are the third or fourth generation to use the weathered headquarters. The membership may be tightly closed and handed down through the various families, treasured not so much for the comforts of the camp but for its location and the long-recorded habits of deer of the area. Near some such camps, a dozen generations of whitetails, clever though they were, have adopted the same crossings, followed the same runways, and leaped the same ancient back-country roads, pushed by generations of hounds which also have learned the country.

From one such camp the hunt begins at dawn, the guns still cased, and the hunters ride or drive a circular route of old logging roads, trails worn by a half century of hunters, and crossings through natural clearings. They look carefully for tracks of deer that moved the night before. There are a number of hunters and they are businesslike in their inspection, hoping to find where deer have entered their chosen area. An especially large track is examined with special care and then brushed over with a pine branch to prevent its being noticed by a member of another hunting party. This is all part of the game.

It takes experience to tell the deer tracks from those of feral hogs but the deer's are much longer and more pointed. Also, the sand is marked by bobcats and foxes and sometimes by black bear. The hunters hope these distracting trails will not be near the deer sign they choose to work, for their hounds are lean travelers, bred for the trail and hard to stop once they give voice, right trail or wrong.

The dogs go down upon a chosen track, large and fresh, and they are followed by a reckless horseman with a buckshot-loaded gun. The hounds bawl and chop musically into the longleaf pine woods and across the switch-grass flats and around the bay heads. There are backwoods vehicles, shortwave radios, and fifty years of deer experience among the posted hunters, but the key is the song of the hound, read in detail. The standers know where the dogs are and where they are headed as the pattern begins to unfold. The hunters change their positions hurriedly but are confident at their new stands, and suddenly there is a changed tone to the Walkers' cry. The game has jumped from his bed and is moving. The buck is not hurried; he can move in leisure ahead of the pack for it is not a sight race and the scent must be gathered from bushes and scrub oak as the dogs go.

The stands are hurriedly taken but long planned and called by old names—the stump stand, the rock stand, the creek stand, the pig stand, the wagon stand. It may have been fifty years since the wagon was a landmark. Sometimes the reason for the name is forgotten, but the title remains. Sometimes the shooting area is small and the hunter must stare relentlessly for a first glimpse. He listens for the rustle of a deer. Even when pushed by a clamoring pack with a smoking trail, the whitetail moves through swamp water and away from grass clumps, leaving a vague and drifting scent. When he reaches a road he parallels it for a hundred yards and creeps past a hunter on stand. When he finally crosses the road, he does so quickly—as he does at the fire trails and the open patches in the pines.

The baying may fade to disappointed yips, or it may rise to fevered squalling. If it rises, the deer may be coming fast, too fast to utilize his usual cunning. He crosses the fire trail in a singing leap as the standers send the buckshot whistling across his path. And now the hunt is over —one way or the other. The deer has broken through the standers—or he has become a trophy. In any event the hounds are caught laboriously, except for a few which continue on the trail; some days and many trails later they will be found emaciated and with bloody feet—for the hound bred to run knows no other way of life.

Even farther south a hunting day begins with a gentle drizzle, a little steam showing in parts of the palmetto flat. The hunters will find a trail in the sand, not yet dulled by rain, and they show it to a single hound. He has displayed little interest in other tracks they have shown him, but now he lifts his head and bays musically.

The two hunters, one with shotgun and the other with rifle, unsnap his lead and follow him on foot as best they can. He goes slowly and thoroughly, with a man twenty yards to either side, watching ahead of the dog. They believe the deer has bedded in the waist-high palmetto and scrub oak of the old burn.

They are right but they do not win the game, for the buck does not jump high in terror. Instead he leaves his bed in a snaking thrust for the cover, the hound's warning in his ears. Once, far ahead, one of the hunters sees a scrub oak shiver. The hound forgets some of his discipline and goes too fast, pushing the deer hard. The running shotgunner loses all hope of getting within range. The rifleman on the other side of the dog looks for an open area the game must cross, but there is none until the deer leaps into the narrow neck joining two grassy ponds. The rifleman cannot shoot the game in the water, and underbrush grows within ten feet of the opposite shore, so he pantingly tries to steady himself. As the deer lunges to solid ground he takes one fruitless shot.

The other hunter whistles for his dog a little frantically, eyeing the lily-padded surface of the deep ponds, and finally stops the hound at the water's edge. As he snaps on the leash there is a small swirl a short way out, unnoticed among the bonnets, and three black knobs disappear silently—the eyes and nose of a nine-foot alligator that knows somehow a barking dog is reptile food. His ancestors learned it thousands of years ago, when the southern swamps were inhabited by doglike animals.

But the whitetail buck does not stop at the sumac along the pond's border. There have been too many hunters lately, and now he travels steadily for another half mile, wades the black water among the cypress knees, and beds anew on a hummock formed by roots of a long-fallen tree. It is nearly noon on Christmas Day and deer season has only a few days to run.

13.
**Bobwhite prefer open fields
for feeding, weedy fringes for roosting,
and heavy undergrowth for escape.
The sly wild turkey ventures more.**

The covey of bobwhite quail has been in the row of camphor trees for more than thirty years. It was a small covey the year the cotton rats were so thick, and one year, because the weather was just right, it appeared there were two distinct bunches. But one covey has always been there.

More than thirty years ago, one of the best wingshots of the South began his bird-hunting career by the camphors. His tactics were a little different then, and he approached the trees in a stoop, as if he were making a stalk, which he was. His shotgun was a single-barrel and old, and as he slipped fairly close to the tree trunks, he watched the small area beneath the trees where the ground was almost bare. He had observed his game before and he knew the quail could run faster near the trunks than in the grass and dog fennel a little farther out. To move along the line of trees, he knew they would prefer to travel in the little open strip and he hoped they would decide simply to run away rather than fly. They did.

The birds gave themselves away with a few tiny, warning chirps and a gentle rustling of leaves, and then paced smoothly into the shaded opening along the tree trunks. There were about a dozen of them and they hurried along in an oval-shaped group, spaced so that each bird had room enough to run and make his quick crouch and jump if the bevy flushed. They paused for an instant for a better look at their pursuer, and at that moment the boy with the old shotgun made his first upland kill and rushed for his prize, never seeing where the other birds went and hardly hearing their muttering roar.

Last winter the Gunner visited the camphors again, but this time he did not stalk the covey. He walked slowly along, fifty yards from the trees, and watched a pointer flailing his tail as he worked the broom sedge some distance from the camphors. Soon the dog caught bird scent on the heavy, humid air, and moved out of sight toward the trees, head high, his random searching steadying to a sure, straight line.

He was as still as a porcelain dog a minute later when the Gunner walked in with a soothing commendation and stepped briskly ahead of the point, swinging his knee-high, snakeproof boots for just a little extra noise in the undergrowth. As he stepped on a dead branch, the covey flushed at his feet, some fifty feet from the tree line, and swung abruptly parallel with the trees, appearing as quick, scattered shadows against the dark green. The slim-barreled bird gun swung up almost lazily and the light quail loads cracked at just the right time. "Fetch."

Subconsciously, the Gunner had faced in just the right direction for his shot and the birds had turned just as he expected, for the bobwhite is a creature of habit and so is the hunter. Next year it will be the same hunter and the same covey, although the individual birds may be different.

The camphor trees were planted to protect an orange grove, and some of them are more than fifty feet high now. Once the camphor was an important producer of medicines in the South; now it is an ornamental and widely scattered. It is neither essential nor traditional in the bobwhite's scheme of things, but the bird adopts it—as it has appropriated almost every other new bit of cover and food it has found—provided the weather is bearable. In other parts of the southern and central United States, it makes itself at home in completely different surroundings, although still liking the fringes between field and forest—the open field for feeding, the weedy edges for roosting, and the heavy undergrowth of swamp or creek bottom for escape.

Its enemies have found the camphors, too. A Cooper's hawk will sideslip into the thick branches and silently wait for a bird to venture into an open spot, prepared to drive down and outward for his kill. The quail nests are likely to be only a little distance away and the camphors are in a snaky area—diamondback rattlers, black-snakes, and gopher snakes, all of them happy to

Opening pages: Bobwhite quail, the aristocrats of upland game, flush in a roaring pod ahead of pointer. Shown here over southern cornfield, bobwhite adapts to wide variety of cover and lives close to civilization.

185

find a quail's nest. When the tiny young have hatched in summer, even a loggerhead shrike is a dangerous enemy which will impale a thumb-sized quail on a thorn. Our Gunner, who visits the area at intervals the year around, is depressed by that, although he regards a transfixed grasshopper or lizard as only an interesting bit of nature study. When he sees a family of tiny quail, he walks a long way around, for they disappear in an instant and are easy victims of a carelessly placed boot.

On one side of the trees, opposite the orange grove, is pasture with a good stand of Bahia grass, whose seeds are good food at an excellent height for quail harvesting. Wild turkeys also like the grass. While quail harvest the seeds with intent peckings and stretchings, a turkey takes the lower part of a stem in its beak and strips the entire collection of seeds with a sidewise motion of its head. But the turkeys visit the pasture edge only occasionally. They, too, have a preferred range, but it is wider and more varied than the bobwhite's.

Waist-high broom sedge, although providing little food, is excellent cover, and one end of the camphor row runs into a field of it. Higher up is a sandy ridge of slash and longleaf pine and turkey oaks. The ridge would be missed by many, for in Florida a "ridge" may be only twenty feet above a swamp; a cypress dome with standing water may be only a few yards from a ridge, and the whole transition from one to another is so compressed that the entire community of habitats can be visited within half a mile. Most of the game varieties of the entire region are found within range of one rifle shot.

The Gunner can look at such an area and tell you where the quail are and about how many coveys there will be. His observation is a thoughtful checklist covering the feeding area, the roosting sector, the place for nesting, and the sanctuary for quick escape. The camphor row has all of these things nearby.

The orange grove is kept clean of heavy

undergrowth. In February, when a stranger comes to the camphors, he runs his dogs along the row and through the broom sedge, and goes on to the sandy ridge, but he never considers the turned ground of the orange grove where the very small green shoots of new grass make their February appearance, and where the quail, eager for a different diet after a winter of dry seeds, acorns, and camphor berries, spend much of their time. No one should hunt in a grove of valuable oranges, but at morning and evening the borders of the grove may hold more than one covey.

The camphors are a busy place, nearly always harboring a few blue jays, which frequently are victims of the hovering or hidden Cooper's hawk. The kills are marked by dying shrieks, some convulsive rustlings, and a silence that probably causes the quail to stop their feeding and crouch a little. Noisy fish crows like the camphor berries, and gray squirrels make frequent visits for them, too, although the squirrels prefer other residence. Frenzied squirrel activity is sure indication that the wild world is awake and moving.

Large flocks of northbound robins swoop into the trees late in winter. For some reason, the robins are fairly tame during these feeding orgies, very different from the furtive flights that arrive from the north and disappear deep into the forests.

The shooters who regularly work such individual coveys as the camphor bevy are called "brush hunters" by most southern sportsmen. The other extreme is plantation gunning, where the sportsmen ride in rubber-tired shooting wagons drawn by matched mules, and dog handlers ride Tennessee walking horses over fields and ridges planted especially for bobwhite, with predators carefully controlled. Most quail hunting is somewhere between the two, often done with a four-wheel-drive hunting car carrying two or three shooters and a box of several bird dogs.

If he covers enough territory with proper equipment, a hunter makes his bag of quail with-

Bobwhite cock (left)
holds tightly under nose
of belled pointer. New
Jersey quail (above),
flushing almost
under hunter's feet, will
head for woods. Plump
handfuls, bobwhite
are often hunted
with double-barreled guns.
Not all bird dogs
are steady. One opposite
has been startled
into frantic pursuit
of buzzing quail.

out bothersome study of the birds, leaving the hunting to efficient dogs, but the best quail hunter utilizes both equipment and knowledge.

Out of sight of his master part of the time, a big-going pointer sweeps the edges—edges of the fields, edges of the scrub oak patches, edges of the draws that groove the pine woodlands, and edges of the bay heads, those clumps of loblolly bay trees that make the transition from highland to swamp. He is scarred by years of palmetto cuts and he goes tirelessly with the reach and pull of one who knows his trade. Two scents will stop his drive—that of the game and that of the diamondback. The snake is the hazard of his profession, and a downwind bound into a spot of sandy shade can end his hunts forever. But he has missed the killer a hundred times and the bobwhite is first on his mind.

Closer in is a slower-working dog, and near the car, which wallows slowly over the uneven ground, is a puttering, cautious fellow, not really very enthusiastic at the moment, but waiting hopefully for the time when singles will be marked down. This is an almost perfect canine combination and many hunters constantly try to achieve it.

Within a few sweeps the farthest dog can encompass a bobwhite's entire range, and he ignores all but the margins of the complex cover; if the birds should happen to stray to the center of a field, he might miss them, but if the breeze is steady and damp, he will wind them from the field's border.

On the pine ridges the foraging quail likes the heavy stands of wire grass that can give him instant protection. As the grass lengthens, the tops sweep down to the ground, making a thousand little tunnels through which a quail can dart away from almost any predator; it is the kind of hiding he prefers, for if pursuit comes too close he can change locations without ever showing himself. The overhanging grass or tips of fallen branches also cover the bobwhite's nest.

I once hunted quail where a large covey of bobwhites flushed from a narrow creek to what appeared to be a completely open field. It was an area that had not been hunted for years and the situation seemed almost unsporting—more than a dozen birds spread out in a wide area, and a careful dog to find them one at a time. But on closer examination, the little field proved to be covered with tall weeds and grass that had been flattened by heavy rain and wind. The entire covey refused to fly and no bird was seen again, although they could occasionally be heard scampering beneath their shelter, while the dog gave up his classic pointing style and behaved like a backward cat seeking imaginary mice. We yielded and went to look for another covey.

To the quail hunter, the sweetest scent is one he could never detect himself, but which leads his dog to the game. An imitation of it, which might cause all but the most experienced dog to go astray, is a stench to be abhorred though never received by the hunter's dull sense. Thus, the pleasant-mannered little field sparrow becomes a "stink bird" because it puts forth a scent easily mistaken for the bobwhite's, and the tense shooter relaxes in disgust as the little fraud flits up ahead of the embarrassed dog.

The field sparrow can either dart among the grass clumps and other cover, or hold tightly to prolong the travesty, and its efforts at insect control go without commendation, the hunter wishing nothing but ill for its innocuous tribe. The bird's short flights and drab appearance make no impression on the consciousness of a hurried walker. The meadowlark, whose scent also approximates bobwhite's, is accepted more gracefully by hunters because it at least faintly resembles a quail in appearance and size.

Bobwhite quail move most in early morning and late evening. Their presence near the edge of heavy cover leads some observers to believe they roost in the cover and come out only to feed. It is true they may spend much of the day in heavy brush, but it is likely that they make their evening foray and then roost in weeds or grasses, some distance from higher growth.

Quail roost in a circle with their heads pointed out. During cold weather the circle is tightened, and it appears that in the coldest northern edge of their range some birds are actually suffocated in their protective formation. Circular ground-roosting is used even in warm weather and the places are quickly identified by the round concentration of droppings. The plan gives the covey a 360-degree view of predators, and enables it to flush explosively with a sound likely to freeze a creeping intruder into a moment of indecision.

In sand, quail prospectors often have difficulty in telling bobwhite tracks from those of other birds, but a number of dusting beds in a tight area is a strong indication of quail, the individual bed being about the size of a man's fist and deep enough to be visible, even after a rain. A hunting hawk is another indicator, if observed following transitional edges of various kinds of cover; he is probably tracing a route he has covered before and he may have taken quail there.

On warm days in central Florida, many hunters will not put their dogs into quail cover; in southern Florida the rattlesnake is a calculated risk and it seldom becomes so cold that his strike is sluggish. In northern Florida, southern Georgia, Alabama, Mississippi and Louisiana, it would probably take unseasonably warm weather to make rattlesnakes dangerous in midwinter quail hunting. A friend once came south with beautiful dogs, looked at Florida's palmetto and scrub oak, and went back to Illinois without uncasing his gun. Perhaps he was right, for his dogs were inexperienced with big rattlers. How much dogs learn and how much is instinct is a constant topic of discussion among quail hunters.

The ability of a big diamondback to kill a man or dog quickly is not to be doubted, but the man covers much less ground and most of the man is higher than the snake is likely to strike. Most

bird gunners in dangerous country wear tough fang-proof boots or leggings.

It is the individual temperament of the rattlesnake that makes the great difference, for there are noisy snakes, quiet snakes, and snakes that flee. There are snakes that coil for low, defensive moves, and others that rear high from a tight, springy coil and can snap to their full length with fatal accuracy. The expert can release a hundred rattlers in a pit and point out the most dangerous ones immediately. Some he will treat with disdain, but others command his respect and he will not turn his back to them, snakeproof boots or not.

Perhaps it is the traveling snake that is most dangerous of all, for he may be confronted in an unusual spot by an unprepared victim. In the southern bobwhite country a long dry period will turn shallow ponds into overgrown basins, perfect spots for cottontail and swamp rabbits and cotton rats, which move quickly to the new growth, followed promptly by lesser snakes and the diamondback himself.

Then comes high water, often in the fall, after a series of summer rains; the creeks flow and the little basins fill and push back into the shallow draws, driving the diamondback ahead of their shorelines. His days of plenty are gone and he must find a new hunting ground. It is during this migration that the hunter is most likely to meet him, because once he begins his trip few obstacles are allowed to interfere.

A rattlesnake crossing a river or lake is unmistakable, even at a distance. He floats incredibly high on the water, like an inflated rubber tube, and he keeps his rattles dry most of the time; you can see head and rattles moving rhythmically as he swims. He appears even larger than on land for there is no grass to hide part of his bulky body. When he is tired of swimming he will crawl aboard anything dry and will often head straight for a duck boat, assuming from experience that the other occupants will leave

1

2

3

4

Opposite: Nesting bobwhite merges into color scheme of Florida field. Turkey vulture is frequent observer of southern hunting. Camphor berries attract quail in Florida. Cotton rat is a major predator of quail nests in South. This page: Armadillo is noisy wanderer in brush, often mistaken for important game. Diamondback rattler is deadly foe of bird dogs. Wily wild turkey often appears in same region as bobwhite.

when he arrives; thus come the stories of the great snake that attacked the fifteen-foot boat. Washed through an inlet he intended to cross, a rattlesnake may be found miles at sea, still high on the water but completely lost.

"Bay head" and "cypress head" are southern terms that refer to clumps of bay or cypress trees in low areas. Water often stands about the trees, usually draining into a creek or river swamp. It is the edge of the head that is most important to the quail hunter. Vegetation there appears as a wall of foliage, the bay or cypress trees thrusting higher in the background.

Around the edge of a bay head I know there is a fringe of sumac and some scattered blackberry bushes. At the very brink of the wet area is an almost solid wall of palmetto and the rank fringe of vegetation grades away uphill, thinning into a burned-over area, where the old trees have died out and a little scrub oak is coming up. There is a variety of weeds and plenty of seeds for quail, so a covey can be found there every year, probably within a hundred yards of the head; often within fifty feet.

The dogs point the birds and the hunter has a choice. He can walk them up from the direction of the bay head and hope the covey scatters to give him a chance at singles, or he can drive the birds straight toward the bay head. Almost certainly the birds will go into the bay head anyway, and if he approaches them from that side they will simply fly in his face and over him, which makes awkward shots. Generally, therefore, he decides to face the head and walk into the covey, knowing pretty well where the birds will go and being able to shoot from a good balance. These things he weighs with the mounting excitement of a man who is soon to fire at whirring feather balls that go fast and seem to go much faster, so if his judgment is wrong he may be excused. (Quail hunters who do not have quivering knees as they approach birds soon turn to other pastimes.) The birds rise in something of a scatter because they have been spread out in feeding, a tardy one usually leaving from near his feet after his gun is empty. The unharmed quail generally fly into the bay head, boring through tiny openings, banking to fit narrow gaps, and possibly even breaking straight through a wall of leaves. Sometimes they stop at the palmetto fringe and the hunter can put them up a second time, although he is unlikely to get a shot then, as they bore deeper into the foliage.

He gathers his dogs and his senses—and his birds, if he has bagged any—and looks for another covey half a mile or a mile away, on the other side of that bay head or along the edge of another. He and his dogs know where the birds are to be found, but he calls them "one-shot coveys."

In the dank twilight of the bay head, the birds are scattered and safe, for no enemy has ever followed them there, but there is no feeding to be done, and soon individual quail are looking for company. It is almost time to gather for evening feeding and roosting. An hour or two after the covey has disappeared into the trees, one of the birds will flutter out through the fringe brush and land not far from where they were flushed. Others will appear silently over a considerable area, and after a short while there will be an assembly call. It is the exact situation the hunter hoped for earlier: scattered game that can be hunted up as singles. But by that time he is miles away, and another hunter, who comes upon the arrangement by accident, will have shooting and later will tell his friends how strangely the quail behaved and how lucky he was to find them scattered. Such a performance is not guaranteed, but very likely.

Whitetail deer range along the high ground only a few yards from the bay tree swamp. Their tracks, showing in sand along the edge, suggest that they live in the deep cover; but actually, like the quail, they use the low swampland as refuge rather than residence in normal times.

Pushed by hounds from higher ground, a deer may slip through the wall of vines, ferns,

shell producing rustlings befitting stealthier but much larger citizens.

Expecting a buck, I hear and finally see signs of the armadillo's approach, coming so slowly I discard my deer hope and imagine anything from panther to opossum. Finally, the fake wanders into the open and peeks about at his own eye-level, evidently surprised to have come into full light after the darkened palmetto patch. My presence ten feet ahead of him goes unnoticed and he roots industriously in search of insects, working toward me until a scant two feet from my boots. Without moving, I make a clucking sound and he stops in a dim-witted version of alertness, somewhat resembling a miniature, dehorned rhinoceros. Slowly deciding he was mistaken about the suspicious sound, he resumes his prospecting. When he reaches my foot he goes through a series of false starts in other directions, then sits on his hindquarters and ponders the whole situation as if one number nine boot constituted an insurmountable obstacle. He drops to all fours again, explores the boot toe with some apprehension, and walks away, puzzled.

A relative newcomer to this Florida area, the armadillo has defeated numerous athletic pursuers. A man can outrun him but is often surprised to find the little "armored pig" a master of evasive action. Armadillo succulence at the dining table is not yet well known and his harmlessness has, thus far, eliminated him from consideration as quarry to be intensively hunted.

Standing near the palmettos, the turkey oak carries the name of "scrub oak" as well, but its turkey-track leaves are unmistakable. Southern woods hunters call all short, dense oaks "scrub oaks," even though they may be juvenile live oaks that could reach great height and spread in hundreds of years of life. Identification is hard because crowded oaks hybridize freely. In youth they crowd each other into bushy insignificance, but provide almost hopelessly dense cover with small feeding openings where groups of quail can

and palmetto and skirt the edge of the head, just out of sight. A standing rifleman at the high end of the bay swamp hopes he will break out, but may hear only his quick, rustling progress. The hounds give an extra burst of tongue when they strike the edge and catch the full scent on the high, damp growth, and the deer, going easily ahead of them, will move faster toward his final refuge—the cypress swamp, where water may be deep enough to force a laboring hound to swim.

Palmetto rustlings do not always mean deer. The swinging fronds will produce suspicious sounds even when moved by a small bird or a chocolate-hued swamp rabbit. The armadillo is the most exciting of the counterfeits, his hard

Nesting bobwhite in North Carolina is protective parent and reluctant to leave eggs. Wide-ranging pointer is preferred bird dog in South. Marsh rabbit is member of hare family. Above: Hunter bags a rail.

live their lives in safety from hunters. Dogs might locate birds in these oak flats, but no one could find them pointing, and most hunters turn away from such places.

Not far from the bay swamp is a live oak and laurel oak hammock, where individual trees, through centuries, have shaded out less ambitious seedlings and left open forest ground with heavy leaf cover and little grass. The quail visit there, too, scuttling into palmetto patches when they hear danger approaching on the dry-leaf sounding board. The palmetto patches, appearing in sunny breaks of the high forest, have a part in quail life as they have in the career of the white-tail deer.

On a chilly day, a sunny opening in an oak hammock is an ideal spot for dog and man to nap at noon, when little game is moving anyway. Awakening from such a snooze, the hunter looks into the high sky and watches the slow orbits of turkey vultures, possibly little more than specks, sometimes quite close.

If the birds are low he will be able to see their turning heads as they examine some possible carrion below, and then may realize with a rueful start that he is the tentative target of their critical reconnaissance. That makes him sit up foolishly although he knows there is little likelihood of being consumed in his sleep.

The very opening in which he rests may have been provided by the vultures, which kill the trees they rest on. Their droppings contain an acid that sterilizes their roost and can eventually destroy limbs, letting the sun through to dormant seeds on the floor of the hammock and thus beginning a new procession of growth.

The smoothly gliding black birds are the turkey vultures; the black vulture is less efficient in riding the thermal drafts and its soaring is interspersed with rather rapid wingbeats, as if it had made a miscalculation or had found its short tail inadequate in steering.

Many lifelong outdoorsmen have never seen the roaring dive of the turkey vulture; some who have witnessed it believed the diver to be almost anything but the grim and vulgar specter they have watched quarreling over carrion. I have identified the plunge twice, but have been uncertain of its purpose. A friend was sure he saw one group of buzzards fall to dead alligators, left on an island by poachers.

I am ever amazed at the ability of birds to see small objects on the ground from heights that make the birds invisible to ground observers. The turkey vulture strains credibility even further. When I first heard a diving vulture, I looked for a light plane in some wild maneuver with the throttle cut. The bird came into sight as a speck, roaring louder as tentative identification became possible, the wind vibrating stiff feathers apparently not designed for such travel. Birds of prey may stoop in near silence or with a hiss of speed; the buzzard comes with the noise of a ragged object hurled into trajectory.

Although he has a part in the sanitation of wild places, the vulture has a villainous side, partly because of his lack of weapons. For despite his role as a carrion eater, he will devour a helpless victim alive. Cattlemen in some areas blame him for the death of newborn calves, and the wrinkle-headed shadow which appears too often at calving time is living dangerously indeed. Epidemic livestock disease can be a factor. It will attract buzzards in great numbers, and when the epidemic is ended the starving birds will seek newborn animals for food.

In and near the oak hammock, many a bobwhite, flushed by hunters, dives headlong into thick palmetto and is often quite safe there, for in that tangle a pointing dog could starve before his master found him. But a few reasoning canines have learned the trick and will go into the palmetto thicket, putting aside their pointing instincts for the time. Such a dog will scent the ground-flattened quail and flush it gently with a prodding nose, the bird fluttering upward through the clattering fronds and calling attention to itself before it reaches daylight. It is not in the classic tradition, perhaps, but it is undeniably effective quail shooting.

In cold weather, frost forms in the depression of the bay tree swamp and quail make their ground roost as high as possible, preferring a southeastern slope where sun will strike early. The slope up from the swamp is a good nesting area, but when early spring comes, the covey separates for the mating season. Each pair then rears its young in relative seclusion. All spring and far into the summer the perky roosters, forgetful of their caution, whistle their "bob-white" call, the whistling continuing long after most of the birds have nested and hatched their young.

The Gunner, who hunts many areas in addition to the camphor trees, knows a hundred spots where coveys have lived for years and the places nearby where they rear their young. He can produce the quail's assembly call efficiently and it is enough like the query of an unattached hen to make a noisy young cock forget all caution and work his way rapidly toward it, tooting his mating invitation so enthusiastically that he actually bumbles some of the notes. Seated quietly on a fallen log near the bay swamp, the Gunner continues the soft whistle at intervals until the excited cock bursts into the little clearing, his feet blurring with urgency, and goes on past the Gunner without a glance in his direction.

Another whistle and the little rooster comes storming back out of the weeds and speeds past the caller again in the other direction, his shiny eyes focused at the proper height for lady quail. The game continues until the bird has narrowed his search to the little opening itself and he finally stops dead, standing on the Gunner's boot toe to take advantage of a little elevation in his frustrating search. Next fall, he may be the single who flushes wild, two hundred yards away, when he hears the dog box thump open at the edge of a weed field where luscious partridge pea is especially thick and attractive to a hungry bird.

The paired birds continue their association through the nesting season. Scattered as the quail are, many an energetic hunter uses this time to observe them and compile a sheaf of notes he is sure will make his hunting certain the next fall. Although both male and female attend the nest, they will leave briefly to feed together; the note-taker will sight them crossing the sand road or even the interstate highway. He knows that a new covey is a family group and is confident that he will find them when the season opens.

But the Gunner no longer has to take notes. He knows the wide scattering of birds ends with fall. Suddenly quail will seem scarce. If the nesting season is ideal, coveys will be a bit larger. If the cotton rats have a good season, they may be a little smaller, but the rats are a safety valve of predation and are taken by snakes and birds of prey which might otherwise concentrate on quail. At any rate, the population will not increase by the number of eggs laid and, as before, there will be one covey on the slope by the bay head, and, of course, there will be a traditional covey by the row of camphors.

In more than one way, the bobwhite is nearly the perfect game, for man has established definite rapport with him. Here the science of game management has won the battle; given ideal conditions, the wild quail can be reared almost as efficiently as a tame bird. His food preferences are known and his range requirements are obvious. It is comforting to know that a reduced population can be restored within two years with land changes, and the question is simply one of how much the bobwhite is wanted.

When winter quail hunting ends in the South, the robins have gathered for their northward migration, and if the weather is warm, the closing day of the gunning season may be punctuated by a loud call from an ambitious bobwhite rooster, out to make an early start on raising his spring family.

14.
Everything that would live in the desert—javelina, bighorn, quail, or coyote—must accommodate to its rigorous demands.

Desert life is a program of long cycles, of silent waits for rain, and of explosive blooming and propagation when it comes. The Southwest is thickly populated with a variety of wildlife species, many of them found nowhere else in America. It is a paradox: The greatest numbers of wild creatures live in what appears to be the most forbidding habitat.

An ocotillo plant growing in the broad Sonoran desert is a synopsis of desert life, for the ocotillo, often called Jacob's staff, may live for two hundred years without growing higher than twelve feet. In dry weather it appears to be a bundle of thorny dead sticks thrust into the sand. It produces small leaves when the rain comes—doing this perhaps several times a year—and becomes sticks again when the moisture is used up.

The generations of Gambel's quail that strut perkily past its base live by the same cruel desert rules, although the individual quail's life is short; it is the annual *crop* of quail that depends upon rain, and the population remains at a low during dry years. Desert game must be as patient as the desert plants.

Some authorities state that any land with less than ten inches of rain per year is desert. In some deserts no rain falls for many years. The game biologist classifies lands by their vegetation and consequent animal populations.

There is game special to the Southwest, such as the scarce and much-prized bighorn, the javelina or peccary, the white-winged dove, and the desert quails. That old friend the whitetail appears as the beautiful little Coues (pronounced *cow's*) deer, flicking his flag audaciously as he tops out at long range from bushy canyons lined by saguaro cactus weighing as much as several tons. He is generally near mountain slopes and evergreens, although he sometimes appears well out on the desert among the mule deer.

The transition from one ecology to another is so sudden in the Southwest that the perspiring outdoorsman can stand on the hot sands amid cholla cactus and twisted mesquite and look toward a conifer-covered mountain slope harboring elk, and higher to a snow-sprinkled crown, where the ecology is actually Arctic-Alpine with no trees, but a growth of low shrubs, grasses, and mosses. Such terrain is found on the peaks of the Sangre de Cristo, Jemez, White, and San Francisco ranges of Arizona and New Mexico.

The Southwest is a geographical sector south of the Rockies, including all of Arizona and New Mexico, most of western Texas, and parts of Utah, Colorado, Oklahoma, and Nevada. Some of the wildlife is primarily Mexican and appears only occasionally north of the border. We saw a gray wolf in southern Arizona, fringe-lighted by a low sun that gleamed through the thorns of a big saguaro. There are many gray wolves left in Mexico, but they are so scarce in Arizona that the natives call them "Mexican wolves." The Southwest is an original home of the coyote, which now has spread its range to most of North America. South of Tucson, my hunting companion gave an expert rabbit squeal through his cupped hands, and three minutes later the pricked ears of a foraging coyote appeared on a nearby rise, followed by the little lupine head which tilted in curiosity and then vanished.

The desert bighorn is the most coveted hunter's prize of the Southwest, perhaps of all North America. It is part of the sportsman's "grand slam" in the four recognized divisions of North American sheep. Only a few permits are issued in the United States and Mexico. The desert sheep is somewhat smaller than the bighorn of the Rockies, carrying a spare frame to match his spartan desert fare. His color is grayer than that of the northern sheep—a gray-tan to match the subdued sandy slopes of arid mountains. It is said that some desert sheep may live out their lives without tasting rain water, although they will frequent water holes when available. Without water holes they get liquid from dew and water-holding cactus and other desert plants.

Opening pages: Desert mountains, difficult terrain for both hunter and pointing dog, are habitat of tremendous wildlife population. This is hunt for Gambel's quail near Phoenix, Arizona.

201

Emaciated and dehydrated, the sheep are transformed as they drink and their dried tissues absorb water. To a keen observer the change of appearance may be obvious within minutes, as the bone-ridged frames fill out before his eyes. But in cool weather, the sheep may not visit a water hole at all.

Desert sheep are usually found near precipitous cliffs and ragged-walled canyons. In Arizona and Mexico the sheep's home is on skimpily covered mountainsides where bear grass (a member of the yucca family) appears as dark green spots on a sere slope among paloverde and cacti. Farther west, in Nevada, the sheep are found near the grotesque Joshua trees. The desert sheep's life cycle is similar to that of the northern bighorn and other wild sheep of America, but the breeding season has adjusted to the different climate. It comes in late summer and early fall, so that the single lambs are dropped in late winter and very early spring, the time when new plant growth is most likely because of winter rains. Lamb mortality is high in the extremes of desert weather.

The sheep is primarily a grazer, but in the absence of grass it will eat shrubs and a variety of dead growth. Its range competitors are mainly domestic livestock, and the roads, homes, and military installations of man which gradually encroach upon the wastelands. Even the bighorn's diseases are contracted principally from domestic sheep; the most damaging has been lungworm. Special areas for preservation of the desert bighorn have been established by the Federal Government, with a hunter's harvest allowed for mature rams. Only a few permits are drawn.

In eastern Nevada a hunter and his guide glass a desert mountain. The scene is very sharp in the clear desert air, and they find their game on a high slope at dawn. The sheep's head appears huge because the body is wizened from the rigors of desert life, the horns curling a bit farther from his head than those of the average Rocky Mountain trophy. The old ram lowers his head to butt over a large barrel cactus, a source of moisture or perhaps a little food. The cactus is pleated like many other desert plants, capable of expanding when water is plentiful and hoarding moisture in shaded folds during dry times. In a short while the ram walks stiffly away and beds down out of sight as the hot sun reaches his slope. His tracks had been found in the sand days before, but the hunters knew that, like lunar tracks, those made in the desert may be years old and still appear fresh. Now, with their first sight of the trophy, they make their stalk, a circuitous route because the rotting mountainside shatters constantly into little tinkling avalanches and occasional thumping rock falls. Eventually they come within easy range of the ram bedded among large boulders, just across a steep, narrow arroyo—but they cannot see him.

As a last resort they toss a stone into the little gorge, fearful lest the ram will leave without showing himself, but a tiny movement becomes the ram's ears and the upper curve of his horns as he looks about cautiously. Another pebble brings forth the entire head and part of the neck. At that range it is enough for the careful rifleman, who fires only once. The head and neck disappear instantly. It is a clean kill. Although the older rams acquire extra caution, curiosity about unusual noises is a characteristic of seldom-hunted wild sheep. L. W. Walker, Arizona naturalist, tells of Mexican hunters attracting bighorns by dragging tin cans behind a truck on a mountain road.

The Nevada ram was more than twelve years old, near the end of his natural career, and when the hunter carried him bodily down the mountain he weighed only a little more than one hundred pounds, although his horns were nearly in the record class. A prime ram might have weighed more than two hundred. His horns were greatly flattened on the butting surfaces, with traces of cactus thorns still wedged in their growth rings. There is little hair on the sheep's nose, its

*Desert ram is most
difficult of America's
wild sheep for trophy hunter
to acquire. Sheep live
in remotest and
most forbidding desert
areas, and game
managers grant only a
few permits, drawn
by lot, each season.*

contact with cactus and other desert plants having left a great callus along the bridge.

In part of his range the desert bighorn competes for food with the wild burro, a castoff of the prospector and pioneer, which has been able to survive on the meager subsistence of the American desert. The burro is a homely waif, sometimes killed by hunters who begrudge him the sheep food he consumes.

The desert sheep has been near oblivion, and is among the most expensive charges of game management, profiting slowly from nearly complete protection. The range is pinched by a growing human population and an animal of the sheep's size requires considerable space.

The collared peccary, or javeiina, belongs to a scientific family related to the pigs. It is a dark gray with a long snout and a collar of long hair. A hunter may spend days in javelina habitat without seeing one, but they leave their marks, not only small, round-toed hoof tracks, but rooted areas of turned earth and shredded prickly pear. The javelina has the democratic tastes of domestic pigs, eating reptiles and insects, as well as plants. It prefers acorns when available but can survive on cacti. One of the more common signs is the partly consumed prickly pear which has been taken into the pig's mouth and raked by the teeth, shredded remains of the cactus remaining on the stem. Apparently the javelina's tongue is impervious to cactus damage.

Most javelinas weigh less than forty pounds, but they have been reported to weigh as much as eighty-five pounds, although proffered rewards have failed to produce one anywhere near the larger figure. They have also been painted as ferocious desert man-killers and as timid creatures, harmless as rabbits. The truth is somewhere between. Semitame captive javelinas have been known to seriously injure humans, as when one caretaker in an animal compound received a badly gashed leg in an attack by a cranky male. I can learn of no case in which a completely wild and unwounded peccary has attacked anyone, but a biologist who hunts with bow and arrow told me of a charging boar which rushed to within an arrow's length with ominous tusk clicking, then stopped to observe the results of his bluff. The archer had been following a herd in undergrowth and the boar evidently had decided to block pursuit. The javelina sometimes lives in mountain caves, and a frightened rush of odorous little pigs toward a cave mouth when an intruder enters has often been interpreted as a concerted charge. Despite the javelina's shy attitude toward human beings, herds generally take over desert water holes from other animals, usually stepping aside only for skunks. Although largely nocturnal in feeding habits in the wild, the javelina is believed simply to have adapted to hunting pressures, since captive animals show no aversion to daylight.

Javelinas carry potent musk glands and mark their travel routes by rubbing against overhanging obstructions. Observers say the rubbing is a casual and routine act, later travelers marking the same spots as their predecessors, thus establishing an avenue marked by odorous rubs.

It was the demand for the peccary's tough hide as leather that did much to deplete his numbers and to diminish a range that once ran as far north as Arkansas. In southern Texas the javelina is now hunted in the fall; in both Arizona and New Mexico the season generally comes in late winter. He is a challenging target for rifleman or archer.

The observant hunter may see the chuckwalla, an edible lizard which can lock itself in a shady rock crevice by inflating its body like a balloon. Desert Indians punctured him for easy removal. The gila monster, a poisonous reptile that was nearing extinction, is now protected by law. There is a variety of rattlesnakes, including the big western diamondback and the sidewinder, a smaller viper whose looping, sidewise gait leaves curved marks in the sand. The kangaroo rat lives in his involved burrow in the daytime, sought by a host of predators, as are the desert rabbits. The elf owl's home is a fortress of cactus. Birds of the desert include the turkey vulture and raven, which can fly long distances to water.

Not all of the desert is heavily populated. There are great areas of sand dunes, wind-heaped and rippled, almost devoid of life. But there are also areas of lush seasonal growth and sudden greenness in rainy seasons. Plants are spaced to divide the moisture among them, and there are even some jealous and combative plant residents, such as the creosote bush, which actually exudes a substance from its roots designed to poison large competitive plants. The creosote bush with its tiny evergreen leaves is a lacy symbol of southwestern deserts, possibly the most widely distributed of all the large plants.

The desert is quail country, much of it capable of furnishing the finest of upland gunning, often more shooting than is found in the most carefully managed eastern bobwhite habitat. The key to satisfactory hunting is to find a desert area with sufficient plant growth to cause the birds to hold rather than run.

Within the true desert, most important of the quail is the Gambel's because of its wide range and large population. The Gambel's is a close relative of the California quail, although his breast feathers lack the bold scaled pattern, and he carries a dark patch on the lower breast. There is little difference in size, both birds having a somewhat longer silhouette than the bobwhite, partly due to a longer tail and the high question-mark crown of intricately formed dark feathers. Several feathers are uniquely shaped to form a nearly rigid plume which thrusts forward and upward. Viewed in flight in profile, the Gambel's has a certain resemblance to the shape of a cardinal or blue jay. Over-all it is about the size of the northern bobwhite and slightly larger than the southern bird.

The Gambel's cock has a chestnut-topped head and a nearly black face and throat with white bands as trimming. Like the other Southwestern quails, the Gambel's lays its blotched eggs in a shallow ground nest. Twelve is an average number of eggs but there may be as many as twenty. Like most quail, the Gambel's is principally a seed eater, but takes advantage of beetles, grasshoppers, and other insects of opportunity. In much of the range, mesquite and deer vetch are important food sources.

It is in the most open and most easily covered terrain that the Gambel's quail has acquired his reputation as an impossible bird to hunt; even then he can be worthy game if an early flush is carefully marked down.

Along a sand-floored arroyo, a wash formed by sudden floods from over-grazed slopes, the mesquite trees grew sparsely and the scanty, hard-cropped grass was broken by barrel cactus, cholla clumps, and prickly pear clusters. There was quail sign: tracks in the loose sand and scattered livestock droppings which had been scratched and pecked apart by birds seeking partly digested seeds. Here the hunter should listen for the variety of calls made by the Gambel's and he must separate them from the sounds made by the cactus wren and larks. If a dog is being used, the birds are generally scented before they are seen, but they usually run, nevertheless. In such terrain the hunter's ability to interpret his dog's movements is invaluable. This open country is not the easiest place to hunt but it is the only type of terrain available to some shooters.

The hunter should not expect to see an entire covey at once. It is surprising how much cover actually exists on this nearly barren ground. He is most likely to sight a single bird in a small opening, either sliding along at incredible speed, seeming to float evenly above the blur of its hurrying feet, or pausing momentarily to assess the situation. In most cases the birds have sighted him long before he sees them. They usually appear unexpectedly tall and slender as they run with necks stretched upward.

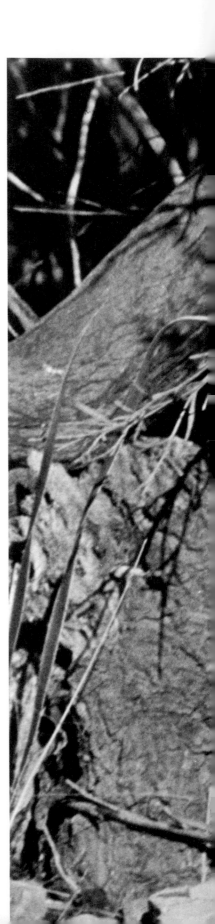

Gambel's quail (top & right) is notable for jaunty plume and splendid markings. A native of Southwest, it runs and flies swiftly. Javelina, or peccary, feeds largely at night, can run surprisingly fast on stubby legs.

Along the dry wash I was startled by the whistling rise of a half-dozen mourning doves, now out of season, and tried to discern quail sounds in the lark noises and the rustling of smaller birds. I thought I sighted a moving quail sixty yards away. I had not looked for birds within range; I hoped to find them already moving and despaired of simply walking upon them while they were resting or feeding. I knew that under the circumstance a first sighting would probably be at considerable distance.

Another quail ran quickly across an opening near a barrel cactus and I quickened my pace toward the birds, sure that an entire covey must be fading before me. As I moved, a single bird called, a certain and welcome sign that my determined pushing had caused the group to scatter. When I felt I had gained a little ground I ran toward the covey in the hope of flushing or scattering it. The birds did not fly as they might have if the cover had been skimpier, but they seemed to have disappeared and I stood panting in a seemingly birdless desert, my noisy charge having silenced even the larks and flickers. I was not completely discouraged for I remembered the single call I had heard earlier; in a few minutes I heard another quail call, somewhat ventriloquial, but not far away. I turned back the way I had come.

I walked back slowly, stopping at intervals, and finally a single quail flushed, the sound not quite so much of a buzz as that made by a bobwhite. As I had hoped, the bird had peeled away from the covey's route, either by accident or personal decision, and had held close while I passed. Then it had become fidgety and finally flew. The performance was repeated twice more—three chances at birds from one covey, although the main group never flushed!

The best shooting is had where walking is difficult and the cover is good. In southern Arizona, about a hundred miles from Phoenix, we drove into mountains with spectacular desert vegetation where cover was thick enough to provide the best of Gambel's quail shooting. Steep slopes were covered with varicolored loose rocks, treacherous to step on but lying among considerable grass. At the bottoms of the arroyos, some of which still held puddles of early winter rain, the brush was thick, growing to the edge of the invariable wash of sand and gravel. In many places there were satisfactory roosting spots for the Gambel's, which spends the nights in trees or bushes, unlike most quails which stay on the ground. The dry wash at the bottom of each arroyo was a clear trail, easily walked by the hunter, and a good course if he could persuade a dog to cover the hostile slopes of cactus around him. Even so, there was little hope of shooting on the first flush. When we finally flushed a flock from a ravine shoulder the birds skimmed low in typical Gambel's flight and fanned out as they descended into a draw, each bird seeking his own hiding place.

We followed them into the brushy bottom and our dog froze near the narrow, sandy wash. Then when we flushed a single bird it started a chain reaction of singles that whirred off in rapid succession from a miniature forest of mountain mahogany, goatsberry bush, and scrub oak, each bird scaling the arroyo walls and flying barely high enough to clear the brush. It was now a bobwhite type of performance, close-range shooting at quick chances—a type of sport rarely reported by Gambel's hunters.

In such terrain, flying birds are hard to mark, since they generally manage to cross at least one ridge. The experienced gunner knows of their reluctance to pass a brushy bottom and knows he is likely to find them in the next ravine, even though he did not see them alight.

Not all Gambel's coveys are large ones, but they seem to gather irrespective of family groups, and they may appear in frustrating numbers, one flushed bunch setting off another flight. We followed a running bunch along a trail at the crown of a steep ridge and lost them some-

Prickly pear is standard element of javelina diet. Bite marks on plant are typical. Thorns evidently do not injure little pig's mouth.

where downwind from our course. Finally they flew, a single bird taking off first, then a large covey plunging downhill into a big valley, and then two more large coveys—more than a hundred birds in all—flew and sailed against the light down into a blue abyss lined by saguaro cactus plants. Some of those mountain plants were thirty feet tall and the backlighting made an aura of their thorns. Just before the birds entered the cover they were glinting specks as the low sun glanced from their glossy wings. We checked our canteens and started down.

More than a hundred birds were scattered over a plot of upended desert land, ravines within ravines, almost half a mile in diameter. Their calls came plainly through the clear air and as we inched down into the valley a few birds flew in scattered bunches. We spread out to take advantage of the occasional flights, stumbling through prickly pear and sidling past the sharp leaves of yucca. Once near the place where the birds had landed, we moved only a few feet at a time, holding quiet for long periods in the age-old ruse that cracks the young bird's nerves and sends it hurtling off within range. Even so, almost as many birds rose behind as ahead of us and

we saw only a fraction of those that had entered the big valley. The dead birds were almost impossible to find without the dog's help. I peered into one bush several times, sure I had seen my bird fall into it, kicked it tentatively and thought I could detect a darker spot at elbow depth. Then I saw a single loose feather, but I was not sure until my scratched hand closed around the dead quail. The dog was handicapped by scattered wraiths of bird scent and the dry air.

The Gambel's quail has been the subject of a long-term study by the Arizona Game and Fish Department, the result of which is probably applicable to many upland species in that it places the usual premium on habitat and de-emphasizes the role of the hunter's kill in game populations. As with much other short-lived game, the Gambel's mortality rate may be as much as ninety per cent during a poor year. The effect of hunting was studied by closing an area to all quail shooting for a ten-year period while leaving a like area open nearby. At the end of the period, hunting success in the closed area was no better than in the area where hunting pressure had been continued. The conclusion is that hunting is not an important factor in Gambel's population.

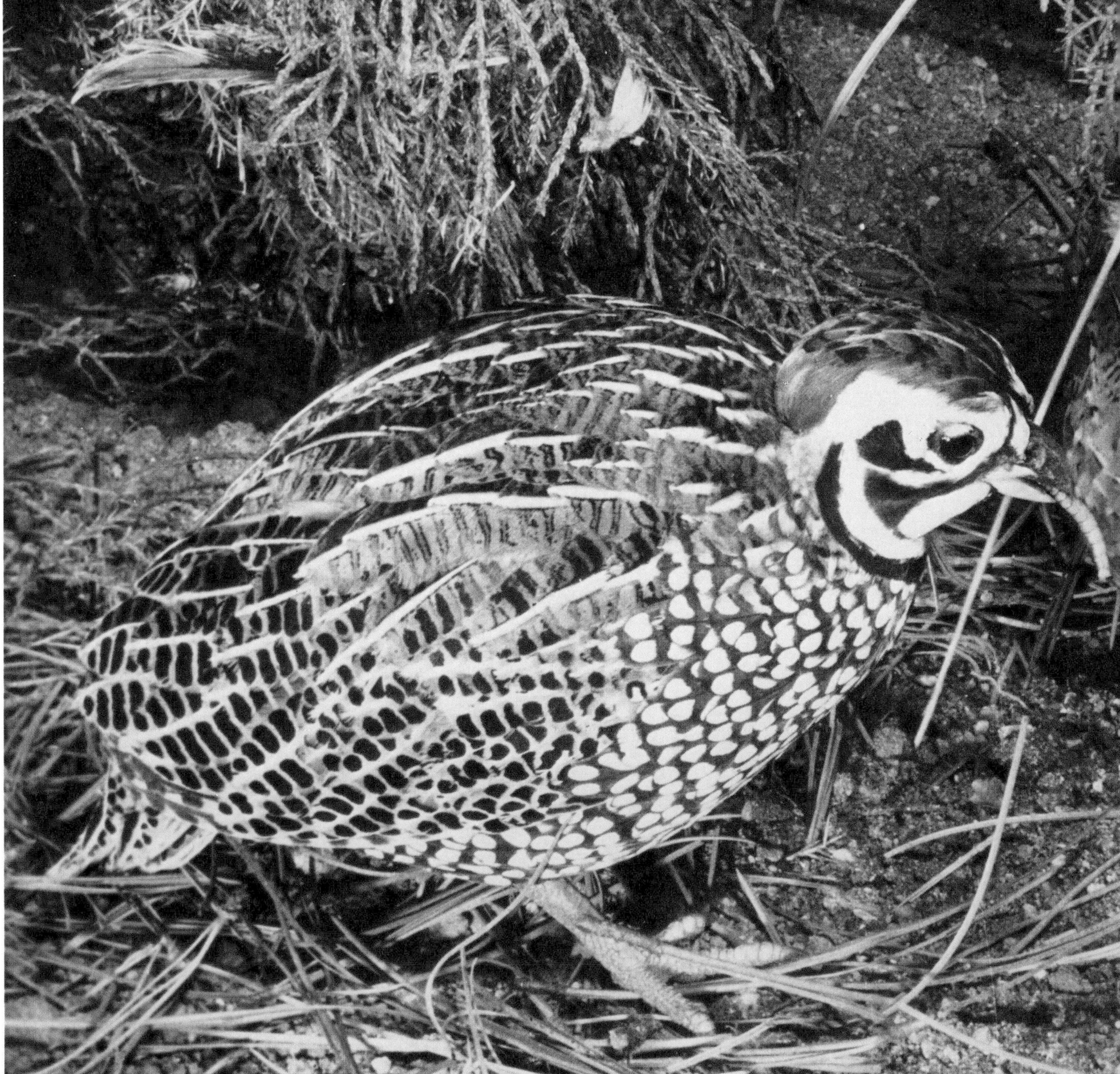

Mearns's quail, also
called harlequin because
of bizarre markings,
are little-known
residents of area near
Mexican border. They
hold and flush
like bobwhite.
Head of Mearns's cock (1).
Scaled quail (2), also
known as blue, has
unique design on head
(3) which gives him name
"cottontop." Hunter
above may find both
species in such terrain.

*Masked bobwhite (opposite)
is species making comeback
in Southwest. Mourning dove
(1) broods young in
tree nest. Kangaroo rat is
food for variety of
predators. Elf owl, with
scorpion, is cactus
dweller, curve-billed
thrasher is cactus percher.*

1

2

3

4

In dry country, rainfall during the winter has a great effect on quail populations. Dry years bring a small crop of food for the birds, and in years when there is little growing vegetation, the reproductive organs of the adult quail actually do not develop for the breeding season. In such years hunting success is relatively small, for lack of birds discourages many gunners and the preponderantly adult population of quail is especially hard to find and shoot; so man, the predator, is effectively controlled by the natural conditions.

The scaled quail will live in more northerly grass country than the Gambel's, ranging as far north as Colorado, although it will sometimes share Gambel's territory. It is a ground nester, laying nine to sixteen speckled eggs. The best known of the scaled quail tribe is the "blue quail," or "cottontop," of about the same size as the Gambel's, but of lighter color. When flushed, it tends to fly somewhat higher than the brush-hugging level of the Gambel's. The scaled quail, like the Gambel's, is often hunted without a dog,

1

2

3

6

Desert Life.
White-winged dove (1).
Joshua trees (2). Ocotillo
plants (3) appear as
dry sticks in left
foreground. In rear is
stand of saguaro cactus.
Paloverde trees (4)
shelter desert wildlife.
Harmless chuckwalla (5)
often frightens first-time
desert visitors. Southern
California cholla
cactus (6) has easily
detachable spines which seem
to "jump" onto passers-by.
Barrel cactus (7) has
corrugations that permit
swelling in wet times,
contraction in dry. Swift
roadrunner (8) in repose.

4

5

7

8

and when seen running ahead of the hunter it can sometimes be flighted by sprinting toward it. Sometimes part of a covey will be flushed by persistent following at a walk. At other times the hunter will simply walk into a bunch if there is considerable undercover. A veteran dog may follow and scatter a bevy, then point the individual birds.

A rainy day in the desert, rare though it may be, can help the dogless sportsman. The sound of falling rain will hide his approach and the dampness keeps the birds concentrated under protective bushes.

In a steady drizzle I walked alone after scaled quail, carrying a duck gun, for I thought the shots would be long in the sparse cover I chose. I moved slowly, listening for quail conversation and looking for tracks or signs of feeding in the wet sand, knowing that anything I saw would be fresh. But the birds had evidently sat tightly during a thunderstorm and continued to do so as they waited for the drizzle to stop. I was surprised when a closely bunched covey took off within range, although to one side, so that my first warning was the whirr of their wings. I watched them coast behind a forest of cholla cactus and a few mesquite trees only three hundred yards away, so I made my way to that point and then studied the ground ahead.

Near the point where they had disappeared I found a truly logical landing place, a slight knob a few feet higher than the surrounding desert, covered with grass and thick prickly pear clumps. The whole hillock was perhaps a hundred feet across and looked so superior as a scaled quail hideout that I walked rapidly onto it.

My landing site was well chosen and a gray form buzzed close to the ground between mesquite bushes. Others leaped from their scattered positions and the duck gun, ordinarily a poor choice for quail, boomed successfully. It had been a good guess that wet birds would not run far, that they would choose the thickest cover, and that they would prefer high ground on a rainy day.

Unknown to most sportsmen, the Southwest has a quail—the Mearns's—which rivals the bobwhite for hunting in the grand manner, holds distractingly close for a pointing dog, and lives in rolling grasslands among live oaks where even a southeastern gunner might feel reasonably at home. Comparisons to the bobwhite may show one or the other to be superior, but the arguments are academic and the flight is similar, whether or not one is faster than the other. Both will sometimes change their positions before the pointing dog, but neither sprints like the Gambel's or the scaled. Both rise in coveys with roaring wings, their appearance of speed enhanced by short tails and bullet shapes. But the Mearns's quail occupies only a small range, a section of lush grass near the Mexican border unknown to most American sportsmen. Often called the harlequin because of the male's polka dot plumage, it is also known as the fool quail because it holds tightly in cover. It nests in the grass and lays eight to fourteen eggs.

Near the border we camped in a valley with only occasional cactus plants and a stand of desert willow trees, dangling bare pods in December. Grass was high and the hills were spotted with live oaks, most of them no more than fifteen feet tall, but occasionally growing higher.

It was first a search for quail sign—the gougings for food that appear somewhat like a squirrel's nut excavations and are made by the bird's long claws, and the circular patterns of small droppings that indicate a roosting spot. There had been recent rains and it was easy to tell where a covey had fed that morning. We found stands of a variety of grasses more than waist high, although not thick enough to seriously impede walking; grama grasses were the most important variety. Much quail food comes from underground, with the chufa tuber high among their foods, along with wood sorrel bulbs. They will also eat prickly pear and when there is a good acorn crop it will make up much of their diet. Although the quail did part of their feeding in the high grass, it was along the dry washes that their diggings showed plainly.

The dogs wore bells almost as a necessity, for much of the time the grass hid them completely. Our first sight of quail was a bird that moved almost casually across an open spot while a slavering dog sniffed eagerly behind it. But then the bird disappeared and we never found it again. Later whirring in the oaks probably marked its departure.

Then a dog disappeared and I found him frozen on point, a light-colored blob in the tan-colored grass. I was within five feet of him before I could tell which way he faced. His head was down—within ten inches of a quail, it developed. I walked up to the spot, by a ravine filled with a close stand of oaks. The bird flew like a bobwhite in an upward spiral, its wings blurring like those of a huge bee, so that it could avoid me in its flight for heavy cover. It was a test of nerves to hold my fire until the quail was at proper range, then to shoot before it disappeared.

The dog next pointed a covey that roared into the oaks, giving me only a single hasty shot, and while the dog aided a companion in running down part of the flock on the opposite hillside I stepped into the middle of a covey and missed wildly while they escaped.

Another quail of like habits is the masked bobwhite, similar to the eastern bird, except that the cock has a sooty countenance, almost black. Once the masked quail lived in the southwestern United States, thriving in grasslands which later disappeared under heavy grazing. About 1912 it disappeared from the United States, and fifteen years later was found on the menu of a Mexican restaurant in Sonora. A few live birds were brought back across the border, although no new population was established. As the Mexican habitat was steadily destroyed by overgrazing, it was suspected that the masked bird had become truly extinct. Scientific expeditions from the United States had great difficulty finding any traces of living birds and enlisted the services of the industrious cactus wren, which builds one nest for residence and several as decoys, usually among the forbidding spines of cactus plants. The wren uses the feathers of other birds as nest material and among these the investigators finally found what they were sure were feathers of the masked bobwhite. Ground roosts were then discovered nearby. Birds were trapped and reintroduction is now under way in the United States.

It is midmorning on a desert mountain and the sun is becoming hot for a hunter trudging among barrel cacti, prickly pear, and sotol, over weather-rounded rocks that roll under his feet. A roadrunner, the much-publicized bird comedian of the Southwest, scurries ahead of him in a flowing gait, its body moving smoothly as the racing feet automatically absorb the unevenness of the ground. The runner's head is thrust ahead, as if to reduce wind resistance, and his whole frame appears streamlined. But when he comes to a small gully cut by a cloudburst he calls upon inadequate wings to carry him awkwardly across, showing his mistrust of aviation by continued walking motions with his feet, even while airborne. He is no serious threat to the hunter's game—the desert quail—although he is blamed for occasionally seizing young birds. The hunter has seen him chase a quail, and despite the roadrunner's reputation as a speedster the scuttling Gambel's kept the distance constant. The roadrunner eats insects, lizards, and now and then a small snake.

Some distance away on the mountainside is a concrete water catchment, noticeable only from above and designed to provide water for desert game. Far below is a blue reservoir carrying tiny specks—geese that have completed their fall migration from Canada.

Not all of man's works oppose wildlife.

15.
In southern wetlands, jacksnipe
find switch grass, woodcock probe damp
earth for worms, and wood
ducks locate in high-rising trees.

At first it is lonely in a cypress swamp, and the hollow thump of a pileated woodpecker only emphasizes the quiet. On a still day the breeze is hardly heard in the cypress crowns, and if a fish crow passes high overhead his two-syllable flight report seems to come from some other land. In early morning and late evening the cypress knees stand like strangers in mourning, a little apart from each other. The water is black from tannic-acid stain, but in many places it is covered by duckweed, a flat rug of little floating plants that appear from a distance as scum. In some sections there are clumps of water lettuce. A wader must move carefully, for the bottom is uncertain with slippery roots and sunken sticks.

A whitetail buck, driven by hounds from the swamp's edge, can be heard from far away by a silent listener, the deer's progress marked by the measured plops of his hooves in the water as he lifts his feet high to clear sunken logs. It is really the borders of the cypress swamp that are filled with life. One border is the upward slope to high ground—the edge of the water where foxes, deer, raccoons, and an occasional flock of wild turkeys move at dusk; where the bushes pinch their passage there is a faint game trail. Spanish moss, draped on the cypress trees and an occasional oak, matches the color of a hiding gray squirrel and is used as nest material by a variety of birds.

The other border is the river itself, black water with silent, drifting rafts of water hyacinths, many of which clog the backwaters. Coots and gallinules walk across the larger rafts, which undulate from the wake of a passing boat, but retain their form for long periods until divided through some vagary of current. They continue, piecemeal, toward the sea carrying their minuscule colonies of insects, tiny fish, and reptiles. Other hyacinths—the beautiful curse of southern waterways—will lodge somewhere on their downstream drift and multiply, often aiding in wood duck camouflage and serving as resting place for water snakes.

In very dry weather, most of the swamp will have water only in the lower pockets and in the small creeks. The streams can be traced easily, even in high water, by their winding alleys through the trees. There is a squeal, high-pitched and part whistle, made by a wood duck, either resting in the swamp or looking for food. It is early afternoon and no really serious feeding is likely until much later. The strange call indicates there is more than one duck, for the single bird generally keeps his silence.

A hunter in the swamp takes his bearing on the sound and makes a careful course toward it. As he moves he tries to keep a large tree trunk between him and his objective, but he also chooses a route that will leave some open shooting area to either side of the tree he hopes will hide his approach. He reaches his chosen cypress and peers cautiously around it until he can select another tree up ahead, but they are simply not growing in a helpful arrangement, so he and his dog cross a fairly open stretch of shallow water, feeling huge and out of place, and finally reach a tree which is too small but better than nothing.

He starts at the faint hiss of wings overhead; it is a flicker approaching a dead tree, fifty feet up, and thinking more of invisible grubs than of staring eyes below. The flicker goes straight at the tree in his up-and-down flight, and as it seems he is about to drive into it he pulls up in a sudden stall, extends his feet, and lands gently. He then examines the hunter and his dog, and scuttles sidewise to the other side of the tree where he begins serious pecking.

The hunter is sure he knows where the ducks are, as the creek is only thirty yards ahead, and he is positive they have landed in the wide backwater and swum leisurely back into the swamp to spend midday. When he hears more squeakings and swishy wing testing, he decides to walk briskly toward them, noting carefully, however, the larger openings the ducks might choose for escape.

Opening pages: *Wood duck drake,*
brilliant prize of swamp and forest.
Species has been brought back
from near-extinction by careful management,
can now be hunted generally.

He walks rapidly toward where he is sure the ducks are resting, making no effort at quiet, and they respond with a frantic flailing of wings and frightened squeals. They do not stay together, but leave in all directions. He sees the flickering of wings in two or three spots and then a bird comes toward him in easy range, a gaudy drake in full plumage. It is slanting upward, though not so steeply as to lose speed, and he mounts his gun for a full swing as the bird veers off. The fugitive is on a collision course with a great cypress and, just as the hunter is ready to fire, fans its tail downward in a sudden halt, darts sidewise through some small branches, and drives off through a high opening. The hunter's shot thwacks harmlessly into the big tree trunk and the bird is above the swamp in sunlight before the hunter can locate it again. He laughs, for killing wood ducks is a small part of hunting them, and he has spent the greater part of a day in the hope of collecting a limit of only two birds.

Above the swamp, the dozen wood ducks rendezvous and fly up the river in loose formation, looking for a new resting place. If undisturbed, they are likely to make three important stops during their day—roosting, resting, and feeding. They roost in a small lake, well protected from wind but large enough to keep them safe from foxes and bobcats, and surrounded by thick foliage. Saw palmetto is very dense almost to the water's brink, where cattails and willows take over.

The hunter has found the lake, but most of the ducks leave before legal shooting hours and return in semidarkness. He has waded through the lake's shallows and stood in the gloom after sunset, finally to see growing dots against the rapidly changing western colors, and has heard the ducks in almost vertical dives as they cleared the lake's rim of cypress. They seem to spatter into the water awkwardly and their sounds on the water are squeals, peeps, squawks, and quacks. It is hard to see what they are doing, but they make a constant splashing. A late arrival may miss the watcher's head by only a few feet.

At dawn they fly out to feed, then rest in the river swamp or a similar area, and at evening they feed again. It is a good year for acorns, and the hunter knows there should be a spot where he can intercept the ducks as they make their daily visit to the same oaks. It is a long and involved process, but their flights can be traced. The process is much the same as that used by beekeepers who locate bee trees by following a single bee as far as possible, then take up the route again when another bee passes in the same direction.

One such wood duck hunt was well under way when I was invited to join it. For two days my friends had been marking the flights. They estimated they would be ready for shooting after three more scouting expeditions. I went with them in late afternoon and we parked a 4 X truck in the midst of a field of thick scrub oak. We heard the assembly calls of a flock of bobwhite quail, and watched fish crows and mourning doves making leisurely starts toward their roosting areas.

The ducks came from a river swamp in groups of twos, threes, and fours, with an occasional flock of eight or ten. They flew the same straight course, some fifty yards above the ground, unmistakable in silhouette, with their heads carried high and fairly close in, and their tails quite long, now folded but capable of fanning wide for quick maneuvers. We watched them with binoculars, established a disappearance point, and hurried there for another view, seeing the last of them cross a pine ridge.

My hunting friend watched the vanishing point and thought across the pines to visualize what lay beyond them. He pondered the ducks' route across citrus groves and pastureland, over highways and homes, and stared for a while at a distant television tower by way of judging their direction. A short while later we made out specks in the twilight and knew the birds had finished

Wood duck drake is thought by many to be world's most beautiful waterfowl. Wilson's snipe (above) are worm eaters like woodcock, but prefer wetter environment. Snipe hunter opposite shoots double after approaching within range behind switch-grass clump.

*Wood ducks are encountered
in swamps and forests over much
of U.S. Hunting them
may require wide variety of
observing and stalking skills.*

feeding and were going to their roosting lake. We were very close to locating the feeding grounds. On the next trip, my companion named the spot, although he was still more than a mile from it. One more day and we went to the oaks, driving most of the way by an unused road and walking for a short distance to stand in an opening left by a fallen monster whose decaying trunk was still partly intact. There was little undergrowth, although dry oak leaves and acorns covered most of the ground. I stood and watched open areas as the feeding moment neared, not quite sharing my friend's confidence in the wood ducks' timetable. He paid no attention to the sky after once locating a proper gap for duck descent, but sat on the leaves with an empty gun and toyed with the single wood duck feather he had found there —his assurance he had gauged the flight correctly and that his strategy would be rewarded.

He checked his watch a few times, and ten

minutes after our arrival he loaded and snapped shut his gun, wished me luck, and moved a few yards away to stand with his back to a tree and face in the direction of the distant swamp where, a week before, he had begun to trace the wood ducks' evening flight. There were only eleven minutes until sundown, closing time for legal shooting, but it was less than a minute as he stood by his tree before the first ducks came through the high branch gaps in a whistling dive, tipping slightly on set wings, and the light upland guns cracked at them. A hurtling ball of black, the retriever scattered the leaves noisily to disappear and reappear with the game. In eight minutes, the week-long hunt had ended.

Wood ducks have no difficulty in digesting acorns—or more difficult things for that matter. Their gizzards will break the bitter pecan, a nut as hard as hickory. Duckweed is a major portion of their diet while on the water, and they are lovers of spiders as well as a variety of flying insects. A tree-nester and fascinating subject for the hunter-naturalist, the wood duck is sometimes a migrant, sometimes a year-round resident in the South. Its range is the entire eastern United States and a bit of the Pacific Northwest, and conservationists build nesting boxes for it. Most nests are in holes in trees, perhaps as high as fifty feet from the ground, a free fall that does not seem to harm the ducklings when the time comes for them to walk to water. However the nest may be acquired—the birds do not cut their own holes but rely on abandoned homes of other woods dwellers or natural openings—the mated pairs have methods of confusing watchers. Both of them may swoop near the hole, the male going on past while the hen enters unobtrusively.

Wood duck pairs locate their nesting sites with much peering and peeking, the female apparently the final authority on the spot to choose. Sometimes the opening is no more than four inches in diameter. Outside materials are not carried into the nesting hole, although some down

is employed, and the duck makes the most of what is already inside the opening. Such holes are sometimes desired by the hooded merganser, but observers say the wood duck usually wins arguments concerning property rights. Sometimes more than one duck lays eggs in the same nest and as many as thirty eggs are occasionally found together. A normal clutch is ten to fifteen creamy white eggs.

When the young are ready to leave the nest and walk to water the mother goes to the ground and calls them. Equipped with sharp claws, they seem to have no difficulty in climbing to the opening of the nest.

Today wood ducks are in good supply over most of their range. From 1918 to 1941, with the birds evidently nearing extinction, the season was closed. Their feathers are in great demand for trout flies, and mounted specimens have been sold for considerable sums. Wood duck colors are so complicated in arrangement that few writers will attempt to describe them. Even the hen is more colorful than females of other duck species, and the drakes have both brilliant and subdued colors, enhanced by iridescence.

Not all of the river shore is cypress swamp. Just above where the hunter stalked the ducks it opens to a large lake, three miles across, but with so gradual a shoreline that there is marsh almost all the way around. Only in a few places do strands of cypress follow shallow creeks down to the water; most of the shore simply slopes up gently to pastureland where Brahman cattle are willing to stand knee-deep to feed in wet weather.

When the water goes down, generally in late winter, great flats of stranded hyacinths are left, green at first but dying slowly, and ready to start new growth when the water comes again. Where low areas are slow to dry up there are gatherings of wood ibises, specialists in collecting stranded water life. The storks are called "iron-heads" by natives, an apt description of the naked gray skull and its great dark beak. Standing on the edge of a dwindling pool they are caricatures of birds, but make decorative patterns in the sky as they come down to their feeding places with perfectly regulated spirals, using their wings only to offset the push of an occasional vagrant draft. Sometimes there are blue-winged teal willing to decoy to a cattail blind on the main lake shore.

Near the lake shore there are high clumps of switch grass, and it is the nearly bare mud flats between the clumps of grass that attract the hunter's attention. He is looking for marks which nearly duplicate those sought by woodcock hunters, but in this case on ground where a film of water covers fairly soft mud. Ideally the surface should shine when viewed against the light, but water should not be very deep. An inch of water would be too much to please the hunter's quarry, the Wilson's snipe, or jacksnipe. Sometimes there are patches of otherwise attractive area which the hunter says have "gone bad"—most of the plants being dead and the water stagnant with perhaps an iridescent film. The mud is evil-smelling, and the snipe are gone.

The snipe breed as far south as New Jersey and as far north as Alaska, choosing marshy ground for the simple grassy nest with three or four splotched eggs. The very existence of the snipe is doubted by some nonhunters; an ancient prank is the "snipe hunt" in which victims are stationed at night with burlap sacks and lanterns to watch for birds that never come. Some hunters are simply not aware of the bird, because snipe shooting was forbidden for years. When seasons were opened some time after World War II, a new generation of gunners failed to recognize the twisting little birds, and many hunters have scant interest in pursuing a target which weighs no more than a pair of shot shells. Inexperienced snipe shooters usually expend more weight in shot than they bag in game, and snipe shooting has never proved popular—a state of affairs which pleases the lone marsh walkers with hip boots and shotguns.

Although the shooting may be funny, the hunting has its scientific aspects, and the gunner needs to know a few salient facts. Between the clumps of head-high switch grass, he looks for probe marks where the snipe's flexible beak has worked for worms; the droppings are chalk marks almost indistinguishable from those made by a heavier and more honored relative, the woodcock. If the water is a bit higher or lower, last year's snipe cover will be useless.

The hunter is especially pleased to find sign between the switch grass patches, for the snipe insists on open sky overhead and it is only the occasional clumps of switch grass that enable the hunter to approach him unseen. A hundred snipe may note his approach and take wing too soon, but one bird may dally behind a grass clump and leave within range. Snipe communication is strange, and some gunners say the birds refuse to believe what they themselves have not seen. A panicked flock may leave a few stubborn stragglers, even when the firing is fast and coming from several hunters.

If possible, the hunter walks downwind, and the flushed bird will show its light underside as it turns against the wind to make its escape. Its wings are long and pointed and make only a whisper compared to the roar of most round-winged upland game, and it may take off between the switch grass clumps and twist away unseen until out of range. Almost invariably, it makes a *cheep* or *scaip* shortly after takeoff, but the sound often comes too late to alert a shooter facing elsewhere.

When snipe have had little gunning on their southward migration, they may be fairly tame and even curious about the gunner. Once missed, a snipe may climb until it is a decimal point in the sky and then dive earthward, its wings held so that it has an arrowhead shape. It may come straight at the uncomfortable gunner, who is thus presented with a close and difficult target, then come to a near stop and change

Woodcock benefits from some of nature's subtlest camouflage. In Northeast it is valued game bird. In South, where it winters, it is largely ignored. Right: Round wing tip is typical of quick-flushing birds.

Juvenile woodcock with
earthworm, which is main element
of the species' diet. On
damp ground (right), point may
mean woodcock or bobwhite.

directions abruptly, its head drawn back on its shoulders and its button eyes on the unnerved shooter. *Scaip!*

The experienced snipe gunner prefers to shoot at the snipe broadside rather than straight on, for the bird is so erratic from port to starboard that it may escape a pattern by zigzagging. From the side it appears to be holding a much steadier course. There are some shooting grounds where the birds are forced to live in fairly tall grass, and hence flush close to the gun.

Once a concentration of snipe is located and flushed, the birds are likely to return to the same spot, especially in late evening. The hunter at the lake shore can drive them up and then make himself comfortable in the switch grass clumps just before sundown, watching little and great blue herons, cattle egrets, snowy egrets,

and wood storks come to roost in low bushes along the shore. There may be white ibis and occasionally a flight of fulvous tree ducks, rare in that area. The wading birds seek their roosting spots with considerable quarreling and ill-natured flapping, and the purple grackles and red-winged blackbirds increase activity as dusk approaches. Then the snipe begin to come back, appearing suddenly in the sky, plummeting little forms from which the hunter tries to collect his bag.

The hardest snipe shooting is on the flooded pastures where the coastal Bermuda grass is thick but too short to hide the hunter from the birds. Here they get up wild most of the time, and he resolves to look straight ahead and pay no attention to derisive cheeps from either side, thus seeing the birds turn up against the wind. The flight of an occasional cattle egret seems to coax

the snipe into the air and the hunter makes hurried range calculations until his head aches and his hands sweat around the slim gunstock. He comes to a small ditch with a bit of willow along it and catches a bird by surprise. In one stretch of boggy ground he is partly concealed by the gray winter stalks of some wild hibiscus and finds he has a better chance at the game.

Only a few feet higher than the watery home of the jacksnipe, the hunter will find an occasional woodcock, sometimes not far from the cypress swamp. Along the swamp edge may be red maple, pignut hickory, and water hickory; then the gentle slope goes to pine or oak, and the woodcock, at the southern end of his migration, makes do with cover somewhat different than that of his northern home. There are no old apple orchards, but there is some soft, damp earth and plenty of grass with earthworms below.

In some ways the woodcock duplicates his northern performances. Often he is a solitary fellow occupying the same spot year after year. If a lucky gunner bags him, his territory will be occupied by another bird so soon that there seems something mysterious about the process.

The woodcock, unlike the snipe, is in the main line of hunting tradition. It is an easterner for the most part, although it turns up disconcertingly in areas where it does not belong. It is tagged after ignominious netting, and spied upon during its unbelievable mating-season demonstrations, but enough of its life is beyond observation to make the pattern of its movements difficult to predict.

Most of the southern population is migratory, some of the birds having come all the way

1

2

3

*Swampland inhabitants
include long-necked
Louisiana egret (1),
sandhill crane (2),
raccoon (3), and red-tailed
hawk (4). Crane
arrives from summer home
in Canada as Florida
hunter goes forth
for ducks and snipe.
Raccoons are noisy
nighttime squabblers.
Red-tail, leaping
into flight, is strong
bird of prey, can
carry off large rodents.*

4

from Labrador, flying low in conditions of half-light and sometimes dying in contact with electric wires or buildings. Evidently the woodcock's bulging comedian's eyes are not too efficient. Although it can stand considerable cold, ground that is hard-frozen or dried-out cuts off its worm supply and can lead to a tragic depletion of the woodcock population.

The woodcock's beak is strangely hinged for probing and it is known that the beak has delicate nerves to aid in below-surface investigation. The bird is also credited with superior hearing to detect the subterranean traffic of earthworms, which comprise four-fifths of his diet.

The true woodcock lovers are hunters of the Northeast, and most of them prefer the hillsides to the bottoms—not that the birds are more plentiful, but the hunting is infinitely easier. Willow and alder bottoms are difficult to walk and a pointing dog is hard to locate in such cover, even with a bell on his collar. Most of the good hillsides have grass cover, but the really choice hunting grounds are abandoned apple orchards, where a century of decayed fruit has produced perfect earthworm habitat.

The birds may feed in the bottoms and then rest on sunny hillsides. Briers that are too thick are inconsistent in producing birds for the gunner, and the best of cover is likely to grow too high and thick if unattended. It is the early growth that attracts the birds, and those hunters who can afford to take woodcock seriously will keep the timber cut back and leave openings for the birds' mating performance. In this display, the male struts like a microscopic turkey gobbler, produces strange sounds, and spirals in wide circles up to great height making still other noises, some of them musical, only to return to his takeoff point, where an admiring female may be observing his aerobatics. The four pinkish-brown eggs are laid in a haphazard ground nest, usually near brushy bottoms or wooded tracts. The young hatch in about three weeks. Most

recent observations indicate that the mother does not transport her young between her legs as was once believed.

When the southward migration is under way, there may be great concentrations of woodcock, especially along the eastern coast where bays and inlets may hinder progress. The birds accumulate while waiting for favorable winds—these arriving they may depart overnight. One of the best known of these stopping places is Cape May, New Jersey, and watchful residents have wonderful shooting at times.

It has been estimated that more than half of the nation's woodcock winter in Louisiana. When friends in New Jersey refused to set any specific time for a hunt, I questioned the Louisiana authorities and found that the woodcock would be there, but that a choice date was difficult to set. Unusually warm weather, even in January, might move the birds up into Arkansas, I was told, but there were some especially good covers that nearly always produced, and I finally went hunting with a companion from Ponchatoula. We went to lumber-company land, divided by carefully laid-out dirt roads, a country with so few landmarks and so many turns that it is very easy to become lost. It offered expanses of grassland, pine forests, and small creeks—always called "branches" there—with occasional spots dense enough to be called thickets.

It had rained almost steadily for a week and the morning was gray with periods of drizzle. Crows were making rainy day complaints and hunching against the damp on high trees. Meadowlarks flushed occasionally ahead of our three bell-wearing pointers, and we sloshed along in knee boots. It was early January, certainly late enough for woodcock to be present, but we made a slow start, and when the dogs pointed in open country the game proved to be a single bobwhite quail, no disappointment to my partner, who was not imbued with true woodcock spirit. In Louisiana, it is difficult to interest gunners in woodcock harvest and a bird dog receives little criticism if he takes no interest in them.

We found the first woodcock sign in heavy grass among scattered and leafless hardwood saplings. It was only a few yards from one of the small branches that ran a foot deep and three feet wide. The bird had worked there the night before or in early morning, and had rummaged so thoroughly, turning up such large tufts of grass and dead leaves, that I glanced toward some nearby oaks and wondered if it might have been the work of a gray squirrel. My more experienced partner assured me these were woodcock probings and I was satisfied when I examined the sign more closely.

The woodcock is noted for lying close for pointing dogs. It is also noted for doing unexpected things, and once we heard the light whistle of wings as a nearby but unseen bird tired of listening to jangling bells and sloshing hunters.

When the dogs finally found a woodcock, it was in a grassy and brushy spot, fifty feet across. They pointed and moved and then pointed again. The unseen bird most likely was trundling about in the cover like some spring-driven mechanical toy, his precious bill resting on his chestnut-colored paunch, and his inadequate legs working hard.

At such a time the hunter is likely to look less for the bird than for the route it will choose through the scattered pines, some of them thirty or forty feet high. Especially in the heavier cover, the bird is likely to fly for the largest opening. My friend chose a spot, the right one, and sent the dogs into the clump of saplings and bushes, not exactly classic procedure for pointing dogs, but a very effective one. The bird fluttered in the grass, stirring a few leaves, and flew almost straight up. It cleared the immediate cover, then drove off in horizontal flight.

The birds had shifted from our hunting area and we found only four or five in the entire day's operation, so I went northward. The first foray was unsuccessful, but I was put into an abundance of birds in another lightly wooded area where most of the game held tightly in clumps of wax myrtle and sweet bay to the satisfaction of a Brittany pointing spaniel which had never encountered woodcock before.

The patterns of woodcock flight were very plain; in fact, the day offered a short course in woodcock shooting, with a concentration of birds such as few shooters ever expect to find. When the birds flushed they flew for the most obvious escape route if the cover happened to be thick; if it was sparse, they made a choice, usually at the exact moment the gunner was ready to fire. Boring toward scattered post oak and pine trees, the birds would appear about to pass among the branches but might pull up in an almost vertical climb, leveling off again in the treetops. Once the gunner had solved this maneuver and held his fire until the climb was completed, his next bird —like as not—would continue on through the trees while he stared blankly at the bare sky above them.

While most of America's woodcock winter on the gentle slopes of Louisiana pasture and woodland, the local hunters pay them little heed, watching for blue geese and ducks, unaware of the woodcock's nocturnal passage and his quick movements with the weather changes. Few of them even recognize his softly whistling wings; he is called by a dozen local names, and cheerfully confused with the Wilson's snipe.

A thousand miles to the north, his other home is in the depth of winter, his alder thickets and apple orchards deep in snow, and his worming grounds frozen hard. His most loyal admirers have not sought him for several weeks, knowing that he has disappeared until spring, when he will again present his strange mating tableau. But most of them have never even seen that; they will wait until the following fall to seek him out again. And hardly any of them can visualize the different world he lives in along the branches of Louisiana.

16.
As summer's haze blurs the
eastern hills, woodchuck munch
timothy and red clover,
while foxes red and gray seek
targets of opportunity.

It is late summer—a sultry day with haze separating the Pennsylvania hills, plainly showing their varied distances. The hunt is no spartan expedition. The hunter arrives in a sedan, parking at the high edge of a field of red clover and timothy. One hay crop has already been removed and another cutting is certain before fall; already the solid growth is nine or ten inches tall, with timothy stalks going much higher in places, and the hunter appraises the height carefully before he gently closes the car door, wincing slightly at the loud latch click he cannot avoid. At home he would never have noticed the sound.

The field slopes away to a fence line which, in turn, borders the forest of maple, elm, and thicker undergrowth in a creek bottom. Against that fence is a streak of ripe goldenrod and white-headed wild carrot; the nearest point of the streak is 104 yards from where the car stands.

The hunter's weapon is a heavy masterpiece of rubbed walnut, gleaming metal, and optical glass, stranger to an assembly line and product of a small and cluttered shop where a master builder slowly inletted a treasured slab of figured wood, fitted the heavy barrel to its burnished action, and made a thousand minute adjustments and smoothings.

The craftsman was a Pennsylvania rifle maker. Pennsylvania remains a source of fine rifles, as it has been since the days of the muzzle-loading flintlock, and the man who built the woodchuck hunter's pride may have descended from one who fashioned locks and barrels more than a century before.

The hunter takes an adjustable rest, a few cartridges, his binoculars, and a canvas to lie on, but he goes only a few yards to stop at a familiar spot where the young hay is still partly crushed down from his last visit. On the way he passes three other spots where the hay is flattened. They are slightly crescent-shaped, two small, kidney-shaped beds and one larger one; distinctly the marks of bedded deer—a whitetail doe and her two fawns. The hunter has seen them feeding near the forest in late evening, apparently oblivious to his motionless presence on the upper slope.

When he stepped from his car there had seemed to be a flat silence, but now that the engine murmur and sounds of his tires have died, the hunter is aware that his station is not quiet at all. There is a steady sound of insects and he can hear a juvenile fox barking somewhere in the forest. Several bumblebees move efficiently about the red clover blossoms and he hears a faint whistle as a pair of mourning doves twists past him, headed for evening feeding. Dove season will open soon, but he has no interest in such game now and hardly glances toward the birds. Instead, he studies half a dozen patches of darker green along the slopes of the hayfield.

In those spots the growth is a bit higher, partly because the woodchucks which dug holes there have turned new earth, partly because the mower blade has been kicked up by the mounds. The hunter knows which of the dens are in current use for he has examined them earlier. A freshly used hole is dusty; abandoned ones are rain-washed and may have cobwebs across their entrances. There is more than one entrance to each den, the main opening sloped and with a mound of earth about it. A few feet away, drop holes run straight down, emergency chutes with their openings cleared of any discarded earth.

Livestock sometimes get broken legs from the chuck holes, but a more frequent casualty is farm machinery, especially the front carriage of some tractors, which can easily be broken by a sudden twist when one wheel goes down hard. In one of the neighboring hayfields, the chuck holes are marked by stakes and plastic flags.

There are several round-topped hills in the hunter's chosen field and his position is selected so he can observe as much area as possible. He can see the opposite fence for a long way. To his left along that fence is a dead maple, and it is 224 yards from his rifle rest. To his right along the fence is a wild cherry tree. It is 240 yards away.

The woodchuck is a vegetarian, especially fond of alfalfa, clover, and various grasses, and enthusiastic about a wide variety of garden produce. There are many species of his tribe, and his cousins, the rockchucks of mountain country, are fired at across sheer canyons. But the eastern woodchuck is something of a beloved pest, treasured by the hunter and tolerated in moderate numbers by the farmer. Although a single chuck can do considerable damage to a small garden if he decides to do most of his foraging there, these animals seldom do much harm to crops like clover and alfalfa because their population is kept to a reasonable limit by hunters. Most farmers consider their burrows more of a nuisance than their eating habits. It is the hunter's hope that chucks remain plentiful enough for good hunting, but never reach the point where they are unceremoniously poisoned or burned out by beleaguered farmers. Human control of some kind is necessary, for the big bears and cats that once controlled their numbers have been reduced to the point where they no longer figure as predators.

The chuck is a true hibernator, not a light winter sleeper like the bear; in western Pennsylvania he may be asleep for three to four months. Generally, he disappears around November with the first real cold, sometimes choosing a special den for his winter sleep, selecting the site for maximum protection from the elements and predators. Some of his cousins in high mountain country may sleep for as much as eight or nine months of the year. All of them acquire extra fat as cool weather approaches, sometimes sitting at their den entrances with such obese smugness that it is a surprise when they dive so quickly into their main entrances or plop through grass-hidden drop holes.

The young, usually born in early spring, are generally four to six to a family, and lovers of the game religiously avoid shooting while they

are still dependent upon parental care. In some **237** sections there are protective laws.

The woodchuck is a watcher, sometimes afflicted with curiosity, and his nose is not especially keen. He is easily alarmed by noise, but it is the quick movement that causes him to disappear almost instantly and he is seldom far from his home.

The fox is an opportunist in woodchuck country, taking over abandoned woodchuck holes as homes and converting them to more suitable quarters. A rodent-seeker, the fox has designs on small woodchucks, but his relationship with their parents is rather uncertain since the chuck may weigh considerably more than the mature fox's seven or eight pounds.

A woodchuck, stricken by a hunter's bullet, may reach his hole in death throes and the fox's nose will tell him from some distance that all is not well with his potential meal. He will then go to great effort to excavate his victim, in some cases digging three feet below the surface to reach a large carcass he cannot otherwise drag out. The fox is something of a camp follower of the woodchuck hunter, ready to accept the discarded carcasses which may be tossed into brushy ravines. For some hunters, chucks—particularly young, tender, grass-fed chucks—are a delicacy not to be so lightly done away with.

The woodchuck hunter may well be a fox hunter, too, for the locale is much the same, and the fox season comes after the chucks have disappeared in fall. His hounds may run the same routes year after year, for foxes may travel the same paths through generations.

Gray and red foxes share the Pennsylvania landscape and when there were bounties our chuck hunter was a fox trapper, a task with many of the same requirements as woodchuck hunting. The fox trapper must have the patience and pay the same meticulous attention to detail as the chuck hunter. His traps are blued and boiled in privately concocted solutions, carried painstak-

ingly to his set, untouched by anything that might convey human odor.

Although the fox's diet ranges from grapes to carrion, the scents used to attract him are laboriously achieved, foul-smelling but applied in minuscule quantities. His nose is one of nature's masterpieces, able to find the buried trap if it carries the slightest taint of oil or metal. The trapper swears that the fox smells the steel if it is not thoroughly disguised.

Instead of simply passing the discovered set, the fox is likely to painstakingly uncover the trap and toss it aside, possibly as a favor to brother foxes and possibly, as trappers sometimes believe, as a contemptuous gesture toward man and his labors. The fox richly deserves his traditional reputation as a cunning trickster living among men and their poultry houses with an attitude of cautious insolence.

But the trapper may be even trickier than the fox and he brings a small horseshoe to the set, covering it carefully, but with no effort at disguising the scent of man, steel, or oil. From years of

thwarted effort and rueful observation he has learned where the fox is most likely to step after digging out the metal counterfeit and in that spot he places the real trap, concealed with care. He has no doubt that the fox will come to the set; his only question is whether the rascal will solve its design. Success is never certain.

But often the fox detects the pony shoe immediately, flips it scornfully away, and steps full into the jaws of the real trap. It is then that he may give his death cry—a chilling wail of defeat, far different from the choppy, petulant bark of the hunting fox.

Red and gray foxes are very different animals, although strikingly similar in silhouette. The red is most prized by hunters who run him with hounds, either afoot or riding behind the dogs, dressed in formal hunting attire. The gray runs a shorter race, but can climb trees almost like a squirrel, and it is common to find the hounds stalled beneath a sizable tree, often doing a fairly good job of climbing themselves. A gray fox may scramble to the topmost branches, as high as forty

feet, and he uses his claws to pull himself up the large trunk. His failing is that he is not hard to dislodge and sometimes jumps when a man arrives. The red is not an American native, but was transplanted from Europe by early settlers.

The gray fox is used as a training subject for deer hounds in some parts of the South, since efforts at introducing the long-running reds have seldom proved successful. The grays are creatures of habit in their evasive courses, the same animal usually repeating his route on succeeding hunts. Some believe the fox enjoys the game as much as the hunter and the dogs. At any rate, killing a favorite fox would be a sacrilege.

In the South, after listening to their dogs until midnight, hunters may decide to pick them up and are able from long experience to predict the fox's run. A wild truck ride on a back road may enable the hunters to cut off the chase, and they grab for their dogs in the blackness. Some veteran dog owners know individual foxes almost as well as they know their hounds.

The Pennsylvania chuck hunter calls foxes as well as traps them. For the reds, he imitates a stricken rabbit. For the grays, he uses an electronic imitation of a young fox in distress; at times responding grays will almost overrun his stand. Although the techniques of fox calling are complex and developed through long experience, the exact tones of the rabbit squeal are not so critical as mimicking the fox himself.

On the sultry day at the hayfield, the young fox stops his high-pitched yapping after a few moments and there is a little crow conversation, one of the birds sitting in the dead maple, 224 yards from the man. The hunter considers him for a moment with his binoculars, but abandons his first idea because the tree is high and there might be some danger from shooting in that direction. Besides, he consoles himself, he has come for woodchucks and does not want to make unnecessary noise; he has a duty to the farmer to keep the population under control, for the same farmer will permit him to hunt grouse along the creek in the fall.

He inspects his entire landscape with spe-

1

2

Woodchuck world is populated by gray and red foxes (1, 2), the clever crow, and cottontails—this one lounging at full length. Varmint hunters will switch to crows if chucks are not about. Woodchuck rising to inspect surroundings (3) betrays himself to spotting scope, eventually falls victim to shot, as in unusual picture above.

cial attention to the edge of the fence and the spots of darker green. Once a hen pheasant appears along the fence but stays close to the cover and disappears promptly. He knows there are other birds, for she is attentive to something else in the weeds. In late evening, he has heard the broken cackle of a cock pheasant, but it is the wrong time of day for that now.

He looks, in particular, for two different things—the streak of reddish brown that trims a woodchuck's grizzled coat, and the dark outline of the animal himself as he rises on his haunches to survey the surroundings. In ten inches of clover, the chuck's cautious inspections may actually endanger him, for he will never be seen as long as he holds his squat, four-footed stance and continues munching greenery.

The first chuck appears as a darker spot against the fence line, no more than five feet from it. His burrow is located on the other side, hidden by bushes and weeds, and he sits up and surveys the hayfield. The hunter does not see him immediately for he is sweeping another part of the field with his glasses, but when his inspection swings along the fence, he sights the dark spot instantly. The chuck is not far from the dead maple, almost exactly 200 yards away, and the rifleman moves to take a prone position, inching the heavy muzzle to cover the target, but the chuck is satisfied with his inspection and disappears in the clover, moving toward the hunter who waits for him to sit up again. It is a young chuck and not particularly cautious, so it simply nibbles clover for a time and then goes back under the fence and into its hole, concealed from the hunter, who waits in shooting position long after the target has disappeared.

It is fifteen minutes before the hunter takes his eyes from the spot where he saw the first chuck. He is looking through the rifle's scope and it is fifteen power, focused carefully at where the chuck was seen. Now he sits upright again, trying to stretch his cramped legs quietly, for he had taken a poor position behind the rifle in order to avoid unnecessary movements. He uses his binoculars again and finally he thinks he sees a suspicious spot. The dark object is not far from a deep green blotch on the clover field, but it is well beyond the wild cherry tree in distance and out into the field. He studies the field for reference points but there is nothing except innumerable butterflies. The dark spot disappears and now there is no doubt that it is a feeding chuck. It shows up again; it is only the chuck's head and he does not rise on his haunches to give a textbook view. He is unaware that he is being observed and the hunter decides the game is 260 yards away. The visible target is only three inches of rodent head, but a body hit is possible if the hold is too low and clover does not deflect the tiny bullet.

The hunter moves his rest, places the rifle carefully, and squirms to a prone position. The cross hairs hang dead still and a nearby butterfly is out of focus in the glass and huge in size. There is a glimpse of the chuck's head; he disappears; then his head reappears and holds quietly for a perfunctory look around.

The cross hairs are one and one half inches over the chuck's head, for the rifle is sighted for 200 yards. The trigger is pressed gently, a light, breaking-glass action, and the rifle gives a rounded bang—almost but not quite the sound of a big-game rifle. The recoil is unfelt, only a gentle nudge, and after the rifle's report comes a solid thump from across the hayfield. There is nothing to be seen in the scope and the hunter gets to his feet, checks his landmarks, and begins his walk toward the target.

The chuck seems always to be farther than expected, optical foreshortening eliminating the gentle swales from view, and the hunter sees he has misjudged a little. Finally, he comes to a hole, dusty about the mouth and the focal point for a series of narrow, crushed-down paths that fan out in all directions. He follows two of the paths for twenty or thirty feet, but each is a dead end. They are the routes of the chuck in his feeding forays. At the end of a third trail is the dead chuck, the tiny bullet having struck with explosive force just below the intended point—a minor misjudgment of range but a satisfactory kill. The woodchuck had been doomed since the man with the jeweler's loupe made the final adjustments in the cluttered gunmaker's shop years before.

The dead chuck weighs more than ten pounds. His head is broad and sleek on top and his color is mostly dark gray with lighter hairs, his coat thick in preparation for the months of cold. He is fat in readiness for hibernation and he wears a moustache of clover he had been holding when the bullet struck. His underparts are reddish brown and the long hair ends at his ankles, exposing black feet. The gunner wonders idly just why a grass eater must have such long teeth. Then he stands and checks the exact location. He will pace off the distance to his rifle.

Driving home, the hunter goes slowly along country lanes. Once he stops to inspect another field. This time he parks atop a slag pile thrown up by strip-mining for coal. Green is coming back to the pile, beginning to turn it to game cover. Japanese larch and a few spruce trees have been planted there to start the return to vegetation. Below it is a field of alfalfa and a cornfield. The hunter's glasses find a streak of downed corn where a raccoon has been working from a nearby creek. He even locates the well-worn trail over which the raccoon has made his feeding forays.

Skirting a forested area on a road that separates it from recently cut alfalfa, the hunter finds he has cut off a woodchuck a good seventy feet from his fencerow tunnel. The hunter is only mildly amused and has no desire to shoot at such certain range, so he drives on toward home. On many occasions he has sneaked away from a woodchuck to lengthen the distance enough for a challenging shot.

The hunter's home is on the bank of a small, deep lake, once a limestone quarry, and in a nearby field are traces of the workers' old settlement that gives the hunter's home its name of Ghost Town. The evening is still sultry and unnaturally hazy and the low sun is red. There is an undefined feel of approaching fall and the hunter notices that a few leaves across his little lake have yellowed prematurely. A few feet above the water the sheer limestone rise gives way to earth and at the upper edge some of the tree roots are exposed by erosion. As the hunter stops for a moment at his lawn chair, a woodchuck, thick with his late summer fat and grizzled more than the younger chucks, sits upright, a fuzzy pear shape by his barely visible den high on the bank. He looks across the lake without alarm, turns his head several times, and then waddles off toward his favorite pasture a few feet away from the brink. The hunter continues to wipe the deadly rifle with an oily rag and watches the chuck disappear. He has seen it there all summer.

From his position well above the water, the hunter can see most of his lake. A grebe eyes him impudently before it makes its sleek dive near a weed bed. The hunter does not recall seeing it there recently and wonders if it may have made some sort of premigration move from another area. He hears the unmistakable soft whistle of a widgeon from an end of his lake that is obscured by oaks. The widgeon must have nested nearby, for he has seen them all summer long, but the call now reminds him of chilly blinds and low, dingy clouds that carry snow.

When he has cleaned his rifle, the hunter goes inside past his fireplace where the mounted pronghorn's head seems to be alive in the dull light. As he puts up the rifle, he absently handles his shotgun for a moment.

Thousands of miles away, the caribou have been acting strangely and the ptarmigan flocks are enlarging as they do late in summer. A year of the hunter's world has passed, but it is hard to say when or where it had its beginning.

Bibliography

Anderson, Chester C., *The Elk of Jackson Hole*. Wyoming Game & Fish Commission, 1958.

Burns, William A., ed., *The Natural History of the Southwest*. New York, Franklin Watts, Inc., 1960.

Clark, James L., *The Great Arc of the Wild Sheep*. Norman, Oklahoma, University of Oklahoma Press, 1964.

Collins, Henry Hill, Jr., *Complete Field Guide to American Wildlife*. New York, Harper & Brothers, 1959.

Connett, Eugene V., ed., *Duck Shooting along the Atlantic Tidewater*. New York, Bonanza Books, 1947.

Duffy, McFadden, "Woodcock Hunting." *Louisiana Conservationist,* Louisiana Wild Life & Fisheries Commission, January–February, 1967.

Gallizioli, Steve, *Quail Research in Arizona*. Arizona Game & Fish Department, 1965.

Goodwin, George G., and O'Connor, Jack, *The Big Game Animals of North America*. New York, *Outdoor Life* with E. P. Dutton & Co., 1961.

Harbour, Dave, *Modern ABC's of Bird Hunting*. Harrisburg, Pa., The Stackpole Company, 1966.

Hayes, Tom, *Hunting the Whitetail Deer*. New York, A. S. Barnes & Co., 1960.

Holland, Dan, *The Upland Game Hunter's Bible*. Garden City, N.Y., Doubleday & Company, Inc., 1961.

Kortright, Francis H., *Ducks, Geese, & Swans of North America*. Harrisburg, Pa., The Stackpole Company & Wildlife Management Institute, 1962.

Laycock, George, *The Alien Animals*. Garden City, N.Y., Natural History Press, 1966.

Madson, John, Library of game books for the conservation department of Olin Mathieson Chemic...

Martin, Alexander C., Zim, Herbert S., and Nelson, Arnold, *American Wildlife and Plants: A Guide to Wildlife Food Habits*. New York, Dover Publications, Inc., 1951.

Murie, Olaus J., *The Elk of North America*. Harrisburg, Pa., The Stackpole Co., 1951.

Murray, Robert W., and Frye, O. E., *Bobwhite Quail and its Management in Florida*. Florida Ga... & Fresh Water Fish Commission, 1964.

Ormond, Clyde, *Complete Book of Hunting*. New Yo... *Outdoor Life,* Harper & Brothers, 1962.

Peterson, Roger Tory, *A Field Guide to Western Birds*. Boston, Houghton Mifflin Company, ...
———— *A Field Guide to the Birds*. Boston, Houghto... Mifflin Company, 1947.

Scharff, Robert, *Complete Duck Shooter's Handbook*. New York, G. P. Putnam's Sons, 1957.

Stoddard, Herbert L., *The Bobwhite Quail*. 1931.

Taylor, Walter P., *The Deer of North America*. Harrisburg, Pa., The Telegraph Press, 1969.

United States Government, Department of Interior, *Waterfowl Tomorrow*. 1964.

Van Wormer, Joe, *The World of the Pronghorn*. Philadelphia, J. B. Lippincott Co., 1969.

Weeden, Robert B., *Grouse and Ptarmigan in Alaska*. Alaska Department of Fish & Game, 1967.

Yeatter, Ralph E., *Hungarian Partridge in the Great Lakes Region*. University of Michigan Press, 1934.

Picture Credits

EAB—Erwin A. Bauer   LLR—Leonard Lee Rue III
BB—Bill Browning   JVW—Joseph Van Wormer
KHM—Karl H. Maslowski CFW—Charles F. Waterman

Cover: Bill Browning and Joseph Van Wormer.

CHAPTER 1
10–11: BB. 13: U.S. Fish & Wildlife Service (*1*), EAB (*2*), BB (*3*), Nebraska Game Commission (*4*), LLR (*5,6*). 14: LLR (*1*), BB (*2–4*). 15: John Turner. 16: KHM (*1*), Government of British Columbia (*2*), BB (*3*).

CHAPTER 2
18–19: LLR. 22–23: BB/Montana Chamber of Commerce. 25: Colorado Game & Fish Dept. (*left*), EAB (*right*). 26: BB (*1*), CFW (*2*), George Laycock (*3*), BB (*4*). 27: CFW. 28: BB/Montana Chamber of Commerce (*left*), Steve & Dolores McCutcheon (*right*). 30: Steve & Dolores McCutcheon (*1,2*), BB (*3*), Government of British Columbia (*4*). 31: Mike Browning (*5*), BB (*6–11*).

CHAPTER 3
34–35: LLR. 38: BB (*1*), JVW (*2*), CFW (*3*). 39: EAB. 40: Ontario Dept. of Lands & Forests. 41: EAB. 42: EAB. 43: CFW (*1*), BB (*2,3*). 44: Steve & Dolores McCutcheon. 45: EAB (*top*), Ontario Dept. of Lands & Forests (*bottom*). 46: BB (*1,2*), Montana Fish & Game (*3*). 47: BB.

CHAPTER 4
50–51: BB. 54: Ontario Tourism Dept. 55: JVW (*1*), Ontario Tourism Dept. (*2*), Steve & Dolores McCutcheon (*3*), LLR (*4*), EAB (*5*). 56: Steve & Dolores McCutcheon (*top*), LLR (*bottom left*), BB/Montana Chamber of Commerce (*bottom right*). 58: Steve & Dolores McCutcheon (*1*), BB (*2,3*), Montana Fish & Game (*4*), BB (*5*), John Turner (*6*). 59: BB.

CHAPTER 5
62–63: CFW. 66: BB (*1,2,3*), Montana Fish & Game (*4*). 67: CFW. 69: Nebraska Game Commission (*top*), Colorado Game Fish & Parks Commission (*bottom*). 70: BB (*1,2*), Montana Fish & Game (*3*), BB (*4*). 71: Henry E. Bradshaw (*5*), BB (*6,7,8*), JVW (*9*). 72: BB/Montana Chamber of Commerce (*top*), JVW (*bottom*). 74–75: CFW. 74: CFW (*left*), Montana Fish & Game (*right*), 75: JVW (*left*), BB (*right*).

CHAPTER 6
78–79: JVW. 82: Pete Czura (*1*), JVW (*2*), Walter D. Osborne (*5*). 83: Charley Dickey (*3*), JVW (*4*). 85: U.S. Dept. of Interior (*left*), LLR (*right*). 86: George Laycock. 87: Charley Dickey (*1*), BB (*2,5*), CFW (*3*), EAB (*4*).

CHAPTER 7
90–91: BB. 94–95: All BB, except Saskatchewan Natural Resources Dept. (*3*). 96: Colorado Game Fish & Parks Dept. 98: BB. 99: All BB, except CFW (*5*).

CHAPTER 8
102–103: BB. 106: BB. 107: BB. 109: Government of British Columbia (*left*), EAB (*right*). 110: Montana Fish & Game (*1,2*), Michigan Conservation Dept. (*3*), BB (*4*). 111: All BB, except Montana Fish & Game (*9*). 113: JVW. 114: BB. 115: BB.

CHAPTER 9
118–119: BB. 122: LLR. 123: All BB, except JVW (*1*). 126: All BB, except JVW (*bottom left*). 127: Government of British Columbia (*1*), BB (*2,3*). 128: BB. 129: JVW. 130: JVW. 131: BB (*top*), JVW (*bottom*).

CHAPTER 10
134–135: JVW. 138–139: Paul D. McLain. 138–139: EAB (*1,3*), BB (*2,5*), John Turner (*4*). 142: JVW (*1*), CFW (*2*), BB (*3*), CFW (*4*), EAB (*5*). 143: BB. 146: National Resources Dept. (*1*), LLR (*2*), Tennessee Game & Fish Commission (*3*), George Laycock (*4*), LLR (*5*), JVW (*6*), KHM (*7*), EAB (*8*).

CHAPTER 11
150–151: LLR. 154: LLR (*1,2,4*), Jerry Focht (*3*). 156: LLR. 158: LLR (*1*), Scott-Swedberg (*2*), BB (*3*). 159: BB (*4*), Scott-Swedberg (*5*), JVW (*6*), John Turner (*7*). 160: LLR (*left*), KHM (*right*). 161: LLR. 162: BB (*1*), KHM (*2*). 163: LLR (*3,4*), Government of British Columbia (*5*), KHM (*6*).

CHAPTER 12
166–167: EAB. 170: Charley Dickey (*1*), BB (*2*), Scott-Swedberg (*3*), W. J. Kenner (*4*). 171: BB. 173: KHM (*1,3*), North Carolina Dept. of Conservation & Development (*2*). 174: Ontario Dept. of Lands & Forests. 175: BB (*top*), LLR (*bottom*). 176: LLR (*left*), EAB (*right*). 177: JVW. 178: EAB (*top*), BB (*bottom*). 179: Paul D. McLain.

CHAPTER 13
182–183: Charley Dickey. 186–187: Paul D. McLain. 190: W. J. Kenner (*1,4*), BB (*2*), CFW (*3*). 191: W. J. Kenner (*5,6*), BB (*7*). 193: EAB. 194: North Carolina Wildlife Commission (*top*), Charley Dickey (*middle*), Florida Game & Fresh Water Fish Commission (*bottom*). 195: Florida Game & Fresh Water Fish Commission.

CHAPTER 14
198–199: BB. 202–203: BB. 206: BB. 207: Texas Parks & Wildlife Dept. 209: EAB. 210: Lewis W. Walker/Arizona-Sonora Desert Museum. 211: BB. 212: North Carolina Wildlife Commission (*1*), Western Ways (*2*), Lewis W. Walker/Arizona-Sonora Desert Museum (*3*), JVW (*4*). 213: Lewis W. Walker/Arizona-Sonora Desert Museum. 214: BB. 215: JVW (*6*), BB (*7,8*).

CHAPTER 15
218–219: CFW. 222: W. J. Kenner (*top*), North Carolina Wildlife Resources (*right*). 223: CFW. 224: LLR. 227: CFW (*top*), EAB (*bottom*). 228: KHM. 229: Florida Game & Fresh Water Fish Commission. 230–231: Lewis W. Walker/Arizona-Sonora Desert Museum (*1*), Florida Game & Fresh Water Fish Commission (*2,3*), U.S. Forest Service (*4*).

CHAPTER 16
234–235: CFW. 238: CFW. 239: JVW (*left*), Ontario Dept. of Lands & Forests (*right*). 240–241: LLR.

Index